Discover

# Sardinia

**Rate of exchange.** The rate of exchange used in this book is L2,200 = £1, L1,160 = US$1, L730 = DM1; remember that the rate may change.

*Cover: fishing boats in the harbour at Alghero make a typic Mediterranean picture.*

# Discover

# Sardinia

# Robert Andrews

**Series editor, Terry Palmer**

HERITAGE
HOUSE

## DISCOVER SARDINIA
First published July 1991
**ISBN** 1.85215.0270
**Typesetting** by Anglia Photoset, Colchester.
**Printed by** Colorcraft Ltd, Hong Kong
**Distributed** in the UK and major outlets abroad by Roger Lascelles, 47 York Rd, Brentford, TW8 0QP.
**Published by** Heritage House (Publishers) Ltd, King's Rd, Clacton-on-Sea, Essex.

© **Robert Andrews, 1991.**

**Acknowledgements:**

In London, the Italian State Tourist Office, *ENIT*, provided useful literature and information, while Signora Luciani of the Italian Cultural Institute was kind enough to make some long-distance phone-calls to obtain certain obscure facts for me. In Sardinia, acknowledgements are due to the numerous staff of the local branches of the *EPT, AAST* and *Pro Locos* who gave their time and knowledge in helping me to unravel my problems, particularly the offices of Nuoro, Alghero and Olbia (thanks, Loredana and Dolores). Also gratefully acknowledged are Marina and the family Mereu of Sássari, who extended their warm hospitality to me. And in Bristol, heartfelt thanks to Josephine Morgan, a patient reader and editor who also kept the wheels turning, and to Quincy who provided the distractions.

Titles in the *Discover* series in print or in preparation include:
The Channel Islands, Cyprus & North Cyprus, Czechokoslovakia, The Dominican Republic, Florida, The Gambia, Gibraltar, The Grand Canyon State, Iceland and the Faroes, Malta, Morocco, Poland, Sardinia, The Seychelles, South Africa, Tunisia, Turkey.

# CONTENTS

218-219

SARDINIA

216-217

214-215

**Robert Andrews** has spent most of his life on the move. After travelling in Europe, Asia and Africa, he spent six years in southern Italy teaching and writing, which gave him an insight into this colourful, slightly addictive, slightly dotty country, as well as a fluent understanding of the Italian language. He has contributed articles to London's *Time Out*, *Harper's & Queen* and *The Independent on Sunday*, co-written *The Rough Guide to Sicily*, and also compiled *The Routledge Dictionary of Quotations*, of which an expanded edition is due to be published in 1992.

# 1: WHY SARDINIA?

## Footsteps in the sand

SARDINIA IS THE 'LOST' ISLAND, not yet discovered by the masses. It is the Mediterranean isle *par excellence,* a slice of sunny Italy but exotically different − as D H Lawrence put it, "lost between Europe and Africa and belonging to nowhere."

All islands have a peculiar fascination and Sardinia is no exception. Compact and remote, it boasts a fiercely independent character − yet is still unmistakably Italian. At the same time, as the second biggest island in the Mediterranean, Sardinia has a range of fascinating contrasts, as if it's taken pieces from a dozen islands and rolled them into one. Historically, culturally and geographically, Sardinia's many different faces ensure that there is something here for everyone.

**Location.** The Greeks called it *Ichnoussa,* meaning 'footstep,' perhaps a reference to its shape, or because it a step on the way to Corsica and Provence. In either case, its 4000-year history bears the imprint of a succession of civilisations that touched here − the inevitable result of its central position, 192km (120 miles) from the north African coast at Tunisia, 180km (112 miles) from the Italian mainland, halfway between Spain and the Middle East. Carthaginian and Roman ruins, Genoan fortresses, a string of lovely Pisan churches, a profusion of Gothic and Baroque − all lie strewn across the island landscape, mingling with more than 7000 *nuraghi,* those prehistoric stone towers unique to the island, and which for some people are its most enduring image.

**Area.** Sardinia covers just over 24,000sq km (9,300sq miles), larger than Wales and only marginally smaller than the Mediterranean's biggest island, Sicily (25,708sq km; 9,926sq miles). But with around 1,500,000 people, Sardinia has only a third the population of Sicily, and has the lowest population density of any Italian region − and for tourist and resident alike this means less stress, less pollution, less pressure on the roads.

At its longest, the island stretches 270km (169 miles) from Capo Teulada in the south to Capo Falcone in the north, where it is only 11km (7 miles) from Corsica, and it lies between longitudes 2° 38' and

4° 19' E, and latitudes 38° 52' and 41° 15' N. The town of Carloforte, on San Pietro island (off Sardinia's south west coast) lies exactly on the 39th parallel, about the same as Peking and Philadelphia.

The landscape sees extremes of high mountains (the highest, La Mármora, at 1834m, or 6.016ft) and flat salt-pans, while the coast is fringed by an amazing variety of beach and cliff. As you travel across the island you experience an equally wide range of countryside and culture, from the high interior, where the jangle of goat-bells is a constant melody across the hillsides, to the sleek yachts and glistening beaches of the Costa Smeralda. In between, you will find relics of the island's past, such as the squat prehistoric *nuraghe*, towers that dot the inland rolling plains, and the monumental examples of Pisan church architecture.

What's true for Sardinia is equally true for each of the island's provinces of Cágliari, Oristano, Sássari and Nuoro. Each has the same mix of craggy mountains, swathes of wild *maquis*, forests, rivers, bays and beaches. But beyond these administrative boundaries exists a collection of smaller entities, historical territories each with its different traditions, dialects and historical roots: for instance Gallura, Logudoro, Sulcis, Campidano, Arborea, Barbágia, and others.

At a still more local level, each village flaunts its individuality at the many flamboyant festivals taking place throughout the year. Whether they are stately medieval pageants or smaller, rowdier affairs, or even dignfied religious processions, these festivities are a celebration and a proud assertion, keeping tradition alive in an island where the past is inescapable.

**Island solitude.** And if the time comes when you need a break, there are Sardinia's small offshore islands, from the bustling Maddalena or San Pietro, to the dozens of uninhabited isles brooding in their solitude, possessing tiny beaches, coves and grottos.

With the help of this book, the visitor to Sardinia will come to know all of these different faces, and recognise all those distinguishing features which are still strong today. Whether you are more drawn by the beaches, the mountains, or the wining and dining, Sardinia's rich diversity will guarantee your holiday never lacks interest and variety.

# 2: BEFORE YOU GO

## Paperwork and preparation

THERE ARE FEW PREPARATIONS for normal tourists planning a holiday in Sardinia.

## PASSPORTS AND VISAS

As Sardinia is politically a part of Italy, all Italian entry regulations apply to the island: **EC nationals** need an up-to-date passport, which for Britons can be a Visitor's Passport, valid for a year, or the full ten-year version. In theory you are required to carry this with you at all times, though in practice it is needed only when you register in hotels or campsites and – apart from cash transactions – when you change money; some car-hire companies will ask to see this too, or some other document with your photo on. **Australians, New Zealanders, Canadians and US Citizens** can enter on the same conditions. Foreigners from any country may stay for only three months; after that they must apply for a visa or a permit for long-term stays, the *permesso di soggiorno*.

**Police registration.** Note that while hotel and campsite staff will automatically register you with the police, if you are renting accommodation or staying with friends or family, you are required by Italian law to report to the local Questura (police station).

**Italian translation.** If you are British, and **driving,** and don't have the new pink licence, you'll need a translation of your old licence, normally available from your national motoring association. The option is to have an International Driving Licence.

## EMBASSIES and CONSULATES

Italian embassies and consulates abroad include:

**United Kingdom:** 38 Eaton Place, London SW1 (✆ 071.235.9371); 2 Melville Crescent, Edinburgh (✆ 031.226.3631); 79 Oxford Street, Manchester (✆ 061.236.9024).

**Republic of Ireland:** 63 Northumberland Road, Dublin 4 (✆ 01.601.744).

**Australia:** 61-69 Macquarie Street, Sydney, New South Wales 2000 (✆ 02.278.442); 34 Anderson Street, South Yarra, Melbourne, Victoria

3141 (✆ 03.267.5744).

**Canada:** 3489 Drummond Street, Montreal, Quebec H34 1X6 (✆ 514.849.8351); 1200 Burrard Street, Suite 505, Vancouver, British Columbia V6Z 2C7 (✆ 604.684.7288).

**Germany:** Graf-Spee-Strasse 1-7, 1000 Berlin 30 (✆ 030.261.1591-2-3).

**Netherlands:** Herengracht 609, Amsterdam 1017 CE (✆ 20.240.043).

**New Zealand:** 34 Grant Road, Wellington (✆ 04.729.302).

**United States:** 1601 Fuller Street, NW, Washington DC 20009 (✆ 202.328.5500); 320 Park Avenue, New York, NY 10022 (✆ 212.737.9100); 2590 Webster Avenue, San Francisco, CA 94115 (✆ 415.931.4924).

## Some consulates in Sardinia

**Belgium:** Via Alghero 35; 09100 Cágliari (✆ 070.652220).

**Denmark:** Via Roma 127; 09100 Cágliari (✆ 070.668208).

**Finland:** Viale Diaz 29; 09100 Cágliari (✆ 070.668121).

**France:** Viale Cimitero 29; 09100 Cágliari (✆ 070.307293); Via IV Novembre 10; 07100 Sássari (✆ 079.271135).

**Germany:** Via Garzia Raffa 9; 09100 Cágliari (✆ 070.307229).

**Netherlands:** Viale Regina Margherita 8; 09100 Cágliari (✆ 070.668094).

**Luxembourg:** La Pineta; 07041 Aghero (✆ 079.930159).

**Norway:** Via Roma 127; 09100 Cágliari (✆ 070.659394).

**Sweden:** Viale Diaz 29; 09100 Cágliari (✆ 070.668121).

**United Kingdom:** Via San Lucífero 87; 09100 Cágliari (✆ 070.662755).

# ITALIAN STATE TOURIST OFFICES abroad:

**United Kingdom:** 1 Princes St, London W1 (✆ 071.408.1254).

**Republic of Ireland:** 47 Merrion Square, Dublin 2 (✆ 01.766.397).

**Australia and New Zealand:** c/o Alitalia, AGC House, 124 Phillip Street, Sydney, New South Wales, Australia (✆ 02.271.308); c/o Alitalia, Mercantile Mutual Building, 143 Queen Street, Victoria 3000, Australia (✆ 03.600.0511).

**Canada:** 1 Place Ville Marie, Suite 1914, Montreal, Quebec HEB 3M9 (✆ 514.866.7667−9).

**France:** 23 Rue de la Paix, 75002 Paris (✆ 142.666.668).

**Germany:** Kaiserstrasse 65, 6000 Frankfurt am Main 1 (✆ 69.237.430).

**Holland:** Stadhouderskade 6, 1054 ES Amsterdam (✆ 20.168.244).

**United States:** 630 Fifth Avenue, Suite 1565, New York, NY 10111 (✆ 212.397.5293−4); 500 N. Michigan Avenue, Suite 1046, Chicago, IL 60611 (✆ 312.644.0990); 360 Post Street, Suite 801, San Francisco, CA 94108 (✆ 415.392.5266).

# WHEN TO GO

Sardinia has a typical Mediterranean climate, which ensures that it is never really cold on the coasts, though the mountains of the interior can get quite chilly, some of them snow-covered from November to March. For practical purposes, **summer** lasts for four months, peaking in July and August. Things can get pretty steamy around this time, making it not the best period to visit Sardinia. Not only is the heat enervating and oppressive, making you want to do little more than panting in the shade of a bar sipping innumerable − and expensive − drinks, but this is the season when the island is deluged with tourists from the Italian mainland, making the beaches crowded and accommodation difficult to find. And prices usually rise by about 10% from June 15 to September 15.

On the other hand the summer visitor will find all the tourist attractions guaranteed to be running, while people coming before June and after September can expect to find many hotels, bars and restaurants, and most campsites, closed.

**Low season delights.** It is in **spring,** from about early March to late May, that the island's vegetation is at its most luxuriant and the light at its most sparkling. If you're thinking of doing any hiking on the island, this is the ideal period, when visibility is at its crystal best and the air is equally fresh. Later, the green hillsides turn to shades of brown as the summer deepens.

A **September** holiday finds the sea at its warmest, though there is often a persistent wind that can blow for a week at a time. Late in the month there are usually a few days of rain, and the occasional storm as the hot weather breaks. **October** is the last month for most package tour operators and therefore sees the last charter flights to the island. This is when prices are cheaper and the weather is still warm, though the evenings are noticeably cooler.

## Average temperatures

The following temperatures are in degrees centigrade. For high inland areas take off three or four degrees.

West coast:

|      | Jan | Feb | Mar | Apr | May | Jun | Jul | Aug | Sep | Oct | Nov | Dec |
|------|-----|-----|-----|-----|-----|-----|-----|-----|-----|-----|-----|-----|
| Min: | 0   | 1   | 4   | 4   | 10  | 11  | 12  | 16  | 12  | 10  | 9   | 5   |
| Max: | 17  | 18  | 20  | 22  | 31  | 31  | 35  | 34  | 32  | 30  | 21  | 18  |

East coast:

|      | Jan | Feb  | Mar | Apr  | May  | Jun | Jul | Aug  | Sep  | Oct  | Nov | Dec |
|------|-----|------|-----|------|------|-----|-----|------|------|------|-----|-----|
| Min: | 5.5 | 6    | 7.5 | 9.5  | 12.5 | 13  | 19  | 19.5 | 17.5 | 14   | 10  | 7   |
| Max: | 14  | 14.5 | 17  | 18.5 | 22.5 | 27  | 31  | 29.5 | 27   | 23.5 | 19  | 17  |

# INDEPENDENT OR PACKAGE?
## PACKAGE

Most package-deal holidaymakers who come to Sardinia have very simple requirements: a week or two in the sun in a comfortable hotel, preferably with a pool and some form of evening entertainment, and perhaps with tennis courts and something to keep the children amused. There's no shortage of deals which offer precisely this, guaranteeing good service — often with English-speaking staff — and the minimum of hassle. Several companies offer the option of a self-catering holiday, saving on hotel expenses and giving you more contact with the local population.

**Compromise.** A package tour will always be the most economical way of holidaying in Sardinia, especially if you're travelling *en famille*. Most hotels and operators provide a range of guided tours and excursions, allowing you to see something of the island, but don't expect to see everything unless you're prepared to pay for *another* hotel in *another* resort: Sardinia is too big for day excursions to be covered from any one base.

**Resorts.** Sardinia's tourist areas are concentrated in the corners of the island: Alghero, in the north west; the Costa Smeralda in the north east; Villasímius in the south east, and Pula in the south west.

Of all these areas, **Alghero** is the best bet for those who are keen to

*Images from the past: nuraghic statuettes from Cágliari's Archaeological Museum.*

see more of Sardinia than the inside of the hotel, since it is not only a vibrant resort, with plenty of bars and restaurants, discos, cultural activities and hire facilities, but it is also the island's main fishing port. It's a good idea to find out first if your hotel is in the town or outside – most hotels are shown on the Costa Smeralda and Coral Riviera maps in this book. If it's more than a ten-minute walk from the town this may be just too far for you to come in for the *passeggiata,* the locals' evening stroll, or for market day. I have met package tourists marooned three or four miles (5 or 6km) outside Alghero who were practically dying with boredom.

The **Costa Smeralda,** strictly speaking, is a narrow strip of coast 6 miles (10km) north of Olbia, but for package tour purposes it includes the nearby towns and villages of **Porto Rotondo** and **Baia Sardinia** (sometimes written *Baja* but pronounced the same), and the bays of **Golfo Aranci, Golfo Marinella** and the **Golfo di Arzachena** with the latter's resort of **Cannigione.**

The **Emerald Coast** is one of the most exclusive areas not just in Sardinia but in the whole of Italy, and the prices reflect it. Despite that, among the deals offered here are self-catering holidays in villas or bungalows at reasonable prices – but you must be prepared for higher-than-average prices in the local grocery stores, and in the bars, restaurants and pizzerias. And remember at your peril that while there is plenty of coming and going here in the summer, out of season the area is fairly dead.

**Pros and cons.** The pros for coming to this corner of the island include the opportunity to enjoy some of the most enchanting coastline Sardinia has to offer, and experience at first hand one of the most élite holiday environments in the Mediterranean. The con is a by-product of this, as the costa is a highly artificial creation, made to be admired rather than enjoyed, with local Sardinian life confined to hotel staff and taxi-drivers. But there are plenty of opportunities for getting out to see more of the island, including excursions to the beautiful Maddalena archipelago.

The resort of **Villasímius** has a more spontaneous feel to it, a lively place with some bewitching coastline nearby. This is a popular destination for Italian holidaymakers, guaranteeing fun and vitality, but the more reserved northern Europeans may find it a little frenetic in the summer. Nearby is the exclusive **Costa Rei** zone of luxury villas and 'residence' complexes (see chapter 5 for more on these).

Both Villasímius and **Pula** are within shooting distance of Cágliari, with its comparatively cosmopolitan feel and diverse attractions – handy if you need a change of scene. The hotels south of Pula form a totally self-contained environment, even more so than the Costa Smeralda, secluded and with the best facilities on hand – and at some of the highest prices.

**Tour operators** offering package holidays to Sardinia include:

**Allegro Holidays** 15a Church Street, Reigate, Surrey (✆ 0737.221.323). Resorts are all in Alghero or the Costa Smeralda.

**Cadogan Travel** 9-10 Portland Street, Southampton, SO9 1ZP (✆ 0703.332.661). This group has taken over Island Sun's operations in Alghero.

**Citalia** Marco Polo House, 3-5 Lansdowne Road, Croydon, Surrey (✆ 081.686.5533), or 51 Conduit Street, London W1 (071.408.4120). These Italian holiday specialists have a range of hotels in Pula, Villasímius and the Costa Smeralda area.

**Club Mediterranee** 106-8 Brompton Road, London SW3 1JJ (✆ 071.581.1161). De luxe complexes in Santa Teresa di Gallura and Caprera.

**Costa Smeralda Holidays** 81 Cromwell Road, London SW7 (✆ 071.493.8303). Exclusive holidays in the Costa Smeralda area, including golfing holidays. Hotels and apartments are both available.

**Exotic Islands** 35 High Street, Tring, Herts (✆ 0442.891.551). Hotel-holidays in Santa Margherita di Pula.

**Falcon Sailing** 33 Notting Hill Gate, London W11 (✆ 071.727.0232). Dinghy, wind-surfing and self-catering holidays in Cannigione.

**Halsey Villas** 22 Boston Place, Dorset Square, London NW1 (✆ 071.491.2950. Villas on the Costa Smeralda.

**Horizon** Broadway, Edgbaston, Five Ways, Birmingham (✆ 021.632.6182). Part of the Thomson group, sharing its holiday locations.

**Interhome** 383 Richmond Road, Twickenham TW1 2EF (✆ 081.891.1294). Houses for rent in Stintino, San Pantaleo and outside Olbia.

*Time to relax: a tropical corner of Poetta's beach.*

**Italian Escapades** 227 Shepherds Bush Road, London W6 (℘ 081.748.2661). The company has access to three of the best hotels in the Pula zone.

**Magic of Italy** 47 Shepherds Bush Green, London W12 (℘ 081.743.9555). A wide range in Oliena, Palau and the Costa Smeralda area.

**Quo Vadis** 243 Euston Road, London NW1 2BT (℘ 071.387.6122/ 388.7588). Flights and holidays in Santa Teresa and Golfo Aranci.

**Sardatour Holidays** Glen House, 200-208 Tottenham Court Road, London W1 (℘ 071.637.0281). Holidays off the beaten track in Platamona, Bosa, San Teodoro, Santa Teresa, Palau and Porto Rotondo.

**Sardinian Affair** 34 Lillie Road, Fulham, London SW1 (℘ 071.381.6636). A wide range of holidays around the Costa Smeralda and Nuoro.

**Thomson Holidays** Broadway, Edgbaston, Five Ways, Birmingham (℘ 021.632.6182); London callers can dial ℘ 081.200.8733. A selection of hotels in Alghero.

**Villas Italia** 227 Shepherds Bush Road, London W6 (℘ 071.221.4432). Several hotels and self-catering holidays offered in Porto Rafael and Baia Sardinia.


The areas covered include:

**Alghero** (south west of Sássari): Allegro, Citalia, Horizon, Cadogan, Thomson, Global.

**Baia Sardinia** (near the Costa Smeralda): Citalia, Magic of Italy, Sardinian Affair.

**Bosa** (between Oristano and Alghero): Sardatour.

**Cannigione** (near the Costa Smeralda): Falcon.

**Costa Smeralda** (north of Olbia): Citalia, Costa Smeralda, Halsey, Sardinian Affair.

**Golfo Aranci** (north of Olbia): Citalia.

**Golfo Marinella** (north of Olbia): Citalia, Costa Smeralda, Quo Vadis, Sardatour, Sardinian Affair, Villas Italia.

**Olbia**: Interhome.

**Oliena** (near Nuoro): Magic of Italy, Sardinian Affair.

**Palau** (north Sardinia, port for the Maddalena islands): Magic of Italy.

**Platamona** (coast north of Sássari): Horizon, Sardatour.

**Porto Rafael** (near Palau, northern Sardinia): Magic of Italy, Villas Italia.

**Porto Rotondo** (near Costa Smeralda): Citalia, Sardinian Affair, Sardatour, Villas Italia.

**San Pantaleo** (inland from the Costa Smeralda) Interhome.

**San Teodoro** (south of Olbia): Interhome, Sardatour, Sardinian

Affair.

**Santa Margherita Di Pula** (south of Cágliari): Citalia, Exotic Islands, Italian Escapades, Sardatour.

**Santa Teresa di Gallura** (on Sardinia's northern tip; port for Corsica): Club Mediterranee, Sardatour.

**Stintino** (Sardinia's north-western tip): Interhome.

**Villasímius** (on Sardinia's south eastern corner): Citalia.

## INDEPENDENT

If you have itchy feet and are interested in seeing something of Sardinia and the Sardinians, then you might prefer the independent option. Given the excellent internal transport links, and with the help of the numerous Italian tourist offices well distributed all over the island and equipped with information on hire-agencies, timetables and accommodation, you should have plenty of chance to discover Sardinia for yourself, with every opportunity to find the perfect beach, or come upon a charming church or local festival, with no other tourists in sight.

The main drawback is, of course, financial. Eating out, sleeping wherever you find yourself, and particularly car-hire can all work out extremely costly, and though you can economise by camping, and taking public transport for the longer journeys, you may still find yourself running into the red sooner than you anticipated.

**Few single rooms.** Another consideration is the availability of accommodation. July and especially August can find the island ill-equipped to deal with the huge influx of tourists that descends then, and you should always look for a hotel early in the day — which limits the time you can spend on the road. And single rooms are often more difficult to find than doubles in the cheaper hotels in towns due to demand by businessmen and commercial travellers or government employees in temporary accommodation.

## DISABLED

Italy has made some gestures towards providing for the disabled, though in practice these don't amount to much more than adapting telephone kiosks for the use of wheelchair-travellers and reserving parking places for drivers — usually in the centre of towns or at the head of ferry queues. There are few lavatories for the disabled in airports, or anywhere else, though at least there are no stairs to be negotiated in any of the island's three airports.

In common with the rest of Italy, Sardinia can be a fast, rather aggressive place, especially in areas popular with blasé Italian tourists from the mainland. But for the most part it has nothing like the traffic frenzy associated with large Italian cities, and Sardinian motorists are noticeably more willing to stop at a zebra crossing than are drivers on the mainland, and pedestrians will often help someone across the road.

As a rule, disabled visitors to Sardinia can be sure of the best services as part of a package tour, in which all special needs are catered for.

Disabled drivers should take their orange badge issued by their local authorities back home, and make sure it is well displayed if they want to take advantage of special parking regulations.

For further information, contact Radar, 25 Mortimer St, London W1M 8AB (✆ 071.657.5400).

## FAMILY HOLIDAYS

Italy is still a country where the family is the greatest gift and asset that one can have, and Sardinia is no exception to this. Children will be treated to lashings of attention and entertainment by both men and women to an extent unknown in Anglo-Saxon countries, while pregnant women are regarded with a touching mixture of awe and concern.

**Children welcome.** This makes Sardinia an ideal place to enjoy a family holiday given its acres of beach and the cleanliness of its seas. Nor need you be afraid of using public transport, for in the short distances involved the local people will tolerate childish tantrums. And most car-hire companies provide a baby-seat for about L25,000 a day extra.

You'll find the best facilities provided by the tourist hotels, which is a good argument for going package if you need some time off from the demands of infants, but Sardinia's smarter non-package hotels often have crêches and play areas for children. I also saw excellent arrangements of this kind in campsites, which are a good environment for young children, especially if the site is on a beach – as they almost all are.

In the shops, you can expect to find everything that you might need: all the major brands of nappies (diapers in American English and the imported word *pamper* in Italian) are available in chemists (drugstores or *farmacíe*) and other stores – and you will find a gorgeous selection of children's clothes in the *Prénatal* chain of stores for mothers and infants as well as in *Standa* or *Upim* supermarkets, though the prices of some of these may cause you to blink.

## YACHTING

With more than 1,000 miles (1,600km) of coastline, Sardinia is an ideal island to cruise around, and its proximity to the French and Italian rivieras has made it one of the smartest yachting destinations in the Mediterranean. The prevailing north-westerlies are agreeably gentle for most of the summer, and there are endless alluring anchorages, especially on the Bonifacio Strait between Corsica and Sardinia.

On the whole, **facilites** are good, with more details available from the numerous tourist offices in Sardinia's ports. For **navigation,** consult *Mediterranean Pilot* Vol 1. Sadly, **hazards** include some degree of pollution around the oil refineries at Porto Torres and Cágliari, and the tunny-fish nets laid out in May and June are to be avoided, especially around the island of San Pietro.

All boats with engines must carry **number plates,** available from your local yacht club.

**Formalities.** If you tow your own boat down to Sardinia behind your car you can leave it for six months in Italian territory without needing special customs papers. But if the boat is not brought by car and its engine exceeds 6hp, it must have **insurance,** which otherwise is not necessary, though on first entering Italian waters *all* craft must be inspected by a port official at the Capitaneria del Porto. The official checks the boat's papers and the owner's passport, then issues a *Costituto* which must be shown at all subsequent ports and which allows you to buy fuel free from tax. Staying long? Then you'll need a Navigation Licence from your country of origin.

**Taxes.** You, the boat owner, are liable for the **tax** which must be paid by all owners at all Italian ports; for boats carrying an auxiliary engine the tax is L60 daily per ton up to 50 registered tons, and L75 for

*There's always room to breathe on the beach at Nora.*

more than 50. For boats with an inboard motor the rate is L120 daily per ton up to 50 registered tons, L150 for more than 50. Tax is reduced by two-thirds in the case of a two-month subscription between June and September, and there are further concessions.

Vessels may be left in Italy for up to one year exempt from tax.

**Driving licences** are not required for: vessels of **length** not excceeding 5m, **engine** not above 20hp and **sails** not more than 14sq m. And **sailing boats** for navigation within 20 miles from the coast with auxiliary engine, or with engine not exceeding 3 BRT inboard or outboard, and not above 20hp.

Foreigners carrying an **Ability Document** from their country of origin may sail the craft for which they are qualified.

For more **information** contact the Federazione Italiana Vela, Viale Brigata Bisagno 2-17, Rome (☎ 06.717924), or the Federazione Italiana Motonautica, Via Piranesi 44b, Rome (☎ 06.717924).

Relevant **reading** includes: H.M. Denham's *The Tyrrhenian Sea*, part of the *Companion Sea Guides* series published by John Murray; *Round the Italian Coast* by P. Bristow (Nautical Publishing), and *Italian Waters Pilot* by Rod Heikell (Imray Laurie & Wilson Ltd).

If you want to find out about **dinghy, surfboard and yachting holidays** contact *Falcon Sailing* 33 Notting Hill Gate, London W11 (☎ 071.727.0232).

## HEALTH

Although Sardinia was bedevilled by malaria until the end of the Second World War (the word *mal'aria* is Italian, meaning 'bad air'), there is no trace of it now. True, there are still mosquitoes, but no worse than anywhere else in the Mediterranean. The bites from these are about the worst health hazard you can expect to encounter in Sardinia, though keep a wary eye open for sea-urchins (*ricci*) which loiter on rocks and can sting like mad if stepped on. There are no poisonous snakes or spiders on the island.

**Water.** As in the rest of southern Europe, water is savoured in Sardinia like wine. Most Italians drink the bottled variety which, in bars and restaurants, is available as 'still,' *naturale*, or 'fizzy,' *gassata*. Tapwater is not *un*drinkable, but if you prefer this kind it's always worth checking first. Sometimes, you will see a sign: *da bere* for drinkable, or *non potabile* for not drinkable, or some variation of the two.

Many towns and villages have public fountains, and in some of these you may find that chlorine has been added. But in mountain villages the water is likely to be of high quality; in some places of such quality that you'll see people queuing to fill their bottles with water that is as prized as the best commercially-bottled stuff.

Otherwise Sardinia is a risk-free zone, though obvious precautions should be taken to prevent overexposure to the sun.

**Precautions.** European Community citizens should consider applying for form E111, available one month in advance in Britain from the Department of Social Security and entitling you to free use of the Italian health services: apply for the form a month before you go abroad. And you *do* need to have have some kind of travel insurance as well.

Doctors are available in all towns and villages, though if you have only a minor ailment you'll find the chemist − *farmacía* − is usually well-informed and helpful.

**Emergencies.** If you have a more serious problem and there is no hotel manager on hand to help, either phone the emergency number ℘ 113 and ask for *ambulanza*, or go to the nearest hospital where there is a *pronto soccorso* (casualty department). **First aid** services, also known as *pronto soccorso*, are avaiable at all airports, and bus and rail stations.

**Dental problems.** Try not to develop any dental problems while you are away: Italian dentists are not covered by the health service there, and charge exorbitant fees.

***Número Verde.*** In 1990 the Tourist Authority in Sardinia initiated an **emergency scheme operational between July and October,** that may be repeated in future years. The service − *Número Verde* − is for the exclusive use of tourists and provides free medical consultation, payment of medical, pharmaceutical and hospital fees, and breakdown and transport service following a road or undersea accident. The number to ring is ℘ 1678.29063, which connects you to an "Operations Centre" available 24 hours a day, manned by English-speaking personnel.

To qualify for the scheme, you must have your travel documents, proof of where you are staying, and a passport, and you must contact the Centre as soon as the accident or incident occurs, or within three days of admission to hospital. Check with the Italian Tourist Board, at home or in Sardinia, if this service is still available.

# ETIQUETTE: HOW NOT TO MAKE A *BRUTTA FIGURA* IN SARDINIA

Social conduct in Sardinia is not much different from the accepted modes on the Italian mainland. Following a few simple rules, not only should you be able to avoid making unnecessary social gaffes but you will enhance what for Italians ranks higher than money: your *figura*, or the impression you make on other people.

The persona one projects is a highly important part of Italian life, to the extent that people will endure all sorts of social privations rather than appear, for example, in a creased dress or an inferior car. And where appearance counts for everything, it goes without saying that rowdy behaviour of any kind is frowned upon. It is as rare in Sardinia to see people openly drunk as it is to see violence in the streets: whatever there is happens behind closed doors.

**Women's behaviour.** Although people on the coasts and in cities have become accustomed to much of what would have been considered unacceptable 20 years ago, in the remote interior, and especially in the mountains, certain behaviour can still raise a few eyebrows. For example, a woman sitting alone in a bar will be regarded as something of an oddity. In fact women alone *anywhere* will attract a degree of attention that they may find unwelcome, though there is less harassment in Sardinia than in many other parts of Italy. And as a rule, the less a woman is wearing, the greater the attention she attracts.

**Offensive dress.** Shorts or tee-shirts – or less – on either sex are certainly not the correct garb for visiting churches, and this is one area where you can actually cause offence. Moreover, if you want to see inside a church, try to make sure it's immediately before or after a service, and not during it. Camera flashes, of course, should be used discreetly. If you come at other times you will often find churches closed, unless they have particular value as tourist sights.

**Topless bathing.** Topless bathing for women is acceptable in Sardinia, though it should be done tactfully. If you are on a crowded beach with families, don't be the only one to go topless. Complaints can be made and in the end it's not worth the trouble. **Nudity** on beaches is not only frowned upon but is illegal under indecency laws, so if you want to chance it, you'd better make sure you're far enough away from civilisation to avoid causing offence – and remember to pack the sun-cream!

When addressing Italians in Italian, remember to use the polite *lei* (3rd-person) form rather than the more familiar *tu*. Being over-familiar is certainly the mark of a boor, though the under-30s can get away with being less formal among themselves, and children can always be given the *tu*. Italians in general adore titles, so if you know someone is a doctor, call him or her *dottore* or *dottoressa* – and this title applies to lawyers, professors and some other professions too. Other men will appreciate *signore;* women who are married or in any case above 'a certain age' are *signora,* otherwise *signorina.*

## MONEY MATTERS

The Italian unit of currency is the *lira,* plural *lire,* abbreviated as 'L,' though it has been many years since anyone has had just one of these in his pocket. The lira may be small but it has not lost value since Italy re-established stable government; today the smallest denomination coin is 50 lire (L50) and notes start at L1,000. At the 1990-'91 rate of exchange L1,000 is a little less than 50p or 20¢ or DM1.50, so L10,000 is about £5, $2.50, or DM15 − and L100,000 is about £50. All those noughts can be bewildering, so for the sake of mental arithmetic, cutting out three of them and dividing by two will give you an approximate idea of the equivalent sterling value; divide by four for an approximation in US$.

Any bank that carries the label *cambio* will change your money, and all those with the Eurocheque symbol will, naturally, change Eurocheques. The fewer times you change money the better, unless you enjoy waiting around in banks. Although tourists often get preferential treatment, they must still go through the same channels, which involves queuing at the *cambio* desk, making the transaction, then queuing at the cash desk *cassa*, and waiting until the cashier comes round to examining your documents. Your signature is required at each stage, and for all but cash transactions you will need to present your passport.

**Banking hours.** Banks in Sardinia are open from Monday to Friday 0830-1320, 1500-1600 (the afternoon times may vary from place to place by fifteen minutes or half an hour). It's worth remembering that the central branches of the Banco di Sardegna in Cágliari and Sássari have outdoor cash exchange machines which are open 24 hours. What's more, they work.

**Exchange offices.** In addition you will find exchange offices in most of the tourist centres, often open straight through from 0830 to 1730, and sometimes into the evening too. The larger hotels will also change money, adding a commision for themselves, and some railway stations and ports have exchange offices. But in the airports, exchange offices are often closed by 1600.

**Credit cards.** All the major credit cards are recognised in Sardinia, and all banks and many shops and restaurants, particularly in tourist centres, will accept them. The major car-hire companies will accept payment by credit card for the deposit and tariff, though it's always wise to confirm this before taking out the car.

**Inflation.** Inflation in Italy is not the scourge that it once was, and it's currently around 6%. There has been much talk in recent years of the *lira pesante* or 'heavy lira,' which amounts to knocking off three noughts so that L1,000 become just L1, but the feared effect on inflation is one reason why this has yet to happen.

**Cost of Living.** In the past few years Italy has ceased to be one of Europe's cheaper holiday destinations and the cost of living is comparable with that in the UK. Sardinia, being an island, is if anything marginally more expensive than the mainland, as many of the consumer goods must be shipped in − yet the visitor will often find prices lower than those at home. Hotel prices are generally cheaper, for example, as is the cost of eating out. Rents and house prices are usually less, and fruit and vegetables, especially if bought in markets, are cheaper and of better quality than we can find in Britain, although this depends on the season. But in areas such as the Costa Smeralda, prices are notoriously high.

**Transport costs.** Public transport is cheaper than in Britain, with trains usually cheaper than buses, though in practice buses occasionally work out cheaper and quicker. But internal flights between airports in Sardinia, or connections with the mainland, are relatively expensive.

**Shopping list.** If you're shopping, you'll find the bigger centres offering the best choice, and within these it is the supermarkets that have the most competitive prices — but the street- markets are always preferable for buying fruit and veg, fish, meat and some other groceries. Here is a selection of prices with the base converted to sterling:

## Clothes

| | | |
|---|---|---|
| Handbag | L95–130,000 | **£43** |
| Jacket, man's (wool) | L60,000 | **£27** |
| Jacket, man's (Armani) | L650,000 | **£295** |
| Jacket, woman's fashion | L330,000 | **£150** |
| Pullover, wool | L250,000 | **£113** |
| Pullover, cashmere | L780,000 | **£355** |
| Pullover at Benetton | L130,000 | **£60** |
| Shirt, man's fashion | L100–140,000 | **£45** |
| Shoes, woman's fashion | L90–120,000 | **£41** |
| Suit, man's fashion | L950,000 | **£430** |
| Tie | L50,000 | **£22** |
| Trousers, corduroy | L140,000 | **£63** |

## Food

| | | |
|---|---|---|
| Beefsteak, 250g | L6,200 | **£2.80** |
| Bread, 1kg | L1,500 | **68p** |
| Butter, 250g | L2,130 | **96** |
| Coffee, 100g | L2,000 | **90** |
| Eggs, 1 doz | L2,800 | **£1.20** |
| Figs, 1kg | L3,000 | **£1.30** |
| Fish, cheapest, 1kg | L8,000 | **£3.60** |
| Lobster, 1kg | L40,000 | **£18.20** |
| Grapes, 1kg | L2,500 | **£1.13** |
| Milk, 1 litre | L1,300 | **59p** |
| Mozzarella cheese, 125g | L1,260 | **54p** |
| Olive oil, 1 litre | L5,500 | **£2.50** |
| Onions, 1kg | L1,000 | **45p** |
| Plums, 1kg | L5,000 | **£2.27** |

Tomatoes, 1kg .......................... L2,500 — L3,000 **£1.36**
Yoghurt, 500g ................................... L2,440 **£1.10**
**Drinks**
Coffee, capuccino (at bar) ........................... L1,200 **54p**
—, espresso (at bar) ............................... L900 **40p**
Coke (at bar) ..................................... L2,000 **90p**
Beer (at bar) ............................... L2—2,500 **90**
Gin and tonic (at bar) ........................ L3,500 **£1.60**
Gin, 70cl bottle Gordon's ...................... L10,720 **£4.87**
Whisky, 70cl bottle Red Label .................. L12,140 **£5.52**
Wine, Vermentino (table) ...................... L3,990 **£1.81**
—, Vernaccia (table) ...................... L3,640—4,640 **£1.65**
—, Séleme (D.O.C.) ........................... L4,150 **£1.88**
—, Dorgali, (D.O.C.) .......................... L4,480 **£2.03**
Mineral water, 1.5 litre bottle ................... L560 **25p**
— —, glass in bar ................................ L500 **22p**
**Miscellaneous**
Cigarettes, 20 Marlboro ........................ L3,150 **£1.43**
— 20 MS ..................................... L2,050 **93p**
(MS is Italy's most popular, state—subsidised brand)
Film, 36 exposure Kodacolor ...................... L9000 **£4.09**
—, 36 processing .............................. L25,900 **£11.77**
Nappies (box of 40) ........................... L17,000 **£7.72**
Petrol, 1 litre 4—star ........................... L1,520 **69p**
Postage, Europe, letters ......................... L750 **34p**
—, —, cards ................................... L600 **27p**
Toothpaste, 150cl tube .......................... L3,000 **£1.36**
Train fare Sássari—Olbia ...................... L7,000 **£3.18**
City bus fare ................................... L700 **32p**
**Large purchases**
Moped 50cc ............................. L1,800,000 **£818**
Vespa 150cc scooter ..................... L3,000,000 **£1,360**
Moto Guzzi 500cc motor bike ................... L6,000,000 **£2,725**
Fiat Panda ............................. L9,000,000 **£4,090**
Apartment, Costa Smeralda (2 rms) ........... L65,000,000 **£29,550**
—, —, rental in Olbia ................... L600,000 per month **£272**

*Basic monthly wages of teacher* .................. *L1,500,000* **£680**

# 3: GETTING TO SARDINIA

## Air or sea

FLYING IS THE MOST CONVENIENT and often the cheapest way of getting to Sardinia, though some would argue that the first sight of an island should be from the sea.

The main ferry ports for embarcations to Sardinia are in France and Italy, but the permutations are almost endless and the main factor is whether you are in a hurry. The most direct ways are through the ports of Toulon or Marseilles in France, or Genoa or Livorno in Italy. Alternatively, you can sail from Corsica, or Italian ports further south, including Sicilian ones, or even Tunisia or Malta. You might consider these routes if you are visiting Sardinia as part of a grander tour, or island-hopping across the Med to Tunisia.

Services, schedules and prices change from year to year, so the following information is only an outline; check the latest facts with your travel agent.

## ARRIVING BY AIR

**Scheduled services.** In summer, only Alitalia flies direct from the UK to Sardinia; with all other carriers you must change at Milan, Rome or Naples. Fares vary according to season: high season is usually a week around Christmas and Easter, and between 1 June and 30 September.

In addition to the normal fares, the scheduled services operate a few special schemes that might suit your requirements. **Eurobudget** gives you approximately 20% reduction if you make reservations and buy the ticket simultaneously. The return flight is open, and there are reductions for children and infants. **Pex** fares must include a weekend away, with reservations, payment and ticket-issue at the same time. Fifty per cent of the fare is refundable, prior to departure date. Discounts for infants and children.

Advanced passenger excursion, known as **Apex,** is similar to Pex except that you must pay and book at least 14 days before departure, and the 50% refund apples only when the booking is cancelled more than 14 days before. Infants only get reductions.

*British Airways* (✆ 081.759.5511) offers **'seat sales'** return flights −

*A site by the sea: the ruins at Nora.*

but staying over one Saturday night and for a maximum of 14 days — to Milan for £136, to Rome £150, rising to £172 and £193 in peak season. Its Apex fares to Milan are £206, rising to £236; to Rome £222−258. BA's Pex fares are £254−311 to Milan, £295−354 to Rome.

*Aer Lingus* (✆ 01.377.777) flies Dublin-Milan and Dublin-Rome and back for 251 Irish pounds, or about £232 sterling.

*Alitalia* (✆ 071.602.7111) flies directly from the UK to Alghero and Olbia. The best offer is its Apex flight to Alghero, at £266 low season, £302 high; its flights to Olbia are fixed at £410 (via Milan).

**Charters.** Britannia and Dan Air are the two main airlines flying direct from Britain to Sardinia, though neither of these lines continues after the end of October — exact dates vary from year to year, obtainable from a travel agent. Typical fares are £150−200 return. Contact your local travel agency for the best deals, or else try *Quo Vadis* (✆ 071.583.8383), *Italflights* (✆ 071.405.6771), *Citalia* (✆ 081.686.5533), or *Italia Nel Mondo* (✆ 071.828.9171) — though there are others.

**Arriving by air in Sardinia.** Flying-time to Sardinia is 2½ to 3 hours. The island has three airports, all small but modern, and all served by flights from the UK. There is a choice of the major car-hire agencies at each one: Avis, Hertz, Budget, Maggiore and others; regular bus-services from all but Fertília (for Alghero-Sássari), and bars and shops at each.

**Cágliari.** Scheduled international flights land at Cágliari's Elmas Airport (✆ 070.40047) from Frankfurt, Munich, Paris and Zurich. The airport also has scheduled connections at least once a day with the mainland Italian cities of Bologna, Genoa, Milan, Palermo, Pisa, Rome, Turin, Venice and Verona. Sample one-way fare: Rome-Cágliari L92,500.

The airport sits beside the city's largest *stagno*, or lagoon, a 15-minute drive from the centre of town. There is a *cambio* and tourist information office at the airport, the latter with maps and information on accommodation. A taxi-ride into town costs around L15,000, and there is a free bus-service every hour or hour-and-a-half to the bus and train station from 0620 until 2055. The air terminal is in Piazza Matteotti.

**Fertília.** Fertília airport (✆ 079.935033-43) serves both Alghero (4 miles, 7km distant) and Sássari (21 miles, 35km). It has scheduled connections with the Italian cities of Bologna, Genoa, Milan, Pisa, Rome and Turin, all once a day except Rome, which has three daily flights (one hour duration). Sample one-way fare: Genoa-Fertília L175,000.

A taxi will cost about L30,000 to Alghero, at least L60,000 to Sássari. There is no regular bus-service, but there is normally a bus of the *Catugna* line leaving after every flight arrival for Alghero, from which there are frequent buses or trains to Sássari.

Fertília's air terminals are at Corso Vittório Emanuele 11, Alghero, and Via Cágliari 30, Sássari.

**Olbia.** Scheduled international flights land at Olbia's Costa Smeralda Airport (✆ 0789.23721)) from Frankfurt, Geneva, Munich, Nice, Paris and Zurich. It also has scheduled connections, usually *less* than one a day, with the Italian cities of Bérgamo, Bologna, Florence, Forlì, Genoa, Milan, Naples, Parma, Perugia, Rome (four times daily), and once daily to Turin, Venice and Verona. Sample one-way fare: Milan-Olbia L184,500.

The airport is only three kilometres from the town, and is connected to the centre by the frequent No.2 bus. The service stops at 2000 but there are always taxis waiting, charging about L15,000 for the trip to Olbia. There is a duty- free shop here.

# MOTORING

The easiest and most comfortable way to see Sardinia is, of course, by car, and bringing your own is sure to work out cheaper than hiring one; petrol coupons available to foreign-registered cars — not rented ones — will also reduce the higher price of petrol in Italy by 15%. You might find it worth investigating some of the deals offered by package companies such as *Citalia*, which pay for the Channel crossing, but not the Mediterranean crossing.

Here are the details on shipping your vehicle over, and see the next chapter for motoring in Sardinia and how to get petrol coupons.

## BY SEA

So you're motoring down to Sardinia, or coming by coach or rail? Either way you'll need to take a ferry for the last stage. There are a number of companies that ply between Sardinia and the mainland, and there are also routes linking the island with Sicily and Tunis, which you might consider as part of a longer tour.

If you're planning to take your car on the ferry, remember that it is essential to *make reservations well ahead*, from January onwards; sailings in July and August especially can be fully booked by May.

### FROM FRANCE DIRECT

Travelling from the French mainland can save you the money that you would otherwise spend on petrol and motorway tolls to reach the main Italian ports, and may also offer greater availability at short notice.

The French company *Société Nationale Maritime Corse-Méditerranée*, SNCM, operates a line from **Marseilles and Toulon** April-September direct to **Porto Torres**, on Sardinia's northern coast near Sássari, though the last Marseilles departure takes place in June. Sailings are weekly and, apart from morning departures in August and September, overnight, taking 9-15 hours. Prices for passengers start at about £25 (half for children up to 11 years old; under-fours travel free), with berths from £10. Cars are carried one-way from £40, depending on size.

The SNCM's UK agency is *Continental Shipping and Travel*, 179 Piccadilly, London W1V 9DB (✆ 071.491.4986).

### FRANCE VIA CORSICA

Another possibility is to sail from either of these French ports, or from the Italian ports of Genoa, La Spezia or Livorno, for Bastia in Corsica, and journey down to the southern Corsican port of Bonifacio. From here there are frequent daily ferry crossings to Santa Teresa di Gallura in Sardinia.

Mainland departures for Bastia with SNCM, Navarma Lines or Corsica Ferries are four or five times a day in high summer, dropping to once weekly in winter. In the summer, there are also departures further south down the Italian coast, if it suits you, from Piombino or Porto Santo Stéfano. One-way prices to Bastia for passengers start at £15 (L30,000), rising to £32 (L68,000) for a berth in a cabin in high season. Cars cost from £15-55 (L30-126,000) depending on size and period.

Bonifacio-Santa Teresa ferries leave all the year round and take just one hour. Tirrenia, Saremar and Navarma are the companies, alternating every hour or two hours from 0900 to 2100 (less frequent in winter). One-way fares are about £6 per person, plus £14 for a medium-sized car.

## FROM THE ITALIAN MAINLAND

**Genoa, La Spezia and Livorno.** Tirrenia and Navarma Lines link these Italian ports with **Olbia**, while Sardinia Ferries lands a few kilometres further north, at **Golfo Aranci**. Average journey-time is ten hours, with frequent departures daily July-August, less in June and September, and once or twice daily most of April, May and October. Other months have twice-weekly departures.

Ferries of the Tirrenia company — Italy's biggest line — also depart from Genoa daily for **Porto Torres**, twice-weekly for **Arbatax**, on Sardinia's eastern coast, and twice or three times weekly for **Cágliari**.

Prices range from £20-£50 (L40-100,000) per person, depending on season, whether or not you take a berth, and which class. You will pay a minimum of £20 for a small car in low season, rising to £80 for a large car in high season. (Prices are slightly higher on the Genoa-Cágliari route.) Navarma and Sardinia Ferries offer 50% discounts for vehicles on certain dates if you book your return when you buy your outward-bound ticket.

**Civitavécchia.** Tirrenia ferries leave Civitavécchia, just north of Rome, for **Arbatax** once or twice weekly taking nine hours. Passenger tickets cost between £12 and £35 (L25-71,000), cars £25-£55 (L57-120,000). There is also a daily **Civitavécchia-Cágliari** service at 2030 (1900 on Fridays between 18 June and 14 September). Tickets cost £16-£45 (L33-96,000) per person, £32-£65 (L67-140,000) for a car.

Italian Railways (FS) also runs a **Civitavécchia-Golfo Aranci** service four times daily during the summer months, less the rest of the year.

**Naples.** Tirrenia ferries sail Friday and Sunday evenings to **Cágliari**, plus an extra Tuesday departure June-September, taking sixteen hours. Fares per person are £15-£50 (L30-110,000), £33-£60 (L67-140,000) for a car.

**Sicily.** Tirrenia leaves Palermo weekly (every Fri Oct-May, every Sun June-Sep) at 1900, arriving in **Cágliari** 0830 the next morning. Tickets cost £13-£45 (L26-98,000) per person, £33-£60 (L67-140,000) for a car.

From Trápani ferries sail every Wednesday at 2100, arriving in Cágliari at 0830 the next day. Prices are the same as those from Palermo.

## AND ON TO AFRICA

**Tunisia.** Tirrenia runs a service **Tunis-Cágliari** every Tuesday, leaving at 2000, arriving Thursday 0830. Tickets per person are from £35, rising to £70 (cabin first class), with £55-£80 for a car.

The **London agent for Tirrenia and Navarma Ferries** is *Serena Holidays*, 40-42 Kenway Road, London SW5 ORA (✆ 071.373.6548/9).

The Elephant Tower still stands guard over Cágliari.

# 4: TRAVELLING IN SARDINIA

## Road, rail, air and sea.

IF YOU INTEND SEEING SOMETHING OF SARDINIA beyond the hotel gate, the best way is to have your own transport, but it's by no means essential. In theory there's no reason why you shouldn't get anywhere you want to on the island, using a combination of public transport and taxis. In practice, the problem lies in linking the bus and train timetables with your own itinerary, and in reaching some of the more inaccessible rural areas.

## INTERNAL AIRLINES

There are frequent daily air links between Cágliari and the island's other two airports at Olbia and Alghero, run by Alitalia's internal arm, ATI, and Sardinia's own Alisarda and Air Sardinia. The high cost of the tickets would suggest that the flights are only intended for the business classes, but quite substantial **reductions** exist on most flights — up to 90% for families, 50% for same-day-return tickets, and 30% for people under the age of 22, for those older than 65, or for anybody travelling during the weekend.

These were the regular basic one-way fares in 1990:

Cágliari-Olbia (30 minutes) . . . . . . . . . . . . . . . . . . L62,000-64,500 (£28)
Cágliari-Alghero (35 minutes) . . . . . . . . . . . . . . . . . . . . . L80,500 (£36)

You can buy tickets at a travel agency or at the airport.
**ATI's** main office in Cágliari is at Via Caprera 12-14 (✆ 070.60107) or call the office at the airport on ✆ 070.240079; ATI has another office in Sássari, at Via Cágliari 30 (✆ 079.234498). For the ATI office at Fertília (the airport for Sássari and Alghero) call ✆ 079.935033. In Olbia, call the airport at ✆ 0789.23721.
**Alisarda's** office in Cágliari is at Via Barone Rossi 27 (✆ 070.669168, 651381), or dial ✆ 070.240169,240111 for its agency at the airport. For Fertília airport (Alghero and Sássari) dial ✆ 079.935043. In Olbia the main office is at Centro Martini, Via G. D'Annunzio (✆ 0789.28016), or call the airport ✆ 0789.52634-00. There is also an area agent on the

Costa Smeralda, at the offices of Sardinia International Travel, La Passeggiata, Porto Cervo (✆ 0789.92225).

**Air Sardinia** has a Cágliari office at Piazza Cármine, 22 (✆ 070.666921,651951), or ✆ 070.240458 at the airport. The Olbia airport number is ✆ 0789.69191.

All of the larger towns, including Nuoro and Sássari, have free bus services between the main office and the airport, details of which should be checked on the spot.

## BUS SERVICES

**Intercity buses.** The most diffuse and widely-used public transport network in Sardinia is the bus and coach system. There is only one island-wide company: **ARST** (Azienda Regionale Sarda Trasporti), its blue-coloured buses linking all the major and minor centres and villages. All towns have ARST bus-stations, *autostazione,* centrally-located, where timetables are clearly written up and there are usually waiting areas and left-luggage offices.

The private company **PANI** provides a slightly higher standard of comfort, and with slightly more expensive fares, for long-distance runs, but only serving the major towns of Cágliari, Oristano, Nuoro and Sássari, and places between. PANI's local agency-addresses are given in the guide.

In addition, there are smaller **local services,** such as Fréccia Catalana, between Alghero and Sássari, and more specific ones like the railway's FS line, which fills some of the gaps in the island's transport network. As a rule these buses depart from and arrive at the ARST *autostazzione,* but they also make stops in the centre of the town or village.

In practice, most bus drivers will stop wherever you ask them to — if they can — but don't assume a speeding bus will stop to pick you up just because you're holding your hand out: pick-up points are more strictly defined and you should check with someone where the stop — *la fermata* — is.

As the roads in Sardinia are generally very good, and no distance is over-long, travelling by bus can be a pleasant and relaxing experience. Remember that most last departures are at around 2030, and that there are reduced services on Sundays and festival-days.

Here are some sample fares and journey-times:

Cágliari-Sássari (ARST) ......................... 4 hours, L12000
Nuoro-Oristano (PANI) ......................... 2 hours, L7,200

## CITY BUSES

For most purposes, towns in Sardinia are quite manageable on foot, but there might be occasions when it saves time and reduces fatigue to jump onto a city bus. On the whole they are fast, frequent and cheap – the normal flat fare is around L700 and routes are usually printed on the bus stop. Buy your ticket before boarding, either from bars or newspaper kiosks anywhere in the city, or the ticket booths at the terminus of the route, and you'll have it punched in the machine once on board.

## TRAINS

Sardinia's railway network can't have changed substantially since the English engineer Benjamin Pierce (sometimes called Pearce, or Piercy) laid the first tracks in 1870. There are only three main lines on the island – Cágliari-Sássari, Cágliari-Olbia and Olbia-Sássari – with subsidiary lines branching off to connect Palau, Porto Torres, Carbónia, and Iglésias.

**Narrow-gauge.** There is also a narrow-gauge line which links the smaller centres of Alghero and Nuoro (change at Sássari for Alghero, Macomer for Nuoro), and two much longer stretches weaving inland from Cágliari and Sássari. The former winds north through the middle of the island, dividing at Mandas, one fork burrowing into the heart of the Barbégia mountains as far as Sórgono (this was the line taken by D H Lawrence when he visited Sardinia in 1921), the other ending up at the eastern port of Arbatax.

The line from Sássari follows a similarly tortuous route, zigzagging all the way east into the mountains of Gallura, passing through Témpio Pausánia before descending to the coast at Palau, the port for the Maddalena islands.

Both lines touch on innumerable hamlets and villages, but the going is so slow that they are of interest mainly for the remote and strikingly desolate landscape they cross, which you might not otherwise see. If you are a railway enthusiast with loads of time to spare, and you don't mind the noise and excruciatingly slow pace, then these inland routes are the ones for you.

Otherwise the railway is very much part of the 20th century, the stations at Cágliari and Sássari having been equipped with computerised information systems for the use and amusement of the passengers.

**Rail classes.** Trains in Sardinia are either *Espresso,* fast; *Diretto,* not so fast, stopping at more stations; or *Locale,* stopping at all stations; though you pay for the distance travelled rather than the category of train. Make sure it's the right one! Also, specify whether you want *Prima Classe,* first class, or *Seconda Classe,* second. First class is marginally more comfortable and always less crowded. Here's an outline of the main services:

| Cágliari | 0650 | 0750 | 1200 | 1350 | 1600 | 1820 |
|---|---|---|---|---|---|---|
| Oristano | 0750 | 0922 | 1304* | 1459 | 1653 | 1922 |
| Macomer | 0841 | 1034 | 1406* | 1600 | 1741 | 2017 |
| Chilivani | 0940 | 1134 | – – – – | 1658 | 1828 | 2112 |
| Sássari | 1030 | – – – – | – – – – | 1756 | 1910 | – – – – |

| Sássari | 0510* | 0700 | 0952 | 1425 | 1625 | 1915 |
|---|---|---|---|---|---|---|
| Chilivani | 0552* | 0745 | 1044 | 1506 | 1705 | 1959 |
| Macomer | 0650* | 0839 | 1158 | 1602 | – – – – | 2105 |
| Oristano | – – – – | 0928 | 1246 | 1650 | – – – – | 2153 |
| Cágliari | – – – – | 1025 | 1400 | 1800 | – – – – | 2255 |

| Sássari | 0510* | 0545 | 0700 | 0952 | 1245* | 1425 | 1625 | 1735 | 2033 |
|---|---|---|---|---|---|---|---|---|---|
| Chilivani | 0552* | 0637 | 0745 | 1044 | 1329* | 1506 | 1705 | 1826 | 2115 |
| Olbia | 0714* | 0756 | 0857 | 1248 | 1439* | 1622* | 1819 | 1947 | 2225 |

| Olbia | 0540 | 0640* | 0718 | 0759 | 0930 | 1420 | 1545 | 1740* | 2005 |
|---|---|---|---|---|---|---|---|---|---|
| Chilivani | 0641 | 0741* | 0828 | 0933 | 1046 | 1526 | 1702 | 1901* | 2117 |
| Sássari | 0743 | 0828* | 0920 | 1030 | 1134 | 1610 | 1756 | 2007 | 2205 |

Services marked ✽ run only on normal working days.

**Other services.** Frequent trains between Sássari and Alghero and Porto Torres; less frequent between Cágliari and Carbónia, with a branch-line for Iglésias leaving from Villamassárgia.

Some Olbia trains run as far the the main ferry terminus at Isola Bianca, saving some lugging around of heavy baggage if you are travelling by boat.

Bear in mind that timetables may vary and that the winter timetable is always modified, so the above times may vary. And be prepared to change trains at Macomer or Chilivani, the two great transport junctions in the centre of the island.

**Fares.** Here are some sample fares:

Cágliari-Sássari L26,700 (1st class); L15,700 (2nd class)
Cágliari-Nuoro L23,500 (1st class); L13,400 (2nd class)
Oristano-Nuoro L11,000 (1st class); L7600 (2nd class)

**Reductions.** There are reductiòns for tourists who plan to spend a lot of time on Italian railways, possibly useful if you are visiting Sardinia in a wider Italian tour.

The *Biglietto di Líbera Circolazione* gives unlimited travel for a set period: e.g. eight days second-class costs about L140,000, or £65. A *Chilométrico* ticket is valid for 3,000km (1,860 miles) and costs about the same. You can buy both of these at frontier stations and outside Italy.

*The Romanesque church of Santa Maria at Tratalias.*

Other offers include a *Circolare,* 'circular' ticket, for at least 1,000km (620 miles) and valid for one month. Restrictions include not travelling through any place twice, and since the cost is not much less than normal rail fares, these tickets are not very attractive to tourists.

Day-return and three-day-return tickets qualify for a discount of 15%, for a maximum of 50km (31 miles) and 250km (155 miles) respectively. A family-card, available for £5 from all BR offices in Britain and at similar prices from other European rail systems, gives half-fares for up to eight people living at the same address, though these should be accompanied by one adult paying the full fare; it's valid for a year. Ten to 24 people travelling together can get up to 30% reduction outside peak travelling times, such as Christmas, Easter and from 25 July to the end of August. The *Carta Verde* gives a 30% reduction to under-26s, available at all Italian stations for L8,000.

## DRIVING

Having your own transport in Sardinia obviously gives you maximum independence to get the most out of the island, especially in the interior where archeological, architectural or scenic attractions are scattered across the countryside.

Apart from some obvious trouble-spots such as the centres of Cágliari, Sássari and Olbia, Sardinia does not share the perennial Italian problem of having too many vehicles in too small a space, so driving need not be the mega-headache that many visitors to Italy find.

The drawback is, of course, financial. Bringing your own car involves costly ferry expenses, and renting is not cheap anywhere in Italy. And then there is the fuel; Italian petrol prices are among the highest in Europe, currently L1,575, or 75p, (DM0.25) for a litre of four-star, or £3.42 per Imperial gallon, $5 per US gallon, though diesel costs considerably less than in the UK. These prices are fixed by the government so are the same everywhere. Your main consolation is that there are no toll roads.

## COST-CUTTING.

There are several ways in which you can reduce your motoring costs:

**In your own vehicle.** Bear in mind that when ferrying your own car over to Sardinia, the smaller it is the less you pay. Also, some companies offer discounts if you buy your return ticket when you get your outward-bound one.

Drivers can also make considerable savings by investing in **petrol coupons,** which give discounts of 15% on petrol and diesel, and on mainland motorway tolls. Coupons are available for all cars bearing non-Italian number-plates at all entry-points into Italy, and at any of the main offices of the Italian motoring organization ACI, the *Automobile Club d'Italia,* but known as 'Atchy,' as well as at some of the larger tourist offices. In Sardinia, the main ACI offices are: Via Carboni Boi 2, Cágliari; Viale Adua 32B, Sássari; Via Piro 9, Olbia; Via Cágliari 50, Oristano; Via Sicilia 32, Nuoro. Their opening hours are 0830-1230 Monday-Saturday.

There are four types of coupon booklet, with numbers 2, 3 and 4 covering Sardinia. The difference is in how much fuel you want to buy; no.2, for example, gives you L120,000 worth of petrol, no.3 L300,000, no.4 L400,000, saving you respectively L74,400, L130,200 and L161,200. Unused coupons can be redeemed at ACI offices, or the larger tourist information offices.

**Hiring a car.** If you rent a car, you can bring down the cost in a number of ways. To begin with, investigate what's on offer before leaving home; some tour companies include a rented car for a period as part of the package; some agents (Pilgrim, for example) also offer special low rates for pre-booked car hire.

Sharing a car is an obvious saver. Using a car for shorter, specific journeys is another expedient, going back to buses and trains for the longer hauls where you can enjoy the scenery without the distraction of remembering which side of the road you're meant to be on.

Finally, pick your car-rental company with care. With all the competition that exists in this field in Sardinia, there is a range of deals on offer from which to choose. For example, if you know you will only be covering a limited distance, it's worth paying less on your daily hire fees and opting for the companies that charge per kilometre; some of them give you the first 100km free. The larger firms may give you unlimited mileage but they also charge higher daily rates. And you may find several firms, such as ACI, Budget, Maggiore and some independents, offering special low weekend rates, from midday on Friday to nine o'clock Monday morning. You can cover a lot in two and a half days.

The major companies well-represented in Sardinia include Avis, Hertz, Budget, Eurodollar, ACI and Maggiore, all of which have agencies at all the airports. As well as these, independent hire companies proliferate in each of the island's major centres and resorts; along with the bigger firms, these have been listed in the guide.

Here are some specimen charges for cars in the cheapest category, i.e. for a Fiat Panda: L30,000 per 24-hour day plus L350 per kilometre; L40,000 a day plus L400 per kilometre but the first 100km free; L85,000 for 12 hours with unlimited mileage; L100,000 per day inclusive with unlimited mileage; L75,000 for a weekend with unlimited mileage — though rates including extras such as tax and insurance waiver generally cost more.

**Hidden extras.** Where prices are not all-inclusive, the customer is expected to pay extra for the Italian equivalent of VAT (IVA, at 19%), and has the option of paying L10-15,000 per day extra for an insurance waiver (*kasko,*) excusing him or her for any damage incurred to the rented car for which he or she is responsible. All other insurance is usually included in the rental fee. Note that the petrol consumed is always at the driver's own expense, though any other maintenance bills such as oil or spare parts, can be claimed back on production of receipts. Also bear in mind that cars taken from an airport usually attract a slightly higher rate, and that most companies — exceptions are Avis, Hertz and ACI — charge up to L40,000 for delivering the vehicle to the airport or any pick-up point other than the office where the car was hired.

**Age limits.** The minimum age for taking out cars is usually 21, sometimes 25, and drivers must have held a licence for at least a year. Deposits are sometimes required, though a blank credit-card payment will often do.

**Driving in Sardinia.** Drivers must carry their driving-licence and **car documents** with them at all times. The wearing of **seat-belts** is compulsory, though many islanders don't appear to have heard. Cars must also have a red **hazard triangle** on board; you can hire one at any ACI frontier office for a nominal fee. Italian **speed limits** are the source of much confusion, most of all to Italians. In 1989 they were changed to 90kph, or 56mph, on all out of town roads, 50kph (31mph) in towns.

The upper 110 and 130kph limits only apply on motorways, which don't exist in Sardinia.

Despite the absence of motorways, roads on the island are very good. All but a few of the minor ones are asphalted.

Here is a selection of Italian road signs:

| | |
|---|---|
| *Alt* | Stop |
| *Senso Unico* | One way |
| *Strada senza uscita* | Cul-de-sac |
| *Senso Vietato* | No entry |
| *Sosta Vietata* | No parking or waiting |
| *Sosta autorizzata* | Waiting only within certain times (indicated) |
| *Passo carrabile* | No stopping — access in regular use |
| *Rallentare* | Slow down |
| *Lavori in corso* | Roadworks ahead |
| *Passaggio a livello* | Level crossing |
| *Entrata* | Entrance |
| *Uscita* | Exit |

**Service stations.** Petrol stations (*un rifornimento* in the singular) are everywhere. Their hours are fairly standard: 0900-1230; 1530-1930. They are closed on Saturday afternoons and all of Sunday, though there is usually one in the area that's open *a turno* — on a rota system; ask a local if you're stuck. In the cities, there is usually at least one station with a cash machine. These are signed *24 ore* and take L10,000 notes; make sure they're not folded or torn or the machine won't operate.

One final point regarding filling-up: don't get the wrong stuff. Petrol is *benzina*, unleaded is *senza piombo*, four-star is *super*, and diesel is *gasolio*.

In the larger towns, particularly Cágliari, **parking** is often difficult and when you find a space in the centre you may have to pay for it. Look around for a meter or a warden issuing parking permits, to be displayed on your screen. The wardens are very observant and can strike seconds after you leave your car, fining you on the spot, but as a permit costs only L500, it's worth being honest at the outset. But if you leave your car too long it will be towed away, and that means a hefty recovery fee.

**Warning.** A few words of warning: never leave objects of value visible in the car when you park it, day or night. This applies to radios too, so if possible remove it and compress the aerial. Most Italians carry their radios under their arms when they leave their cars, provoking much hilarity from foreigners — until they get *their* radios stolen! This is quite a contrast to the other Mediterranean islands of

Malta and Cyprus where car theft is virtually unknown.

Staying in a hotel? Ask the manager where best to leave your car. Staying at a campsite? You should be safe enough.

**Breakdowns.** Should you have any problems on the road, such as a breakdown, your best advice is to get hold of ACI (✆116) which offers a free breakdown service to all cars with foreign number-plates. Otherwise get hold of a mechanic and negotiate a price for the repair – if possible, before he starts; call-out fees can be extremely high.

# TAXIS

Taxis are generally to be found outside bus and train stations and airports, and in main squares. Make sure that the meter is working, or else agree a price beforehand for a longer distance. **Charges** are L2,500-4,000 for the hire, plus L1,000 per kilometre. There are extra costs for carrying luggage, journeys outside the town area, and hire at night-time, Sundays and public holidays.

# ON TWO WHEELS

Sardinia offers some exhilarating terrain for **motor- bikers**, as squads of Germans and Swiss have already discovered. Wearing of helmets has been compulsory in Italy since 1989, and though many Sards ignore the rule, you can expect a heavy on-the-spot fine if you meet the wrong kind of policeman when you're not wearing one. The speed limits for bikes are the same as for cars, i.e. 90kph outside towns, 50 in.

**Push-bikers** (pedal-cyclists) too are much in evidence on the island, despite the sweaty climbs in some of the hilly country. But the manageable distances and numerous shady pausing places compensate. Choose your season well, however; August is probably going to be too hot.

**Hiring cycles.** Outside towns and resorts, there are few hire shops for motor- or pedal-bikes; ask at the local tourist office, or failing that at a retailer. Charges are around L50-70,000 per day (12 hours) for a Vespa; L25,000 for a moped; L18,000 for a mountain-bike; L12,000 for a normal pedal cycle; L20,000 for a tandem. For motorised bikes, insurance is included, petrol isn't, and you must sometimes leave a passport or money deposit as security.

# HITCHING

Most of the people I saw hitch-hiking (*fare l'autostop* is the verb) in Sardinia were schoolchildren on their way home to lunch: very few tourists. There is no reason why you shouldn't try it, though, for there's not the same fear of crime on the island as there is in other parts of Italy. Girls should find it easier, but may attract a certain amount of hassle.

# BOATS

You will need to take a ferry if you are thinking of visiting one of Sardinia's minor islands, San Pietro or La Maddalena. There are frequent crossings, though many more in summer than winter. On foot or with a bike you should never have any problem getting aboard, though with a car you should always buy a ticket and lodge yourself in the queue at least 30 minutes before sailing — more in August. In theory it's first come, first serve, though some Italians have made an art of queue-jumping, and island residents have priority.

Palau is the embarcation-point for **ferries to Maddalena**, with sailings every half-hour or three quarters of an hour. For **San Pietro** you can embark either at Portovesme, near Carbónia, or Caletta, on Sant'Antíocho island. which is joined to the mainland by a causeway; sailings are every hour or two hours. Both crossings take about 40 minutes, and the one-way fares are L1,000 per passenger, L4,000 for a small car.

At all of the major coastal resorts **boat-trips** are available to visit some of the more inaccessible isles off Sardinia's coast, or to explore some of the rocky, indented littoral that you would not otherwise see; you should go on at least one of these trips to get some idea of what you're missing by not having your own yacht. Sardinia has an exceptionally interesting coast, the best bits of which are visible only from the sea. In summer there is a variety of tours on offer, fewer in winter: tickets start at L10,000, increasing according to the length of the ride, and whether it includes a meal — *cena* or *spagghettata* — or some other allurement.

*Away from the crowds: plenty of space on Bithia's beach.*

# 5: WHERE TO STAY

## From holiday village to campsite

SARDINIA HAS A VAST RANGE of tourist accommodation, and your choice will reflect the kind of holiday you want. Once package tourists have made their decision, they need not think any more about it, but independent travellers too can plan ahead and make reservations before departure, either with the help of this book or by finding the relevant details from the Italian Tourist Office. This will at least solve the problem of having somewhere to dump your bags and put your feet up on arrival in Sardinia, and you may also be able to arrange to have transport waiting for you at the airport or port of arrival.

Alternatively, you can ask the local tourist offices when you arrive on the island; in the bigger towns and resorts they generally have English-speaking staff on hand. Even if they don't, they can supply you with a free *annuario,* or directory of available accommodation in the region, with prices, addresses and telephone numbers. Annoyingly, these lists are invariably a year out of date, but usually only the prices change, increasing annually by no more than the rate of inflation.

All prices of accommodation in Italy are strictly regulated by the local authorities, as are basic standards. Do not hesitate to take the matter up with the tourist office if there is any discrepancy.

## HOLIDAY VILLAGES

Holiday villages are large, self-contained complexes set apart from the rest of the island. Also known as tourist villages, they cater for those people who demand the minimum of fuss and bother to satisfy their holiday requirements. Basically they are hotels on a large scale, which offer the fullest range of services, with self-catering options, shops and stores, bars, restaurants and discos. Every convenience is laid on to provide the most soothing environment possible, and even the fatigue of going to the beach is removed by the presence of one or more swimming pools. Guests are unlikely to see much of Sardinia, but they are guaranteed a stress-free holiday.

If this appeals, it is best arranged through a package deal at home: the prices will be a lot less than those paid on the spot, and companies can provide a wad of glossy brochures to give you all the info.

## RESIDENCES

Almost a hotel and a bit less than an apartment, a 'residence' offers small, self-catering apartments in holiday locations, and is comparable with the apart-hotel or hotel-apartment of other countries. It has become an increasingly popular choice in recent times.

For some people this is the ideal combination, not as expensive as a hotel but providing room-service and all the best hotel facilities. The fact that you must do your own shopping will allow you to absorb much more of local life.

Residences are usually only bookable by the week, averaging between L650,000 (£310) and L950,000 (£450) a week for a two-roomed, three-bed apartment, according to season.

## HOTELS

Hotels in Sardinia range from the luxury five-star to the humble *pensione*. At the top end of the market, the five-star establishments are as smart as any you'll find on the continent, and, in the Costa Smeralda region especially, can offer imaginative blends of modern and rustic architecture.

Alas, as elswhere in Italy, the *pensione* has ceased to be a cosy family-run inn, though it has gained in professionalism what it has lost in familiarity. Classified as one- or two-star, it can vary enormously in style and standard of comfort: in Cágliari, for example, the *pensiones* tend towards the seedy, while in other places you might find them providing just the right balance between informality and personal attention.

Sardinia also has a few 'unofficial' hotels which are unclassified in the hotel-directories because they don't advertise themselves as hotels for tax reasons. These are often a godsend when all other possibilities have been exhausted, though they may present problems when it comes to tracking them down. Enquire at other hotels, and even the tourist office will sometimes point you in the right direction if you look pathetic enough.

**Prices.** As for prices, these can vary significantly within one category, and there can also be distinctions between high and low seasons – *alta* and *bassa stagione*. These periods vary from resort to resort, and are marked in the accommodation list supplied by the tourist office; normally, high season can be taken as covering a week over Easter and Christmas, and the period between the beginning of July and the end of August. For the most exclusive five-star establishments, you can pay up to a million lire per night for a double room in high season, dropping to about L650,000 in low. Other sample prices for a double room with bathroom are given below, though bear in mind the wide fluctuations occurring from place to place:

|              | High season | Low season |
|--------------|-------------|------------|
| Four-star    | L190,000    | L150,000   |
| Three-star   | L65,000     | L50,000    |
| Two-star     | L45,000     | L38,000    |
| One-star     | L40,000     | L36,000    |

For half-board (*mezza pensione*) expect to pay the above prices *per person* – plus another 15%; full-board (*pensione completa*) is about 30% more per person.

Note that by law – and this is clearly marked in four languages in the *annuario*, to be flashed in the proprietor's face if necessary – the hotel must provide you with a receipt for the room, and that one person using a double room due to the unavailability of a single need only pay 85% of the full double-bed price. Sardinian hotel-keepers are generally quite scrupulous about this and I have never found one trying to cheat, though of course there is no way of checking whether all singles really are booked up.

## CAMPING

The many campsites in Sardinia are often in the best seaside locations and they are well used by Germans, Swiss and French, although the Brits have yet to discover their attactions. All accept caravans and campervans, and many of the bigger ones have other options available, for example small bungalows, with or without bathrooms. As well as stores, bars, restaurants and pizzerias, the campsites often have tennis courts, discos and play-areas for children.

The problem is that in July and August Sardinian campsites can be extremely packed and hardly the tranquil places they are supposed to be, but the months of June and September see them in a quieter mood. Few are open all the year round: most open around May and close in mid-September. The *annuario* lists from the tourist offices give exact times of opening and closing, but these are not always strictly accurate since campsite owners tend to close when they decide it is no longer economical to remain open.

**Costs.** Prices vary according to their star-category. On average, for a three-star campsite, expect to pay per night around L3,500 for a camping fee, plus L4,000 per person and L3,000 for a vehicle. Under-12s are usually charged about L3,000, and under-3s are not charged. Electricity for a motorised or trailer caravan is an extra L2,000, and hot showers in the communal washrooms are about L1,000 when they are not free.

Bungalows with beds for four plus fridge, cooker, sheets and blankets can be L50-70,000 per night without a bathroom, L60- 80,000 with. Four-berth caravans are sometimes available for rent for about L75-100,000 per night.

Outside the campsites, sleeping out is illegal, though if you do it far enough from sight it may be tolerated provided that there are no complaints.

## YOUTH HOSTELS and *RIFUGI*

Youth hostels — *ostelli* — tend to come and go in Sardinia; you may find most of them closed for indefinite periods due to rebuilding work. It's worth checking in advance which are currently functioning: only three were open in 1990 — in Alghero, Porto Torres, and Bosa, all in the north-west of the island.

Standards of cleanliness in hostels are high, and charges are around L9,000 a night, whether or not you belong to a youth hostelling association. (Note that in August, the hostel at Alghero is almost invariably full.)

Sardinia's highest mountains, the Gennargentu, have at least one *rifugio* or mountain refuge (there's one on Bruncu Spina), available for a small sum. They are little more than huts with rudimentary dormitories and basic cooking facilities, and are of principal interest to walkers. The snag is that they must be reserved in advance: contact the Club Alpino Italiano at Via Foscolo 3, Milan for bookings (✆ 70202.3085 or 7202.3735). On the other hand nobody is likely to turn you away if you arrive without warning. Prices are about L12,000 a night for non-CAI members.

## *AGRITURISMO*

This 'country accommodation' scheme is relatively new in Italy, and so far little-used. *Agriturismo* is comparable with the French *ĝite* system and would be the equivalent of British farmhouse bed-and-breakfasts, though with other meals available too. On the Italian mainland, many *agriturismo* farms offer board-and-lodging in return for some light labour, but in Sardinia the scheme is regarded as part of the tourist industry, and accommodation is more like neat and unpretentious hotel lodging than the tumbledown peasant shacks you might expect.

Although the point appears to be to lure people away from the coasts and into the relatively untravelled interior, in practice many *agriturismo* locations are quite near the sea and within easy reach by car of some attractive beaches. Some of the more enterprising farmers work with local tour groups to offer excursions to caves or archeological sites in the area, or pony treks and walking itineraries.

Those lodgings buried deep inland are perhaps the most interesting, providing outsiders with fascinating insights into the island's rural heart, and giving them the chance to meet farmers and peasants away from the regular tourist circuit. Guests are treated to as much attention as they could possibly want, part of the traditional Sardinian

*The Pisan front on Cágliari's Duomo is newer than it looks.*

hospitality which is still taken very seriously in the country areas.

**Prices.** The prices work out quite economical too. You are offered the choice of basic bed-and-breakfast, *pernottamento e prima colazione;* half-board, *mezza pensione;* or full-board, *pensione completa,* for prices averaging L21,000, L30,000 and L41,000 per adult respectively. Children aged 3-6 pay L13,000, L24,000 and L27,500, while the under-threes pay L9,000, L11,000 and L11,000.

There are scores of houses and farms in Sardinia offering the *agriturismo* option, but they do not advertise themselves and unless you are directed by someone on the spot, it is seldom possible to turn up on spec without a booking. For further information and bookings either consult a local tourist office, or apply to one of the following bodies, in English if you can't write in Italian:

Cooperativa Allevatrici Sarde; Casella Postale 107; 09170 Oristano, Sardinia (☎ 0783.51040/418066).

Terranostra; Associazione Regionale Sārda per l'Agriturismo; Via Sássari 3; 09100 Cágliari (☎ 070.668367/660161).

Turismo Verde c/o Conf. Coltivatori; Piazza San Giuseppe 3; 09100 Cágliari (☎ 070.651909/662501).

It is pointless to supply a list as the cottages frequently come and go from the market.

## ROOMS TO RENT

Rented rooms exist in some seaside resorts, advertised as *camere in affitto.* Normally these come under the eye of the local tourist authorities and so must conform to set standards of hygiene. The advantage is that they are more flexible than hotels, especially with regard to children, but few provide food. Prices vary enormously and are subject to seasonal adjustments; expect to to pay a little less than an equivalent hotel room in the same locality.

# 6: DINING OUT and NIGHTLIFE

## From trattoria to passeggiata

LIFE IN ITALY IS AN OUT-OF-DOORS AFFAIR, and Sardinia is no exception. Whether you are sipping drinks at a pavement bar, or joining the *passeggiata*, the boisterous evening promenade, or sitting down to eat, you are in the full-flow of Mediterranean culture, in which the twin pleasures of seeing and being seen are paramount. Every summer evening the same rituals are observed, when people slip out of shorts and beach-wear and into more formal clothing, suitable for gliding around the piazza or waterfront or main Corso, before settling down at a bar or trattoria. Even the smallest mountain village hums at dusk with the parade of chattering strollers, and though cold weather might dampen their enthusiasm, Italian evenings are often the high-point of the whole day.

## BARS

In summer especially, you will always find yourself in and out of bars. This can be an expensive business, with beers and soft drinks costing around L4,000 if you sit down and have waiter service; you can expect to pay around half this if you go 'self-service' by ordering from the cashier, usually seated opposite the bar, then showing the receipt to the barman or -woman.

What are you going to order? If you just want to slake your thirst, there is nothing more refreshing than a glass of **water,** *un bicchiere di acqua*, which usually means chilled mineral water, either fizzy (*gassata*) or plain (*naturale.*) This costs roughly L500 a glass, so a bottle, for about L1,200, may be more economical. On the other hand you might specify that you want it from the tap, *dal rubinetto*, which is free.

**Coffee** is to the Italians what tea is to the British, and it comes in various forms. *Espresso* is thick and black, *capuccino* milky and frothy. *Espresso* with a drop of milk is *macchiato*, with a drop of spirits, *corretto* − and specify whether you want brandy (*cognac*), whisky (untranslated), the fiery *grappa* (see below), or anything else.

As well as the usual range of **soft drinks,** you can have a sugary fruit juice — *succo di frutta* — or a fruit squeezed in front of you, usually orange or grapefruit — *spremuta di arancia, di pompelmo.* Other drinks in cans include *chinotto,* a sort of Italian Coke, and of course, beer, *birra.* Beer can also be served draught, *alla spina,* and is almost always lager; if foreign brews are available they will be displayed. These are relatively expensive.

Many bars also have a variety of snacks to munch, typically sandwiches, *tramezzino;* rolls, *panino;* or slices of pizza, *pizzetta.* Others have hot-dogs, *wurstel;* chips, *patatine;* or microwaved snacks like pasta and lasagne.

At breakfast time most Italians choose a *cornetto,* a sweet bun either plain or filled with jam or custard. This is not to be confused with a cornetto ice cream — the word means 'horn,' referring to the shape — which is also available in many bars. Another treat you might occasionally indulge in is a *granita,* a crushed-ice drink usually made with coffee — *di caffé* — and topped with whipped cream, *panna,* but sometimes available in lemon, *di limone,* or strawberry, *di frágola,* flavours.

## EATING OUT

Eating out is an important part of any Italian holiday and for some people the best reason for coming to Italy. Food, in fact, is probably the most talked-about subject in Italy, even more than football, and is a guaranteed conversation-opener in any situation. If you want to gain the sympathy of an Italian, just praise his country's cooking, after which you can steal his wife, abuse his country, insult his politics — even laugh at his football team — with impunity. Once again, Sardinia is no exception, and on the whole the *cucina,* cuisine, here — both food and wine — is superior to that of Corsica and much of mainland Italy.

You have a broad choice between the pizzeria, trattoria and ristorante, though many restaurants serve pizzas alongside their main menus. If you opt for a **pizza,** try to find a place that has a wood-burning oven, *forno a legno,* for the crispiest pizzas with a hint of charcoal-flavour.

These are the usual choices, ranging in price from L5-10,000:

*Pizza Margherita,* Cheese and tomato.
*Pizza Napoletana,* 'Neapolitan,' with tomato and anchovy.
*Pizza ai Funghi,* Mushrooms.
*Pizza Cardinale,* Ham and olives.
*Pizza Quattro Formaggi,* 'Four cheeses,' two of which are usually mozzarella and fontina.

*Pizza Quattro Staggioni*, 'Four seasons,' the pizza split into four with a different topping on each section.

*Pizza Frutta di Mare*, Sea food, including mussels, prawns, squid and clams.

*Pizza Cappricciosa*, 'Capricious' – the chef's choice.

*Calzone*, Not, strictly speaking, a pizza at all. Literally, 'sock,' with the dough folded over to enclose a cheese and ham (sometimes tomato) filling.

The difference between a **trattoria** and a **ristorante** is roughly one of style. The ristorante is generally smarter, more formal, giving you linen napkins and waiters in suits. A trattoria is just as likely to be run by a grandmother in an apron. The ristorante will give you a better choice on the menu and will cost more, but the fare need not be any better. In either, you may be offered a fixed-price meal, or menù turístico, generally three-course and giving you good value, though choice of items may be limited. In any case, expect a service charge of about L2,500.

Many places in tourist resorts provide a menu in three languages, but this is a breakdown of what you can expect if you are confronted by just Italian:

*Antipasti*, or **starters,** can include melon *melone;* ham, *prosciutto;* octopus, *pólipo* – either alone or in a seafood salad – or just about anything else, and usually comes to about L6,000.

Your **first course,** *primo piatto*, will usually be a soup, *zuppa*, or rice or pasta dish, costing L6-8,000: *Brodo* is clear broth; *Minestrina* is a light soup with pasta while *Minestrone* is a rich vegetable soup. *Zuppa di pesce* is fish soup, sometimes containing up to a dozen kinds of fish; *Risotto* is a rice dish with vegetables and meat; *Gnocchetti*, the commonest pasta dish in Sardinia, contains small pasta shells, often in a sausage sauce.

*Penne*, in the plural, are small pasta tubes; *Tagliatelle* are pasta strips; *Tortellini* are pasta rings, filled with meat or cheese; *Culurrones* are the island version of ravioli, stuffed with ricotta, mint or spinach.

**Sauces.** The sauce that goes with it can be as simple as butter, *burro*, or tomato, *pomodoro*. If the sauce is not specified, it will usually be a meat and tomato mix, the commonest type served with *Gnocchetti alla Sarda*. Don't expect to find *Bolognese* in Sardinia. If you do, it probably won't be what you expected.

Other sauces include:

*Arrabbiata*, literally, 'angry,' a tomato sauce spiced with chillies;

*Carbonara*, a butter or cream, with ham and beaten egg;

*Pesto,* a dish from Genoa, made with basil, pine kernels and garlic;
*Funghi,* made from mushrooms;
*Frutta di Mare,* a seafood sauce, usually mussels and clams still in their shells;
*Marinara,* also a seafood, with squid, baby octopus and prawns;
*Vóngole* is a clam sauce;
*Arselle* is from mussels, and *Bottarga* is fish roe, usually of grey mullet.

**Second course.** Your *secondo* may be meat, *carne,* or fish, *pesce.*
Here are the commonest **meats,** ranging from L8-15,000:

| | |
|---|---|
| *Scaloppina* | Cutlet, or escalope |
| *Vitello* | Veal |
| *Agnello* | Lamb |
| *Bistecca* | Beef-steak |
| *Bracciola* | Steak or chop, usually grilled |
| *Costata* | Sirloin steak, usually grilled |
| *Involtini* | Meat slices rolled and stuffed |
| *Ossobuco* | Shin of veal |
| *Salsiccia* | Sausage |
| *Pollo* | Chicken |
| *Tacchino* | Turkey |
| *Coniglio* | Rabbit |
| *Cinghiale* | Boar |
| *Capretto* | Kid, often roasted on the spit |
| *Porceddu* | Roast sucking pig |

*The rugged beauty of Capo Fico, San Pietro.*

*Porceddu* is a speciality in Sardinia, sometimes known by its Italian (as opposed to Sard) name of *porchetto*. Traditionally it was cooked in a hole in the ground, lined with burning coals and covered with soil. This method was conceived, so they say, by shepherds to conceal the smells of cooking ill-gotten gains.

**Fish** Fish dishes are often seasonal and, surprisingly, no cheaper than in Britain; they are often much dearer. They may be sold by the plate or according to weight. *Don't be deceived into thinking the prices by weight refer to the whole dish!* The price *all'etto* (100g) is usually about L6,000, and a normal dish would be about four *etti*. Lobster costs twice as much, while a plate of squid might be about L10,000. Here are the commonest on offer:

| | |
|---|---|
| *Acciughe* | Anchovies |
| *Aragosta* | Lobster |
| *Calamari* | Squid |
| *Gámberi* | Prawns |
| *Cozze* or *Arselle* | Mussels |
| *Vóngole* | Clams |
| *Spígole* | Bass |
| *Céfalo* | Grey mullet |
| *Orate* | Gilthead |
| *Saraghi* | Sargo |
| *Triglia* | Red mullet |
| *Pescespada* | Swordfish |
| *Tonno* | Tunny |
| *Anguilla* | Eel |
| *Sógliola* | Sole |
| *Trota* | Trout |
| *Frittata* | Mixed fry-up, usually including squid, prawns, sometimes crab and lobster. |

Fish and meat dishes can be done in a variety of ways: grilled, *alla griglia;* fried, *fritto;* boiled, *bollito* or *lessato;* barbecued, *alla brace;* smoked, *affumicato;* roasted, *arrosto;* baked, *al forno;* on the spit, *allo spiedo;* well-done, *ben- cotto* or under-done, *sangue* or *meno cotto;* stuffed, *ripieno;* or cooked in tomato, *pizzaiola* – on the other hand they may be frozen, *surgelato*.

Main courses never come with vegetables, which must be ordered separately as a side-dish, *contorno*. Most side-dishes cost around L4,000, and the main ones, (mostly given here in the plural), are:

| | |
|---|---|
| *Patatine* | Chips |
| *Insalata verde* | Green salad |
| *Insalata mista* | Mixed salad, with tomatoes, olives etc. |

*Even Sardinia has its heavy industry: this is Portovesme.*

| | |
|---|---|
| *Cetrioli* | Cucumbers |
| *Cipolline* | Little onions, pickled and sweetened |
| *Finocchio* | Fennel |
| *Carciofi* | Artichokes |
| *Asparagi* | Asparagus |
| *Melanzane* | Aubergines |
| *Funghi* | Mushrooms |
| *Fagioli* | Runner or French beans |
| *Fave* | Broad beans |
| *Zucchini* | Courgettes |

**Bread.** Bread, *pane,* will be served whether you ask for it or not — it's included in the cover charge — but butter is separate. Make sure you sample the very thin, crispy stuff, known as *carta di música* in Italian, *carasau* in dialect and 'music paper' in English, so-called because of its wafer-thinness. It's a Sardinian speciality, used by shepherds because it keeps for ever, and can be softened by adding a few drops of water.

**Dessert.** Lastly, you will be offered fruit or a dessert, both around L3,500. Fruit, *frutta,* is seasonal, and not all will be available at the same time of year. The main fruits, given here in their plural forms, are:

| | |
|---|---|
| *Mele* | Apples |
| *Pere* | Pears |
| *Banane* | Bananas |
| *Arance* | Oranges |
| *Mandarini* | Tangerines |
| *Uva* | Grapes |
| *Ciliegie* | Cherries |
| *Fichi* | Figs |
| *Fichi d'India* | Prickly pears |
| *Albicocche* | Apricots |
| *Pesche* | Peaches |
| *Cacchi* | Persimmons |
| *Frágole* | Strawberries |
| *Melone* | Melon |
| *Anguria* or *Coccómero* | Water melon |

You may also be offered a *Macedonia*, or fresh-fruit salad. Other **desserts** – *dolce* – are usually either ice cream, *gelato*, or one of the pre-packaged sweets from *La Sorbettiera di Ranieri*, a very successful line currently flooding the market. These include brown or white *tartufo*, truffles, and *Tiramisù*, a sort of trifle, literally 'pull-me-up.' Another popular line is *Antica Gelateria del Corso*, whose products are a bit classier. Some restaurants may have tarts, *torte*, or gateaux.

Alternatively, you may prefer a plate of cheese, *formaggio*, of which the types most often on offer are *pecorino*, *fiore sardo*, (both hard, crumbly sheep's cheese) and *fontina*, a bland northern Italian cheese.

## DRINKING OUT

What do you drink with your meal? Most Italians automatically order a litre of mineral water, *acqua minerale*, plain (*naturale*) or fizzy (*frizzante* or *gassata*,) often drunk alongside the wine.

The cheapest wine is the local stuff, *vino sfuso* or *locale*, which is about L4,000 a litre. It's worth sampling this as it's different everywhere you go. On the other hand you're never absolutely sure what's gone into it, or whether it's been watered down.

To be sure of quality, ask for the corked and bottled sort, *vino imbottigliato*, which can cost anything from L8,000 a bottle upwards. There is tremendous variety, and you will have the choice between table wine, *vino di távola*, and D.O.C. – *Denominazione di Origine Controllata* – wines which meet certain Italian quality standards. In fact there's no guarantee that a D.O.C. wine is superior to a *vino di távola*, due to the idiosyncratic methods of classification, and it's always worth experimenting, or asking advice.

Among the better D.O.C. wines for less than L10,000 are: Cala Luna, Terre Bianche, Torbato, Seleme, Ladas, Rosato Thaoà, Rosé di

Alghero (both rosés) and Cannonau di Dorgali (red). More expensive wines (L12-15,000) are: Vermentino di Gallura, a slightly sparkling white, excellent with fish or just as a refresher on a hot evening, Anghelu Ruju ('red angel'), strong and sweet, and Brut Torbato. Perhaps the best-known Sardinian wine is Vernaccia – a strong (14°), amber-coloured brew, quite expensive and best from the Monte Ferru area north of Oristano.

Sardinia produces a variety of sweet dessert wines too, usually called *malvasia,* and best from the Cágliari and Bosa areas. *Moscato* is also produced in the Campidano area north of Cágliari.

**Après-Dîner.** And after the meal? You could stay to try something at the restaurant, or you might prefer some fresh air and exercise, in which case you could always work your way round to a bar to have an ice cream or coffee or what the Italians call *un digestivo* – something to settle your dinner. This can be anything, but is usually an *amaro,* literally 'bitter' but in fact quite a sweet liqueur. Everyone has his or her favourite brand: the most popular are *Averna, San Marziano, Vécchio* and *Fernet-Branca* – this last having a real medicinal flavour. If you want something stronger try that Italian fire-water, *Grappa,* guaranteed to jolt you back to life, or one of the indigenous Sardinian stomach-warmers, *Acquavita* or *Acquardente,* widely distilled illegally but a speciality of Villacidrò, Domusnova and Santu Lussúrgiu.

## NIGHTLIFE

If you're still feeling frisky most of the resorts offer some form of nightlife. You want to dance? Then dress up and drop in on a discotheque. The music varies, but is normally the hottest sounds from the continental disco scene. Entrance charges start at L10,000, or if they're free they charge double for the drinks. In the summer, most discos in the towns close up and transfer to the coast, but you would be lucky to find anything happening in the resorts outside the summer.

Some resorts offer other kinds of entertainment during the summer, in the form of open-air films or classical concerts, and these are often free. Consult the tourist office or local newspapers for details.

# 7: FOLKLORE AND FESTIVALS

## And a touch of culture

THE REMOTENESS AND INSULARITY OF SARDINIA and its people have given the island a rich and distinctive culture which has not only survived centuries of oppression but been reinforced by them. Whether it survives the pressures of 20th-cent life is another matter: the gaudier aspects of its folklore are being vamped by the tourist industry to an extent that some might find contrived and repellent. But as yet, there is still enough of a pure rural culture alive in this notoriously introspective island to keep the unique Sard customs and ways authentically alive.

Traditionally, Sard culture has been split between the old shepherds' society and the farmers and town-dwellers. The latter were often outsiders who introduced their own foreign ways into the island, often Spanish, Pisan or Genoan, while the peasants had their own world-view shaped by the cycle of the year's seasons — death and re-birth, growth and harvest.

As you get to know the island and its people you can still find hints of the old animosity between these groups, but nowadays it shows itself more openly in a fierce loyalty to local traditions.

This has made the island's culture a highly-seasoned cultural stew, seasoned by its diverse local ingredients. To the lively exuberance of the mountain-villages have been brought the old Catholic and pagan ways of the agriculturalists and the medieval traditions of the towns and villages.

To the outsider, group-identity is most conspicuous in the local dialects, customs and cuisine. Traditional **handicrafts** are another expression of true folk-culture, such as embroidery, carpet-weaving, basket-making in the Castelsardo area, and the fashioning of cork and coral goods in Gallura and Alghero, where they have become important consumer-items for the tourists. On a day-to-day level, local styles are apparent in the bread, in an island which can boast around 300 varieties — or in the many types of sweets, such as the *sospiros* of Ozieri.

Visitors can gain an insight into the living culture by watching how Sards entertain themselves. **Poetry,** for example, seems to have an enduring place, especially among the shepherd communities, where the long mournful recitations are often accompanied by **music,** traditionally on the *launneddas,* a set of triple pipes particularly common in southern parts of the island. Another rustic recreation is **dancing,** either the slow *ballo tondo,* round dance, in which participants join in a wide circle, or in faster numbers performed in linked pairs.

**Costume.** These dances are often formal occasions when the local costume is worn, recalling bygone days when flamboyant suits and flouncy skirts were the normal costume, though there are still a few elderly folk in mountain villages – in the Gennargentu especially – who wear their distinctive clothes as daily dress. Different in every locality, but often black and white for men, brighter scarlets and greens on women, these costumes are best displayed in the Ethnographic Museum in Nuoro, but if you want to see them worn as everyday clothing, you have two choices: *either* spend time in some of the island's remoter hamlets, *or* preferably, catch them at one of Sardinia's many festivals when the costumes are hauled out of wardrobes, dusted down, and aired in the streets with less self-consciousness that one might expect.

Richly embroidered, heavy with jewellery handed down and accumulated through generations, each elaborate costume might be worth hundreds of thousands of lire, and is the product of a tradition which has borrowed something from every culture that has touched the island, from Punic to Spanish.

**Festivals.** Whatever the brochures might have you believe, Sardinia's local festivals are by no means spectacles staged solely for the tourists. Most have been annual events for hundreds of years, and are still today carefully planned, prepared and talked about for months beforehand. Of course, there is always a commercial element and you can expect to see business in the form of street vendors, stalls and amusements – but there has never been a time when these things weren't present, however pious the occasion.

Some festivals are overtly religious, others have little of religion about them: indeed, some seem to be defying the Church by featuring age-old games and competitions, weird masks and role-reversals, and often revealing some of the old pagan ways lurking at the heart of Sardinian culture. Above all the festivals show the Italian love of everything theatrical, of dressing up and being outrageous, and of overturning the strict codes of normal social behaviour. Even the most solemn of religious events are performed with the same flair for the spectacular, and there's no reason why outsiders shouldn't also join in.

*Maquis, mountains, and a lonely watch-tower on Sardinia's southern coast.*

**Village festivals.** You want to see a little of the real Sardinia? It's well worth going out of your way to catch a festival, even if it's just a small village fair. The fixed events, celebrated almost everywhere on the island, are Carnival, 40 days before Easter; Easter itself; and *Ferragosto*, the feast of the Virgin Mary on 15 August. Apart from these, each town and village has its festival in honour of its patron saint's day, or the harvest, or some event far back in the community's history.

Some celebrations take place on the same date every year, others on, for example, the last Sunday of the month, but remember that changes in schedule can occur at the last minute, so check with the local tourist office for up-to-date information.

**What's happening when?** Sardinia's most famous Carnival carousals are at Mamoiada, Oristano (*Sa Sartiglia,*) Bosa and Támpio Pausánia; May sees the greatest parade of costumes on Sant'Efisio's day in Cágliari, and the medieval pageantry of La Cavalcata in Sássari; August sees Sássari's *I Candelieri* and a host of entertainments at Ferragosto, while Nuoro's display of local costume takes place on the penultimate Sunday of the month. But the smaller affairs can be just as interesting. Below is a list of all Sardinia's main festivities, some of them described more fully in the second part of this book; the list is by no means exhaustive, so you should keep your ears open for other happenings while you're on the island.

## January:

**16–17;** Sant'Antonio's (St Anthony's) day is celebrated in dozens of Sardinian villages, usually with bonfires, since the saint is supposed, Prometheus-like, to have given the gift of fire to men, after he had stolen it from hell. The liveliest celebrations are at the villages of **Abbasanta,** near Oristano, and **Bitti, Lodè, Orosei** and **Lula,** all between Nuoro and Olbia. In Abbasanta, four bonfires are lit, while in Orosei and Lodè, the villagers erect a greasy pole which contestants must climb to reach the prize — a suckling pig at the top.

**19–20;** Among the villages commemmorating Saint Sebastian's day are **Turri** and **Ussana,** both in Cágliari province, and **Bulzi,** inland from Castesardo. Again, bonfires, processions and holy singing are the order of the day, usually ending up with wine and food being shared around.

## February:

**3;** San Biagio's day in **Gergei,** near Barumini (north of Cágliari), sees the festival of *Su Sessineddu,* named from the *sessini* — reed frames on which sweets, fruits and flowers are hung and then tied to the horns of oxen. This is mainly a children's festival, which involves seeing who can eat the most sweets before staggering home.

**Carnival.** Traditionally the Carnival period starts with St Anthony's day on 17 January, but in practice most of the action takes place on the three days ending with Shrove Tuesday. There is nothing specifically Sardinian in Carnival, nor is it confined to any one place on the island. Children everywhere raid their family trunks or, in richer households, get stuff hired or bought for them to wear as fancy dress. A feature of Carnival is the use of masks, of which Sardinia has an impressive range, always producing a somewhat sinister effect. Most Carnival celebrations are unashamedly pagan, though strictly the occasion is meant to be a prelude to Lent, marking a time when 'meat is no longer on the menu. The very name, *carne vale,* means 'farewell to meat.'

In **Mamoiada,** just south of Nuoro, the three-day festival features music, dancing and the distribution of wine and sweets, climaxing in the ritual procession of the *issokadores* and *mammuthones,* repre-senting hunters and the hunted; the *mammuthones* are primeval spirits of nature, clad in shaggy sheepskin jerkins, their faces covered in chilling black wooden masks. On their backs they carry dozens of sheep-bells which they shake, making a jangling, discordant clamour. Meanwhile the 'hunters' lasso bystanders who are forced to give them drinks of wine.

*Sa Sartiglia* in **Oristano** is wildly different, a medieval pageant with much horseback racing, and a jousting competition in which masked and mounted 'knights' try to thrust their swords through a hanging ring, called *sartijia* – a Spanish word which gives its name to the festival. The whole three-day event is directed by the *componidori,* a character hiding behind a white mask and dressed in a fanciful frilly costume.

You may find other strange goings-on during this time at **Bonorva,** between Oristano and Sássari, where a six-day affair includes masked processions, dances and ritual burnings of puppets; at **Bosa,** south of Alghero, another six-day event features theatrical funeral processions and costumed searches for the *Giolzi,* the spirit of Carnival and sexuality; at **Témpio Pausánia** in Gallura, where masks and floats invade this normally quiet mountain-village and another symbolic puppet is burned; and at **Santu Lussúrgiu,** in the mountains north of Oristano.

## March:

March is traditionally a period with little merry-making as it is so close to Lent, but the month does have a rustic festival at **Muravera,** on the coast east of Cágliari, then there's the *Sagra dell'Agrume* taking place on a Sunday (the date otherwise unfixed) to mark the citrus fruit (*agrumi*) harvest. Peasant carts trundle through town, and the people perform traditional Sardinian dances.

## April:

**23;** Several villages on the island celebrate St George's day, notably **Bonnanaro,** south-east of Sássari, which features religious processions and prayers conducted entirely in the Sard dialect; **Bitti,** a mountain village north of Nuoro, which has a horseback procession in traditional costume and performances of the mournful songs of

*The grape-harvest: a tractor with its precious cargo.*

shepherds; and **Onifai,** inland of Orosei (east of Nuoro), with horseback processions, traditional dances and poetic competitions.

**Easter.:**

Easter usually occurs in April and sees various holy processions taking place throughout the island. One of the most dramatic is at **Iglésias,** where processions file through town almost daily for a week, beginning on the Tuesday before Easter. The highlight is a re-enactment of the Passion, with all the local guilds represented.

Other places with distinctive rites include **Sássari; Oliena,** near Nuoro, and **Santu Lussúrgiu,** north of Oristano, where 15th-cent Gregorian chants are sung on Good Friday.

On the first Sunday after Easter, religious processions and musical events take place in **Alghero** and **Valledoria** (near Castelsardo), and the Sunday following sees the climax of three days of events in **Dolianova,** outside Cágliari; **Gavoi,** a village in the Barbágia region south-west of Nuoro; **Mogoro,** south of Oristano; **Sant'Antíocho; Ulássai,** south of Lanusei, on the island's eastern seaboard, and **Villasor,** north-west of Cágliari. This is the feast-day of the black-skinned Saint Antiochus, so festivities should be at their liveliest in the town named from him.

**May:**

May's biggest event, if not the whole year's, is **Cágliari's** feast day in honour of the martyr Sant'Efisio. In one sense this festival belongs to all Sardinia since groups of people in costume, and extravagantly decorated ox-drawn carts come from dozens of villages throughout the island to accompany the image of the saint through the streets of the capital in memory of its delivery from plague in 1656, supposedly the saint's doing. The saint and his colourful entourage make their way as far as his church near the Roman site of Nora, 25 miles (40km) down the coast, the site of his martyrdom. The journey takes two days and is the best chance to see a good selection of the island's costumes on show at the same time − and to join in the fun.

15; **Olbia's** yearly extravaganza commemmorates another martyr, its patron saint San Simplicio, and features fireworks, the distribution of sweets and wine, and various games and water competitions.

**Ascension Day.** The penultimate Sunday of May sees yet more costumed revelry, this time in **Sássari,** though without any of the religious overtones of Cágliari's *festa.* Many of the same costumes that appeared there can be seen at this pageant, *La Cavalcata,* which, as its name suggests, has a distinctly horsey flavour to it, ending in a grand *palio,* or horse-race, in the afternoon. The celebration began with the successful repulsion of Moslem raiders around the year 1000.

**29;** In the countryside outside **Onanì** north-east of Nuoro, traditional Sardinian dances take place for three consecutive days and nights.

**Pentecost.** Another moveable feast, Pentecost Sunday sees the climax of four days of celebration at **Porto Torres,** including an impressive parade carrying the plaster images of martyred saints from the clifftop church of Balai to the famous Pisan basilica of San Gavino. The next day the saints are carried to the sea and there's a huge fish-fry-up. One of the high-points of this festival is a boat-race involving teams from five of the main seaside towns on Sardinia's northern coast, and there is also a costumed parade.

**Suelli,** north of Cágliari, also spreads its celebration of Pentecost over several days, beginning the Friday before, when everybody leaves the town and spends the night in the fields gathering wood, singing, and dancing. The people bring the wood into the town, and light a bonfire on Pentecost Sunday, amid costumed processions and games.

## June:

**2;** the island's most important horse-fair takes place outside **Santu Lussúrgiu,** north of Oristano, around the Romanesque church of San Leonardo.

**15; San Vito,** outside Muravera (on the coast east of Cágliari), honours its saint with three days of spirited feasting.

**24;** St John the Baptist's day, which has taken over a pre-Christian feast-day marking the summer solstice, is celebrated in more than 50 villages all over Sardinia with the usual processions, dances, songs and poetry competitions. Among the villages are **Bonorva,** between Oristano and Sássari; **Buddusò** in the Galluran mountains between Olbia and Nuoro; **Escalaplano,** a mountain village between Cágliari and Lanusei; **Fonni,** Sardinia's highest village, south of Nuoro, and nearby **Gavoi.**

Fonni hosts another festival on the second Sunday in June devoted to the 'Blessed Virgin of the Martyrs' – *Beata Vergine dei Mártiri.* Costumes and processions on horseback are the main items on the menu.

**29;** Saints Peter and Paul are commemmorated in a score of Sardinian villages, notably **Ollolai** and **Orgósolo,** both south of Nuoro; **Terralba,** south of Oristano, and **Villa San Pietro,** on the coast south of Cágliari.

## July:

**6–8;** Sards celebrate their love of horses with characteristic gusto in the three-day *S'Ardia di Costantino.* In honour of the Eastern Roman emperor Constantine, this *festa* is held at **Sédilo,** between Oristano and Nuoro, and attracts thousands of fans, not least because of the reckless horse-racing that takes place, guaranteeing plenty of thrills and spills.

**25; Orosei,** on the coast east of Nuoro, holds one of the most important of the island's many poetry competitions, in which contestants recite or sing verses, usually mournful dirges about shepherds

*Tranquility on the quayside at Carloforte, San Pietro.*

and wounded honour.

**31;** there are three days of frolics at **Musei,** just off the Iglésias—Cágliari road, in honour of the founder of the Jesuit order, Saint Ignatius of Loyola *Sant'Ignazio;* it has all the usual festival paraphernalia, usually beginning on the nearest Sunday to the 31st.

**August:**

This is the month when tourists flood into the island, emigrés return for the summer, and all the resorts devote every last *lira* to entertainment. The high-point comes in the middle of the month with Ferragosto, a bank holiday that is celebrated more exuberantly than Christmas.

**First Sunday;** on the first Sunday of the month **Bosa,** between Oristano and Alghero, hosts various events in honour of Santa Maria del Mare, with an emphasis on the water, including a river procession and various water-sports.

**15;** mid-August, or *Ferragosto,* is the day when villages all over Italy erupt with dazzling fireworks displays to mark the festival of the Madonna: the Assumption, or *Assunta.* In Sardinia, some traditional Ferragosto celebrations are coupled with another festival, as in the case of the most spectacular of them all, at **Sássari,** which had its origin in a vow made in the 15th cent when plague was averted in the city by divine intervention. The event starts on the 14th and takes its name – *I Candelieri* – from the huge church candles carried through thronged streets amid much dancing and delirium. Each candle represents one of the city's main guilds, whose traditional colours are emblazoned on the candlesticks as well as on the members themselves, along with various tools and symbols of the trade.

A similar *festa* is held in the nearby village of **Nulvi,** also starting on the 14th, but with just three candles (here representing shepherds, farmers and craftsmen) which are preceded by 12 monks representing the apostles, singing medieval hymns. In Nulvi the Madonna herself is wheeled around town on the 15th, and there follows some sort of religious ceremony every day until the 22nd.

In **Golfo Aranci,** north of Olbia, the regular Ferragosto festivities are combined with a *Sagra del Pesce,* a sort of fishing *festa,* when much seafood is eaten.

Other Ferragosto shows worthy of mention are at **Dorgali** and **Orgósolo,** both in the Nuoro region, and **Guasila,** north of Cágliari.

**Penultimate Sunday** of August; this is when **Nuoro's** annual festival features a procession up to the statue of Christ the Redeemer on top of nearby Mount Ortobene. The biggest of the festivals in Sardinia's mountainous Barbágia district, it includes the most important of the local costume competitions.

**29;** St John the Baptist has a second holy day celebrated in several villages, notably **Orotelli,** west of Nuoro, and **San Giovanni di Sinis,** on the lip of land west of Oristano.

**September:**

Formerly the first month of the year according to the old Sardinian calendar, September marks the return to work and is the traditional time for contracts to be sealed and marriages made.

**First Sunday;** the lagoon town of **Cabras,** near Oristano, re-enacts the safe delivery of the statue of the local saint from raiders in the 16th cent, when an army of young men slip off their shoes and, dressed all in white, sprint the five miles (8km) from the saint's sanctuary into town with the saint borne aloft.

**7;** two separate processions take off from **Bortigali,** near Macomer, to a sanctuary six miles (10km) away in the mountains, the location for dances, picnics and poetic competitions over the next nine days.

**8;** the Madonna is venerated again in **Ales,** a village south-east of Oristano, when she is brought out amid much fanfare no less than six times in three days.

**Second Sunday;** not for the first time in the year, the banners and bunting are strung across the narrow lanes of **Bosa's** old centre, in which, once the religious formalities are out of the way, tables are laid and the celebrants eat and drink their fill.

**Last Sunday;** the end of five days of festivities takes place at **Decimomannu,** outside Cágliari, which is said to attract more than 100,000 devotees every year to pay their tributes to Santa Greca.

*The castle of Monreale is a postman's nightmare.*

### October:

**4;** nestled in the mountains between Nuoro and Olbia, the villagers of **Alà dei Sardi** take to the fields and pass two days attending open-air masses, eating and feasting in honour of St Francis.

**Last Sunday;** the *Sagra delle Castagne,* or chestnut fair, is held at **Aritzo** in the heart of the Barbàgia mountains. The smell of the cooking nuts fills the air around here for days.

### November—December:

The end of the year is a lean time for outdoor festivals, though there are a few saints remembered, notably St Andrew on the last day of November.

**1—2 November;** this is *Tuttisanti,* or All Saints Day, a public holiday, and is followed by the Day of the Dead, a time of mourning observed all over the Catholic world. Families troop to the local cemetery and the graves of their loved ones; in parts of Sardinia, the table is laid and the dead person's favourite dishes are served up and left overnight. Apparently, just the odours are enough to satisfy them.

**Christmas.** Christmas Eve and Christmas Day, comparatively recent introductions, are important dates in the island's calendar, though not the big commercial affair they are in some countries. It is primarily a family event; fish is normally eaten on Christmas Eve, and lamb is the traditional fare on Christmas Day, followed by *panettone,* a dry, sweet cake.

# 8: LANGUAGE and DIALECT

## An island of islands

IT IS ONLY A LITTLE MORE THAN 100 YEARS since Italy became a united country, and what is now known as standard Italian was originally the *parole* of an educated elite deriving from a literary Tuscan dialect. In fact each of the regions of Italy speaks its own local dialect which has only very recently taken second place to 'standard' Italian.

But in the family or informal social circles, the dialect is often the language that is instinctively spoken. The island of Sardinia, splendidly isolated in the middle of the Mediterranean, has a dialect so different that it is virtually a separate language from Italian. Not only the island, but every *area* of the island, almost every *village*, has its own variation, as you might expect in a place that is both mountainous and, from ancient times, poorly integrated. These local strains will include a mixture of ingredients according to each area's particular history.

**Historical quirks.** Thus on the isle of San Pietro in the south west of Sardinia, a strong Ligurian dialect is spoken, a reminder of its settlement by a colony of Genoans who came in 1737 at the invitation of King Carlo Emanuele III. Around the same time there was a wave of immigration from Corsica into the northern region of Gallura, which still retains a dialect close to that spoken in the southern parts of Sardinia's sister-island. And the people of Alghero still speak a variety of Spanish Catalan 500 years after the Aragonese king made the town his main base for the conquest of Sardinia and flooded it with Catalonians. Visitors there cannot fail to notice the 'foreign' street-names in the old quarter, even if they cannot distinguish the differences in speech.

**Spanish in Sardinia.** The influence of Castilian Spanish is widespread throughout the island — hardly surprising in a place that was a colony of Spain for 300 years. Spanish permeates all the various dialects, but the evidence is also on maps, where you will see examples such as *rio* used for a river, where the Italian would be *fiume*.

*The elegant Palau Reial, an old Jewish palace in Alghero.*

**Latin in Sardinia.** Interestingly, the Sard dialects often have large chunks of Latin in them, a residue of the much older Roman occupation. 'House,' for example, which in Italian is *casa*, is called *domus*, the same as in Latin. The words for 'the' in northern Sardinia – *su* and *sa* in the singluar, *sos* and *sas* in the plural – are derived from the Latin noun-endings. In the south of the island, 'the' is *is*, from the Latin *ipse*. Again, you'll find many examples on the maps.

The region which has the greatest use of Latin in its dialect is Logudoro, once covering the north-eastern quarter of Sardinia. Its people boast of speaking the purest form of dialect, which in effect means the form least corrupted by later influences.

**An island of islands.** Added to the insularity of islanders, Sards have a particular reputation for being *isolani,* meaning that they are not only insular but a closed and introspective people, with little interest in anything beyond immediate concerns. Whether or not this is still true today, the trait has influenced – and been influenced by – the local variations in speech. Within the artificially imposed provincial boundaries of Cágliari, Sássari, Olbia and Oristano, Sardinia is a mixture of diverse regions – Campidano, Arborea, Logudoro, Gallura, the Iglesiente and Barbágia, among others, each with distinct traditions and a fierce awareness of its differences from the others.

The use of dialect became not just a colloquial mode of speech but a symbol of local solidarity, and Sards have always been able to identify each other's birthplace just by listening.

**Italian in Sardinia.** The result of this linguistic mix is that Italian has become the only means for people of different areas of the island to communicate effectively, and they have learned it, as a foreign language is learned, to perfection; some people claim that Sards speak the most correct form of Italian anywhere. Television, of course, has also played its part, and it is extemely improbable that you could now find a non-Italian speaking Sard.

**English in Sardinia.** But what about visitors who don't speak Italian? The average islander's knowledge of English is not great, at least among the older generation, partly because there has always been a stronger tradition of studying French in the schools. But this shouldn't pose a problem: for a start it's pleasantly surprising how much can be communicated by the use of body language alone — hand and face movements, shrugs, smiles, and miming — and *that's* an art at which Italians excel.

But in all the tourist areas, staff in bars and hotels know enough to understand your basic needs, while the larger hotels always have some staff who speak English. Tourist offices in the main centres too will usually have someone around who speaks broken English, though remember that they also have German and French to contend with, so don't be too impatient! In any case they have reams of tourist literature printed in English, enough to provide most of the basic information you could want.

**Learn some Italian!** At the same time, tourists who are interested in Sardinia and the Sards will find their experience greatly enriched by some attempt to learn the basics of Italian. Even if you learn only a few sentences from a phrase book, and can just about ask for a glass of water, it makes you feel less helpless. Not only that, but your efforts are appreciated by the islanders, who will view you more like an individual, and less like another faceless holidaymaker.

You will have found the odd word and phrase slipped into these pages which I hope may prove useful, but there is too much basic vocabulary to be included here. Your best bet is to pick up a cheap pocket-sized phrase book, available at airports and some book-shops in Sardinia itself. The rules of pronunciation are easy: pronounce each syllable of every word, and the louder and clearer the better. Italians are by nature an effusive people, and they can never understand why the British are always muttering instead of singing out whatever they have to say (remember that opera is an Italian invention).

The stress on a word normally falls on the penultimate syllable: if not, there is an accent to show where it goes. Thus it is not Cagli*ari* or Sas*sari*, but C*á*gliari and S*á*ssari. (But note that vowels are always sounded separately even when they're together, so that the stress in *pizzeria,* for example, falls on the second *i,* the last syllable but one as well as the last vowel but one.) It's not customary to put accents on capital letters, so I've not done it either.

*Immaculate carving on the splendid Romanesque church of Santa Trinità di Saccárgia.*

# 9: SARDINIA THROUGH THE AGES

## From *nuraghi* to NATO

NOBODY KNOWS WHERE THE ORIGINAL SARDS CAME FROM. Were they the followers of Sardus, claimed to be the son of Hercules? Or were they descendants of the Libyan Shardana people? The island's name could have come from either of these sources, or neither – we don't know. But the earliest history of island, the part we know least about, is also the most intriguing as it saw the building of the *nuraghi,* the mysterious remnants of which are still scattered across the landscape of modern Sardinia.

Of all the vestiges of Sardinia's 4,000-year history, only the *nuraghi* truly belong to the island in the sense that they are unique. Dating back to a time before the island was a prey to foreign invaders, they have become enduring images of the true, unconquered Sardinia.

## A PREHISTORIC LANDSCAPE

So what *is* a *nuraghe?* In simple terms, it is a stone-built dual-purpose fortress and home, with a circular ground plan but tapering inwards towards the top and so looking like a cone with the point cut off. The majority of such structures were built between 1500 and 500 BC; the bigger ones have several chambers on two or three levels, but all are crudely built of the same rough stone yet strong enough for them to be still standing today after some 3,000 years.

You can see nuraghi are everywhere in Sardinia – on roadsides, perched on hills, stranded amid a sea of *maquis,* often in places which seem to have been chosen for their pointlessness. All this adds to the mystery surrounding them and deepens their hold on our imagination. Although the island is thought to have about 7,000 of these cones, archeologists have estimated that up to 30,000 could have been built, the majority pulled down to provide material for later houses.

So we in the 20th century must close our eyes to visualise a landscape dominated by these structures that appear so curious to us, but which must have been the normal architecture of the time, whether as houses, shops, palaces or castles.

**Giants' Tombs and Fairy Houses.** Traces have been found in Sardinia of older cultures too, notably from cave paintings of the paleolithic era, and the so-called *Domus de Janas,* literally fairy-dwellings but actually tombs, hollowed out of the rock and most common in the **Sássari—Alghero** zone. The biggest is the **Anghelu Ruiu** complex outside Alghero, dating from about 1750BC.

The other major phenomena from this dawn of Sardinian history are the 'Giants' Tombs,' *tombe di giganti,* thought by the locals to have been the burial places of their gigantic ancestors; actually they were collective burial-grounds for the Nuraghic culture and are common in the area around **Macomer,** and you can also visit some near **Arzachena** north of Olbia.

**Statuettes.** Probably the most pleasing traces left to us of the Nuraghic civilisation are the statuettes and other pieces which are now in the island's museums. Diminutive, full of charm and character, they are without doubt the most exciting things to be seen in Cágliari's rich archeological museum.

But the most numerous and most conspicuous relics are the *nuraghi* themselves. The biggest ones are all in the heart of the island: at **Su Nuraxi,** outside Barumini; **Losa,** near Abbasanta, and **Sant'Antine** between Macomer and Sássari. These are usually fenced and locked up outside set opening times, and two of them were closed for repairs on my last visit.

The smaller *nuraghi* are always open to anyone with the determination to find them. Among the more interesting are Peppe Gallu in Uri, near Sássari; Palmavera, west of Fertília; Serra Orrios, near Dorgali, and Bruncu de Madili near Gésturi (north of Cágliari), though a little enterprise and the ability to go a few kilometres off the beaten track will reward you with many more.

**Power struggle.** The culture reached its peak between the 10th and 8th cents BC, trading abroad and cultivating at home, but its fate was sealed when Sardinia became caught up in the commercial and military rivalries of other Mediterranean powers. Henceforward, the island was rarely to be left in peace, an inevitable consequence of its position in the middle of the busy trading routes between Italy, North Africa and Spain. From Italy came the Etruscans and Romans, later the Pisans and Genoans; the African coast was the springboard for the Carthaginians, then Moslem raiders, while Spain held the island in its grip for 300 years.

## THE CLASSICAL ERA

From the eastern Mediterranean, **Phoenicians** first began trading in Sardinia around 900BC, and soon established peaceful commercial bases. Carthaginians and Romans later settled in some of these outposts and enlarged the most important sites which are still to be seen today at **Nora,** south-west of Cágliari, and **Tharros,** west of Oristano.

From the 6th cent BC onwards, the main protagonists on the scene were the much more warlike **Carthaginians,** whose capital was less than 160 miles (200km) away across the Mediterranean, near present-day Tunis (see *Discover Tunisia* in this series). Intent on drawing Sardinia into their sphere of influence, the Carthaginians proceeded to wipe out as much as they could of the Nuraghic culture, and were stopped only by the need to concentrate on the new military threat to their power, the Romans. The few Carthaginian traces on the island include the two necropolis sites at **Cágliari** and **Sant'Antíoco,** and the fort at Sirai, near Carbónia.

Eventually, in 259BC, the thrusting new power of **Rome** was turned against Sardinia itself, and the Sards struggled against the new aggressors as fiercely as they had against Carthage. Their inevitable defeat occurred in 177BC, in a battle during which 12,000 of the islanders were slaughtered. The survivors who refused to yield to Roman supremacy fled into the impenetrable central and eastern mountains of the island where they kept their independence, in an area the Romans called *Barbaria,* known today as Barbágia.

## THE ROMAN OCCUPATION

Under the Romans, Sardinia became a *provincia* and was bled of its tax revenue and its resources – minerals and agricultural produce mainly, especially grain – without any great benefit going to its people. Although the island was rewarded for supporting Caesar's side in Rome's civil wars, little was done during seven centuries to instill Roman values or develop the island. The attitude of the Romans was summed up in the use they found for it as a place of exile for 'undesirable elements,' including 4,000 Jews sent by the emperor Tiberius, and early Christian subversives; these latter helped to spread the Gospel in Sardinia.

Apart from some impressive remains at Nora and Tharros, traces of Roman building on the island are few when compared with Sicily. The most notable are at **Porto Torres** – including a bridge that is still in use – and the amphitheatre at **Cágliari**, then called *Karalis*. But Rome's greatest legacy to Sardinia is probably the strong Latin element that can still be heard today in the Sardinian dialect.

## THE MIDDLE AGES

With the disappearance of the Roman empire in the 5th cent, Sardinia shared the fate of other former territories in becoming vulnerable to barbarian raids and plundering that reached far inland.

For a short period the island was held by the Vandals, then, after 552AD, by the **Byzantines.** It was too distant an outpost of far-off Byzantium (present-day Istanbul) to benefit greatly from this new rule, though the island received some help in fighting off raiding Goths and Lombards from the European mainland, as well as the Saracens from north Africa. The only significant monument of the Byzantine era is the church of **San Saturnino** in Cágliari.

**Dark times.** Raids from the new Moslem empires on Africa's northern shore were to continue sporadically for more than 500 years, and had the long-term effect of driving the people away from the island's coasts; today, travellers in southern Sardinia in particular can hardly fail to notice the scores of **watch- towers** along the shoreline, built to warn against these attacks. Most towers date from a later era, when the Spanish ruled the island, but fear of sudden death or slavery at the hands of the corsairs was a fact of life in Sardinia and other mid-Mediterranean islands throughout this period; see *Discover Malta* in this series for some extreme examples.

Another reason for the move inland was the increasing prevalence of **malaria** on the coasts and lowlands, encouraged by neglected irrigation works, deforestation, and the silting-up of rivers. From this combination of marauders and malaria dates the downgrading of agriculture on the island, and the rise of sheep and livestock farming in the safe highland pastures of the interior.

**The *Giudicati.*** One survival of Byzantine rule was the system of *giudicati* into which the island was divided for administrative purposes. There were four main *giudicati:* Cágliari, Arborea, Torres (or Logudoro), and Gallura, each a small kingdom with an elected monarch — originally a judge, which is the meaning of *giúdice.* The *giudicati* survived all through the Middle Ages and became the focus of resistance to the Spaniards when they first arrived.

**Pisa and Genoa.** In the meantime the Sards were finding themselves out-manoeuvred in a game of alliances played between the two competing Mediterranean trading cities of Pisa and Genoa. The **Pisans** were first on the scene, having been granted ecclesiastical rights over Sardinia in the 11th cent. Their influence was mainly in the south, based in Cágliari where the defences they built around that city's citadel still stand. But the other Pisan remains in Sardinia — a series of remote and beautiful churches — can be found throughout the island. Among the most striking are **San Gavino** in Porto Torres; **Santa Giusta,** outside Oristano, and two marooned in the middle of the countryside: **Santa Trinità di Saccárgia,** south-east of Sássari, and **San Pietro di Sorres,** a little to the south, both as if transplanted ready-built from mainland Italy.

**Aragon and Eleanor of Arborea.** By the end of the 13th cent, the balance had swung entirely in the favour of **Genoa,** whose power-

bases were in Sássari and the *giudicato* of Logudoro. But when Pope
Boniface VIII gave James II of Aragon exclusive rights over both
Sardinia and Corsica in exchange for giving up his claims over Sicily,
**Spain** entered the scene. The 14th cent saw continual fighting
between Aragonese forces and the alliance between Sards, Genoans
and the mixed-blood aristocracy that held much of the north of the
island. The islanders' cause was led by the *giudicato* of Arborea, the
region around Oristano, and championed in particular by **Eleanor of
Arborea,** who was not only a warrior along the lines of Boadicea or
Jeanne d'Arc, but granted Sardinia its first written Code of Laws, the
*Carta di Logu,* which the Spanish afterwards extended throughout the
island, and it remained in force for the next four centuries.

Despite numerous betrayals, including the defection of her husband to the enemy, Eleanor succeeded in stemming the Aragonese
advance, but after her death in 1404, Sardinian resistance crumbled
and the Aragonese triumphed.

## SPAIN, and the KINGDOM OF SARDINIA

In 1479 the Spanish kingdoms of Aragon and Castile were joined by
the marriage of Ferdinand and Isabella, and Sardinia became a
colony of a united Spain. Like Sicily, the island was ruled by viceroys
who had no interest in the island's welfare and in any case were
unable to make any improvements in their short three-year terms. In
consequence, the three centuries during which Spain ruled Sardinia
left many traces, though few of great significance. The overall result
was a generous infusion of Spanish into the island's dialects and a
heavy sprinkling of Gothic and Baroque architecture in churches and
other buildings.

The most remarkable example of Spanish penetration was at
**Alghero,** where the people still speak a strong Catalan dialect, and
the whole town has the air of an island out of the mainstream. Other
specific traces of Spain in Sardinia are in **Sássari,** particularly the
elaborate baroque façade on the city's cathedral, and the town of
**Iglésias.** Positive benefits included the construction of the defensive
towers that still line Sardinia's shores today, and the foundation of two
universities, in Cágliari and Sássari.

But on the whole Spain had only a superficial impact on Sardinia,
and the period is a barren one in the island's history. Relegated to an
exploited and deprived backwater, abandoned to the malaria that
was sapping its vitality in all but the highest points, Sardinia sank into
lethargy and decay.

**The Kingdom of Sardinia.** As Spain itself declined, events
elsewhere in Europe began to touch on Sardinia's destiny. During the
War of the Spanish Succession (1701-20), an English fleet bombarded
Cágliari in 1708 and briefly occupied the town. The English, with

Dutch allies, also seized Gibraltar during this war (See *Discover Gibraltar*). Treaties followed, first ceding Sardinia to Austria, then, according to the Treaty of London of 1720, to Victor Amadeus, Duke of Savoy, a territory on the French-Italian border. The duke's united possessions became the new **Kingdom of Sardinia**.

Now a period of reconstruction began, with the opening of schools, investment in industry and agriculture, and the building of roads, not least the Carlo Felice highway that runs the length of the island from Cágliari to Porto Torres — today the SS 131. Although discontent simmered constantly, occasionally boiling over into open revolt led by such characters as **Giovanni Maria Angioy,** an aristocrat who championed the rights of the poor against the injustices of the feudal system — even at one stage capturing Sássari — all the same, Sardinia enjoyed a period of comparative prosperity in which the population grew and the economy improved.

**Napoleon and Nelson.** But Sardinia's links with the House of Savoy had certain drawbacks. Savoy's quarrels became Sardinia's, and in 1793 the island found itself threatened by **Napoleon,** who personally led an unsuccessful attempt at invasion. Later, **Horatio Nelson** spent 15 months cruising around the island's coasts in the hunt for the French fleet that led up to the rout at Trafalgar in 1805. Nelson's dispatches showed a strong affection for Sardinia and its people, though he was also interested in the island as a potential British base.

"God knows," he wrote, "if we could possess one island, Sardinia, we should want neither Malta, nor any other: this which is the finest island in the Mediterranean, possesses harbours fit for arsenals, and of a capacity to hold our navy, within 24 hours' sail of Toulon. . ."

Sardinia was not to become British, and at the century's end Nelson had driven Napoleon's troops from their two-year occupation of Malta. "I now declare that I consider Malta as a most important outwork to India. . ." Nelson wrote (see *Discover Malta*).

Sardinia's most noteworthy Savoyard kings in the 19th cent were Carlo Felice (1821-1831) and Carlo Alberto (1831-1849), whose names have been given to streets in practically every village of the island. The first concentrated on modernising the island's infrastructure while the second was responsible for abolishing the feudal system in 1836. Although this led to bitter conflict over the introduction of enclosures to mark the boundaries of private land in the mountains, and so limited the ancient liberty of shepherds to wander freely in search of fresh pasturage, it was an essential prelude to rural reform.

# ITALIAN UNIFICATION and MODERN TIMES

The end of the Kingdom of Sardinia came with the unification of Italy in 1861, when Vittório Emanuele II, son of Carlo Alberto, became Italy's first king (1861-1878). Sardinia played a small part in the unification, the *Risorgimento,* not just because Vittório Emanuele had previously been King of Sardinia, but also because the man who played a crucial role in uniting the country, **Giuseppe Garibaldi,** set out on both his major expeditions from his home on one of Sardinia's outlying islands, **Caprera**. His tomb lies here, in the grounds of his house, which is now one of Sardinia's most intriguing museums.

Sardinia's problems entered a new phase with unification. Adjusting to its role as a part of a modern nation-state has been the main theme of recent times, and attempts to force it to integrate into the new centralised, bureaucratic Italy created a host of resentments whenever old and traditional ways came up against the new. The phenomenon of **banditry,** for example, associated with the hinterland and the Gennargentu mountains in particular, was largely the continuation of old habits into the new age. But the new State ruthlessly suppressed these outbreaks of lawlessness and, as there was little money available to deal with the causes of the problem, and the new rulers had even less interest in trying to do anything, the problem persisted.

**Mussolini.** Ironically, Sardinia had to wait for a ruthless dictatorship before real changes began to make themselves felt. Mussolini saw the backward island as fertile ground for his socal and economic experiments, and in the 1920s began a series of schemes which made genuine improvements. The island's many rivers were harnessed and dammed to provide irrigation as well as power, land was drained and made fertile, agricultural colonies were implanted to exploit the new resources, and the new towns of **Carbónia** and **Fertília** were founded.

**World War and Autonomy.** Sardinia contributed notably to both world wars, with the **Sássari Brigade** in particular achieving lasting distinction during World War II. The island also suffered as a result of its participation, and Cágliari received some of the heaviest bombing of all Italian cities in 1943. Traumatised, the island awoke to a post-war era which seemed all too familiar. Once more it felt itself to be a second-class member of the Italian state, enduring a new form of colonialism within the national frontiers.

Some attempt to offset this came in 1948 when the *regione* of Sardinia received the autonomous status also given to Sicily and two other areas on the Austrian and Yugoslav borders; this gave the regional government direct control over such areas as transport, tourism, police, industry and agriculture.

Two years later the central government's fund to speed up the development of the South of Italy, the *Cassa per il Mezzogiorno,* was extended to Sardinia, which began to receive hefty injections of capital for investment in the island's economy. Perhaps more significantly, through the intervention of the US Rockefeller Foundation, Sardinia was saturated with enough DDT in the years immediately following World War II to rid it once and for all of malaria, the centuries-old scourge that had always undermined every local initiative.

## SARDINIA TODAY

The success of this combined effort to haul Sardinia up from the equivalent of a 'developing' country in Asia, is apparent everywhere, and some areas of Sardinian life are as streamlined and sophisticated as anywhere on the mainland. Today's visitor to the island will see a piece of Italy — the same shops, the same cars, the same language — to the extent that it is getting daily harder to distinguish 'the real Sardinia' underneath the Italian gloss.

But this doesn't mean that the Sards are completely satisfied with their lot. Historically the island has had little in common with events on the mainland, and economically it no longer needs the small change offered by the new prosperous Italy. With Italy's entry into the European Community, Sardinia finds itself more marginalised than ever, and there exists a great deal of rancour directed at the central government which has imposed on the island, among other things, one of the largest **NATO** concentrations in the Mediterranean.

**Action Party.** Campaigning against this presence, and in the longer term for complete independence, is the *Partito Sardo d'Azione,* or Sardinian Action Party, a local separatist party with about the same degree of electoral success as Britain's Plaid Cymru (Welsh Nationalists). After all, they argue, if Malta can exist independently, why not Sardinia?

The island also has its share of internal problems, including the wholesale degradation of its natural environment — the result of hunting, the depredations of industry for short-term profit, and uncontrolled building in some of the most beautiful spots. With the Aga Khan's development of the Costa Smeralda in the 1960s, and the subsequent opening-up of the tourist industry, Sardinia has found a new place on the map, and a new path to follow. But the price for a people determined to preserve its culture and identity is a high one: for all its attempts to harmonise with the surroundings, the average modern tourist complex has little in common with the primitive rugged solidity of the *nuraghi.*

# 10: THE GREAT OUTDOORS

## Wildlife and outdoor activities

SARDINIA HAS PLENTY TO INTEREST the outdoor enthusiast, apart from the obvious attractions of sun, sand and sea.

**Hiking and walking.** The diversity of the landscape, from rocky shore to upland plain, from bare mountains to lush river valleys, plus the vast regions of *maquis,* all broken by stretches of thick forest, holds enough interest for a dozen holidays, and the island is becoming increasingly popular with hikers and nature-lovers from all over Europe. Not only does the terrain offer magnificent walking possibilities in a variety of locations, but pony-trekking is now available, while fishing fanatics will not be disappointed by the many small lakes and the rivers coursing through the mountains.

**Flora and fauna.** The island's proximity to Africa gives it an abundance of brilliantly-coloured plants and shrubs on the ground, as well as some fairly exotic birdlife. The most common animals you will see are of course sheep and goats, whose jangling bells are a constant background music to anyone travelling in the island's mountainous interior, but there are many much rarer creatures which give Sardinia an added attraction. Its island status means that there are several examples of wildlife unique to it, and also that it lacks some species which you might have expected to find.

## WILDLIFE

**The hunters and the hunted.** Although a recent referendum on hunting was inconclusive, and so allowed it to continue by default, Sardinia has still a rich selection of wildlife, much of it protected against hunters. The trouble is, Sardinian men are so extremely keen on bloodsports, seeing them as a symbol of maturity and virility, and it is not uncommon in the open season to see troops of heavily-armed hunters pushing through the maquis in search of grouse or hare.

**Migration route.** As Sardinia lies on the central-Mediterranean flyway, one of the three main bird migration routes between Europe and Africa, anything with feathers travels in peril of its life, though controls are increasingly having an effect on this random shooting, and conservation and ecological issues are gaining a larger audience.

The WWF is well supported, as is LIPU, *Lega Italiana per la Protezione di Uccelli,* the bird protectionists.

In fairness I must add that Sardinia is not alone in this slaughter: birds are shot or trapped in Malta, and shot in Tunisia, but Greece and the Republic of Cyprus (not Northern Cyprus) have banned hunting. In all these areas, public opinion is gradually reducing the slaughter of birds.

**Mouflons.** Many mainlanders must share the Sards' responsibility for the rarity of species that once thrived on the island. The **mouflon**, for example, a species of wild sheep, was a favourite victim whose regally curved horns graced the parlours of many north Italian homes. By the 1950s the mouflon was on the verge of extinction in Sardinia which, along with Corsica, is the last European habitat of these creatures; they're also found in Cyprus. Now firmly protected by statute in all three islands, the mouflon's numbers have risen to more than 1200 in Sardinia — still a tiny number compared with its past profusion, but some improvement nonetheless.

They are confined to the upper reaches of the Barbágia mountains in the centre of the island, and some parts of Gallura, occasionally in groups of 60 or 70. If you're there, keep a sharp eye open for them, perched on the most precarious ledges on what appear to be sheer cliff-faces.

**Boars and pigs.** Another favourite prey for hunters in Sardinia is the wild boar. Again, its numbers have decreased to a tiny proportion of what they once were, though its tamer and less hairy cousin, the wild pig, is a common sight along the roadside of the Gennargentu mountains, snuffling for nuts and acorns.

The drastic deterioration of forest on the island due to charcoal-burning, industrial demands and fire has led over recent years to the total disappearance of the deer, but a species of Sardinian **stag** — smaller, like so many other island species, than its mainland counterparts — has been saved thanks to its being bred in controlled conditions. A reserve where these can be seen is in the southern parts of the Iglesiente mountains, south-west of Cágliari, at Is Cannoneris, a village between Pantaleo and Domus de Maria.

**The albino asses of Asinara.** Unless you commit some serious felony, one curious creature you are unlikely to see on your holiday in Sardinia is the *asino albino,* or **albino ass.** Another species unique to the island, these diminutive white asses are found only on the isle off Sardinia's north-western coast that was named after them, Asinara. This has for many years been used as a penal colony, and is therefore strictly off-limits.

Other asses — also small by European standards, making their burdens look horribly big — are still common on the island, but much less so than previously. Once they were the principal beasts of burden, just as horses or ponies were used for transport by people who could afford them. Happily for the animals, they have now been replaced by the *mácchina,* or motor car. Oxen, too, have been largely superseded, in this case by the tractor, and nowadays donkeys, horses and oxen are mainly to be seen at the island's various fairs and festivals, where they are decked out in colourful ribbons and bows.

**Horses — domestic and wild.** Horses are especially common at festivities in the area north of Oristano, where they are traditionally bred, marketed and raced — particularly in the villages of Sédilo and Santu Lussúrgiu, and Oristano itself. But you have to travel 18 miles (30km) south-east of Oristano to find ponies in their wild state, on the high basalt plateau of Giara di Gésturi, where the boundaries of Cágliari, Oristano and Nuoro provinces meet.

Until comparatively recently these small ponies could be found in the lowland areas of the island too, but gradually they have retreated to one of the few habitats where they can find a reasonably safe pasturage. About 800 of them roam these thick forests above the village-line, an ideal hiking terrain, though anyone hoping to spot these shy creatures will need to use a good deal of stealth to get anywhere near them.

**Pretty flamingos.** A more exotic creature to be found on the island is the flamingo, which has discovered a perfect environment in Sardinia's lagoons. These birds can be seen easily by anyone driving past the *stagni,* or lagoons, outside Cágliari and Oristano. The flamingos alternate between the lagoons, sharing their home with cranes, egrets, cormorants and other lakeside birds.

Other fowl to watch out for are the huge griffon-vulture, which preys upon lambs; and various species of hawk, all found in the high, mountainous terrain.

**The Mediterranean seal.** Sardinia's coasts provide the last remaining refuge of the Mediterranean seal. The *foca monaca* has chosen the deep marine grottoes on the east coast of the island as its last home, though even here it is severely endangered and on the verge of extinction. Frequent tours of the coast sail from the nearby resort of Cala Gonone, but this must be the likeliest way to drive the seals out, and, in summer at least, the celebrated *Grotta del Bue Marino* is the last place you could expect to see them. The species's real whereabouts must remain a well-kept secret, at least until it is off the danger list.

**Absent friends.** Among the species you definitely won't come across in Sardinia are poisonous snakes, which should give some comfort to prospective hikers. None exists on the island, and none survived when scientists, as an experiment, tried to introduce some vipers under controlled conditions. Other animals that you won't see here are wolves, squirrels, frogs, toads, otters and moles, none of which survived Sardinia's separation from mainland Europe.

## FLORA

As the Mediterranean island furthest from the mainland, Sardinia offers botanists a treat of rare plants and shrubs. The non-specialist will notice above all the bushy wisteria and bougainvillea, the spiky cactus, and the palms and other tropical-type vegetation that give an almost exotic feel to the island. Of the lush forests that once covered Sardinia there is a fraction remaining, and though they are still thick enough in parts to offer a sense of real isolation, the most characteristic growth here is the maquis, or *macchia,* that carpets a good part of the mountain slopes.

Maquis has little value for farmers or shepherds but contains plenty of attraction for the nature-lover and the cook, with its thick, colourful and strongly scented plants, such as myrtle, juniper, gorse and broom interwoven with a scattered selection of herbs that are much favoured in Sardinian cuisine.

Mind what you take home with you, though! One parsley-like herb once grown on the island (and possibly still present, but unidentified) was described by ancient Greek and Roman authors. Highly poisonous, it caused those who ate it to die convulsed with something resembling laughter — hence the word, 'sardonic.'

On higher ground, the island's main trees are cork (principally in the Gallura region), sweet-chestnut and holm-oak. Lower down, eucalyptus trees are widespread, while along the coasts the shelter and shade offerd by pine groves are much appreciated by campers.

## HIKING

Sardinia is seeing a gradual recognition of its potential as a choice European hiking zone, its mountainous and scarcely populated countryside making it ideal for gentle or longer hikes. The best time to walk here is in spring — after the snow has melted from the higher peaks and before summer gets into its stride. This is also the period when visibility is at its crispest, and hillsides are adorned with an array of wild flowers.

The only area specially designated for walkers, with numbered routes and picnic areas, is on the Sopramonte plateau, above Oliena, near Nuoro. But there are many villages in the Nuoro region which offer some spectacular unmarked treks, including a longer one along the Gorruppu canyon, leading south to Baunei and Arbatax. You can also follow a parallel route following the wild, rocky coastline. Other areas still relatively undiscovered are the granite hills of Gallura, the coast around Alghero, the Giara di Gésturi, the mining country around Iglésias, and the still-desolate valleys of the Sarrabus, east of Cágliari.

For shorter walks a solid pair of trainers or tennis shoes is adequate, but in rougher country stout boots and a map are essential, as is some knowledge of where to find water.

Wandering the country like this not only gives you the opportunity to meet people you wouldn't ordinarily come across but would be a fun way of attending some of the village *festas.*

Sards, especially those in the interior, share the custom of being hospitable, common to all mountain peoples; the tourist authorities claim that you can find accommodation just by asking villagers to rent you a room. As I have never tried this I cannot confirm it, but some of the smaller centres in the hills do have cheap lodgings. Otherwise you could pitch a tent; in warmer weather, between May and October, you don't need anything more than the protection of a sleeping-bag.

Some starting-off points are mentioned in the guide, but for more information about hiking in the Gennargentu or other areas around Nuoro, the Nuoro tourist office provides an excellent package of trekking information, maps and routes, with details of distances, times, levels of difficulty, and features to look out for. Local hiking clubs in the Nuoro area can be contacted at these addresses:

**Desulo,** Cooperativa Montanara, c/o Comune di Desulo, DESULO (✆ 0784.61019). Sci Club, c/o Francesco Deidda, Via Cágliari, DESULO (✆ 0784.61144).

**Dorgali,** Gruppo Ricerche Ambientali, c/o Gianmichele Porcu, Via Sos Dorroles, Cala Gonone, DORGALI. (or just c/o Comune di Dorgali). Ristorante Monte Viore, Angela Grispu, Località Monte Viore, DORGALI (✆ 0784.96293). Trekking Sardegna, c/o Claudio Sorrenti, Via Marco Polo 13, Cala Gonone, DORGALI (✆ 0784.232613).

**Lula,** Professore Matteo Corrias, Via Marat 13, LULA (✆ 0784.416670) (or just c/o Comune di Lula).

**Oliena,** Cooperativa Enis, Via Aspromonte 8, OLIENA, (✆ 0784.287460),

**Orgósolo,** Cooperativa Rinascita, Via S. Antonio 14, ORGOSOLO, (✆ 0784.402580).

**Urzulei,** Società Televai di Ugo Murgia, Località Televai, URZULEI, (✆ 0782.649057).

Other places from which you can make interesting treks are the villages of Fonni, the island's highest village, south of Nuoro; Berchidda and Témpio Pausánia in Gallura; Cuglieri near Bosa; and Santadì in the Iglesiente. In these areas you can usually get local information at Pro Locos or other tourist offices; otherwise contact the Club Alpino Italiano, Via Príncipe Amedeo 25, 09100 Cágliari (✆ 070.667877).

Stefano Ardito's book on Italian hikes, *Backpacking and Walking in Italy*, (Bradt, £6.95), also has a chapter on Sardinia with some routes outlined.

## RIDING

One aspect of tourism in Sardinia that has recently grown impressively is pony-trekking. This is best done from one of the organized centres; you can find more information at local tourist offices and the following addresses:

**A.N.T.E.** Via Pasteur 4, 09100 CAGLIARI (✆ 070.305816)

**Centro Vacanze Alabirdi,** c/o Hotel Alabirdi, Strada Mare 24, 09022 ARBOREA (✆ 0783.48268).

**Centro Vacanze Su Gologone,** c/o Residenza Turística Su Gologone, 08025 Oliena, NUORO (✆ 0784.287512).

## FISHING

Fishing is a huge leisure industry in Sardinia today, either in the sea or in the many rivers and lakes inland. Fishing clubs are proliferating all over the island, with centres in Cágliari, Alghero, Oristano, Olbia, Nuoro, Sássari, Iglésias and Sinnai.

In the sea, certain regulations exist regarding the number of rods, the weight in the case of particular types of catch, and the use of nets and diving equipment. Underwater fishing also has restrictions on breathing equipment and on the gathering of molluscs and coral. These are liable to vary and are best learned on the spot.

Fishing from lakes and rivers is allowed wherever there is not a sign saying *Divieto,* but you must carry a permit. Three-month permits are available from the Assesorato Regionale alla Difesa dell'Ambiente, Viale Trento 69, 09100 Cágliari.

# 11: THE PERSONAL TOUCH

## In search of the *real* Sardinia

I HAD HEARD AND READ a lot about Sardinia's untamed interior before I went there. In particular, the Gennargentu mountains of Barbágia, the old Roman *Barbaria*, held a special fascination. I had read the works of Lawrence, Satta, Ross and the novels of Grazia Deledda, and studied the the glossy brochures from the tourist office. I had seen the Taviani brothers' *Padre Padrone*, and read of the exploits of outlaws like Graziano Mesina.

And at last I was in the interior. For three days I had crossed the area, by hired car, on the narrow-gauge train, and on foot. Now, driving up from Lanusei on the fourth day, the last before returning to Nuoro and continuing my journey into Gallura, I had to admit defeat. I was no nearer to understanding Barbágia than when I had started out.

The problem was the lack of personal contact. I had talked with waiters and hotel staff, and exchanged pleasantries with my friendly fellow-passengers on the train, but nothing really *essential* had been said, nothing to give me any deeper insight into this closed environment. Not even when I had given a lift to a shepherd-boy near Sorgono did I manage to prise any information out of him. Overjoyed by the prospect of a captive local whom I could probe at leisure, I had fired question after question at him. Where did he come from? Brothers and sisters? How did he spend his day? What was it *like*, but *really like*, spending hour after hour, day after day on a mountain with only sheep for company? Didn't it drive him mad, or did it calm his soul, deepen his wisdom? What about bandits? Sheep rustling, at the very least?

The shepherd-boy, all of seventeen years old, grunted monosyllables, shook his head, shrugged, and gave me as much inside information as a picture postcard would have done; I could have got more from a book jacket. He looked thoroughly bored by my questions, and relieved when his village finally swung into view, throwing a terse *grazie* behind him as he slammed the door shut.

That was in the morning. This afternoon, cruising through an empty landscape of rolling hills, utterly devoid of life, I had to face the fact: I had learned nothing new in four days. I had seen some thrilling landscape, and dropped in on some festive merry-making at a village fair, but the new knowledge I had acquired amounted to zero.

I sighed. The car seemed to sigh too. Or rather, it choked. Then the engine gave a final cough and stopped. As the car slid to a halt by the side of the road, my heart sank. Silence closed in.

I'm no mechanic, so I stared blankly under the bonnet. I checked the oil, tapped the battery, and looked up and down the road. Nothing. It looked like no one had been past this way for centuries. In the distance, the tinkling of sheep-bells, but neither the sheep nor the shepherd was anywhere to be seen. Again my gaze swept up and down the empty road; I looked at my watch, lit a cigarette, and waited.

Twenty minutes later I heard an engine, and saw a car approaching. I braced myself, put on my best smile, and waited for it to pull up. It was almost level, but showed no sign of stopping. I made a little wave as the car sped past, catching sight of a grim, tight-lipped woman in a headscarf at the wheel, determined not to meet my eye.

What was she scared of? I could think of a hundred possibilities, and began to replan my strategy. I was even beginning to consider going off across the fields on foot when I heard another vehicle approaching. It was a truck, with sheep in the back. I didn't smile this time, nor wave. I just stood there, paralysed by indecision. The decision was made for me: the truck pulled up, a scruffy man got down, nodded at me and asked what was the problem.

*Far from the madding crowd in the tiny port of Stintino.*

I explained what was obvious, that the car wouldn't go. The man, in a frayed corduroy suit and peaked cap, unshaven and giving off a sort of animal odour, muttered to himself, giving me a quick sidelong glance. He seemed to be sizing me up. Then, his mind made up, he tried the engine, checked the lights, touched something under the bonnet.

"No good!" he shouted, and showed me both his thumbs down. I thought I saw something like smugness in his face.

He disappeared into his truck. For an instant I thought he was going to drive off but instead he reappeared with a length of stout rope, tied it to the back of his truck and the front of the Fiat, and gestured for me to climb into my car.

With a jerk we set off, my mind full of that nervous suspicion that falls whenever events are taken out of your hands and put into somebody else's — a stranger's. Thoughts raced wildly; I wondered how much ransom a poor travel-writer might fetch, and who would pay it. He drove fast and we soon approached a village. Pulling up outside a yard, he spoke quickly to a man in overalls and, turning to me, bared his yellowed teeth. I later discovered this was a smile. He laid a leathery hand on my shoulder and pulled me away. I tried to protest, thinking I should stay with my car, but he persisted, guiding me with determination down a muddy alley. I saw the light fade and began to think about hotels and dinner, but we were suddenly inside a doorway, in a gloomy corridor so dark I couldn't see a thing.

A woman appeared, looking suspiciously at me. The man exchanged rapid words with her in dialect; she nodded briefly, then she stood aside, and when I hesitated, almost pushed me forward through a door. It was the kitchen. I blinked. If I had thought about it, I would have expected a grimy hovel with an open fire and, perhaps, a kid goat roasting on the spit. Instead I saw gleaming surfaces, a polished gas stove, and even a large-screen colour TV in the corner, all bathed under the dazzling light of a fluorescent bulb.

A door opened and a teenage boy appeared, who immediately bade me sit down, thrust a liqueur into my hands, and began asking me questions. What did I do? Where did I live? Brothers and sisters? Did I enjoy my job? What was it like, but *really like*, living in Britain?

This went on for about 40 minutes, then my saviour came through the door. He was out of his corduroys and cap, no more shaved than when I had last seen him, but no longer smelling of sheep. He bared his yellow teeth again and I smiled back, nodding.

The car was ready. Electric fault. No problem. Come again. As I shook his hand, his son, Leonardo, asked if I could send him a video, and he pointed to the recorder beneath the TV set. During his interrogation he had told me that he was on his way to university next month.

The mechanic asked a nominal payment for his work and I drove on to the next village where I found a hotel. So much for the probing travel-writer. I had been thoroughly turned inside out. I had learned nothing about the old Barbágia, the bandits and the shepherds and the Sardinia of Deledda and Lawrence. But I had learned a hell of a lot about modern-day Sardinia.

*King Vittorio Emanuele strikes a commanding pose in Sássari's Piazza d'Italia.*

# 12: SARDINIAN FACTFILE

### Facts at your fingertips

AS SARDINIA IS PART OF ITALY, it is in the European Community and so follows the EC's rules on trade and frontier regulations. Together with Sicily, it sends nine deputies to the European Parliament in Strasbourg.

## ARMED FORCES

The young men of Sardinia are subjected to military conscription, as are all Italian males aged 18. They join one of the armed services for a year unless they are studying or can show some other excuse such as physical or psychological disability. In the last few years *servizio civile* has become an increasingly popular alternative, involving work in the community or countryside, though for 18 months instead of 12.

Conscription is even more unpopular for young Sards than it is for their mainland compatriots, as it often involves being garrisoned several hundred miles away from home and serving national interests with which many islanders do not sympathise.

Sardinia also hosts one of the biggest concentrations of American troops in Europe, in the Maddalena archipelago.

## BUSINESS HOURS

**Banks:** Weekdays 0830-1320, and generally 1500-1600 — though the afternoon time may vary from place to place.

**Shops:** Food shops are open from 0800 or 0830 until about 1230, then 1600-1930. Saturday is usually half-day, but shops in the bigger towns may stay open. Other stores may open at 0900, sometimes 1000 for boutiques, to 1300, then 1700-2000.

**Supermarkets:** 0830-1300, 1600-2000.

**Post offices:** 0830-1320; every major town will also have a central post office (*Posta Centrale*) open all day till 1700.

**SIP telephone offices:** 0830-2200.

**Museums:** Standard hours in the summer (1 June-30 September) are Tuesday-Sunday 0900-1300, 1600-2000; Monday closed. Winter; Tuesday-Sunday 0900-1300, 1500-1800, but there are variations.

# ECONOMY

After centuries of inertia, the Sardinian economy has changed drastically in the last half-century. In this traditionally rural society, life revolved around the land. Transhumance was practiced for centuries (moving livestock to high pastures in summer), and the peasants led a static life tied to the same plot of land that their forefathers had always ploughed.

The tendency in the past hundred years has been for the farmers to improve their lot at the expense of the shepherds. The long-dormant potential of the land has been realised by a series of major programmes, the first of which was largely started by Mussolini. His efforts to make Italy self-sufficient boosted agricultural output, particularly grain production, while more land was made available by means of massive drainage schemes. Output was also improved by a more efficient system of irrigation, fed by dams in the interior, which also tamed Sardinia's unpredictable rivers.

**End of malaria.** The next improvement was after World War Two when the USA led the destruction of the malaria mosquito which, for centuries, had hindered growth and depopulated large areas of lowlands. Lastly, the government fund for the development of the Italian South, *La Cassa per il Mezzogiorno*, was extended to Sardinia in 1950, stimulating growth and making large sums available for land development.

Other advances came at the expense of the pastoralists. Cork-production, for example, in which Sardinia still accounts for 75% of Italy's total output, requires forest-land which would otherwise serve as pasture for sheep; the papermaking industry based at Arbatax also needs large tracts of woodland.

**Mining.** The only other area in which Sardinia's economy has historically played an important role is mining. This was the lure for more than one invading power, which wanted the island's coal, lead, zinc, silver and even gold reserves. Today you can see everywhere in Sardinia (but particularly in the Sulcis and Iglesiente regions in the south- west) the remains of old quarries and mine-shafts. A certain amount of extraction still takes place, but mining has been largely replaced as the island's leading industry — by oil.

**Black gold.** In the 1960s the famous 'economic miracle' that helped Italy's economy had its knock-on effects on the country's remoter parts. In Sardinia, oil-processing plants were established outside Cágliari, where the mammoth Sarroch oil refinery and petrochemical plant has attracted a host of subsidiary industries. Other refineries have sprung up in Ottana, at the dead centre of the island, and Porto Torres, on the north coast, employing thousands of people and ensuring that the petrochemical industry has a secure future here.

**Tourism.** At the same time that heavy industry was being

established in Sardinia, the island's economy was given a thorough shake-up from a new direction. It was the Aga Khan's demonstration of the potential of tourism as a new source of foreign cash that has altered the economic landscape of Sardinia in a way that could never have been predicted. His development of a stretch of barren but picturesque coast north of Olbia was to be the start of a huge tourist boom that has transformed Sardinia into an island largely based on service industries, including a flourishing construction industry.

The consequences today are readily apparent, and the evening *passeggiata* in Oristano or Alghero can now compete with those at Florence or Bologna for sheer elegance and ostentatious wealth. On the other hand, while the wealth exists in some quarters, much of the new *benessere* is largely a fiction, a facet of the Italian passion for keeping up a sophisticated pretence of being well-off. In fact most of the profits from tourism flow directly overseas, and for native Sards the employment generated by tourism is very much a seasonal affair without long-term security. Across the island unemployment runs at a high 15%, encouraging a steady drain of its human resources in the form of emigration. Further evidence of Sardinia's underlying instability is the sinister appearance of hard drugs in the last few years.

Meanwhile, in Sardinia's neglected interior, some things have hardly changed. Sheep-farming, centred on the great massif of Barbágia, is still important; with 2,500,000 sheep, the island holds a third of Italy's total. And crop-farming produces its customarily low returns, with Sardinia's yield per hectare ranking among Italy's lowest. Perhaps the greatest change of all is that where once there were oxen and mules and horses, today there are cars and vans and scooters. Things are a little faster now.

## ELECTRICITY

The current runs at 220V, and should be suitable for most appliances of 240V. Two-pin sockets for shavers are available in most hotel bathrooms.

With much of the island supplied by hydro-electric generators for which virtually every river on the island has been dammed, electricity reaches all parts of Sardinia and the supply is generally reliable. Tourist areas anyway shouldn't have any problems, though cities can experience occasional blackouts of around five minutes, and campsites with their own generators have been known to lose their supply temporarily. The current in country areas can surge, causing problems for computers and television sets.

## FLAG

The Sardinian flag (see back cover) is a red cross on a yellow back ground, each square showing a blindfolded, ear-ringed negro, or Moor. No one can say for certain what is the origin of this peculiar device, which resembles the Corsican flag, though that has just one negro, and with the bandage around his forehead. The Sard Action Party, *Partitito Sardo d'Azione,* has adopted the Sardinian flag as its emblem, giving it a new political connotation.

The Italian flag has green, white and orange vertical bands.

## GAS

Camping Gaz is available in all sizes at all outdoor shops and hardware shops. Most campsites sell it, as does any seaside-resort shop that sells beach items.

## MAPS

You are unlikely to need any map more detailed than the one provided on the spot by the tourist offices in Sardinia. They also issue excellent town plans for each of the major cities and resorts; drivers might also appreciate the road-map covering the whole of Italy issued by the *Automobile Club d'Italia.* All of these are free.

If you want to take something with you which has a little extra detail, Michelin, Touring Club d'Italia and Bartholomew-Clyde all do excellent maps, including items such as filling stations, *nuraghi* and footpaths, for sale in Britain for about £5. Try *Stanford's,* 12-14 Long Acre, London WC2E 9LP (*✆* 071.836.1321); *Robertson McCarta,* 122 King's Cross Road, London WC1 (*✆* 071.278.8278), or *Daunt,* 83 Marylebone High Street, London W1M 4AL (*✆* 071.224.2295).

**Hikers.** On the more accessible routes, hikers could get by on these, but more serious trails need the better detail supplied by the old-fashioned Italian military maps produced by the *Istituto Geográfico Militare,* or the hiking maps of the *Club Alpino Italiano,* neither of which is always available on the island. Some of the larger bookstores in Italy should have them, otherwise there is nothing for it but to order one though a bookshop, or go direct to the main IGM office in Florence (Via Strozzi 44, Florence) or the CAI at Via Fóscolo 3, Milan.

## NEWSPAPERS

There are two main newspapers covering the island: *Unione Sarda* and *La Nuova Sardegna.* Both are unashamedly provincial, and are produced in Cágliari, Sássari and Olbia, with slightly different editions in each. You'll find lists of local films, concerts and other cultural events in their pages, as well as the most up-to-date train, ferry and flight timetables.

In additon, every area has its own range of publications, from students' free-sheets to specialised cultural and literary magazines.

*Out of the hubbub: Sássari's public gardens offer shade and calm.*

The national newspapers are on sale and widely read everywhere. Foremost among these comes the pink *Gazzetta dello Sport*, guaranteed to be seen in all bars and piazzas on a Monday morning, following the weekend's sports events. Of the other dailies, the main ones are *La Repúbblica*, *Il Corriere della Sera* and the Communist *L'Unità*.

**Foreign newspapers.** Newspapers from Britain, France and Germany are available, usually about a day late, from stations and newspaper kiosks in Cágliari, Sássari, Alghero and Olbia, and some other resorts.

## POLICE

Visitors to Italy are always bewildered by the number of different uniforms worn by the police. In fact there are several types of police, and all but the two main ones have specific areas to cover. The main ones, *Polizia* and *Carabinieri,* are themselves confused about their separate roles and there exists a sharp rivalry between them. Partly, their overlapping responsibilities were a deliberate policy by the founders of the Italian state to prevent one force becoming too powerful.

The Carabinieri, wearing a smart uniform of pale blue shirt, worn open, and dark blue trousers with a red stripe down each leg (in winter, officers wear a darker jacket and trousers, white shirt and black tie), are a military force, billeted in barracks and coming under the control of the Ministry of Defence. The Polizia, whose less fashionable uniform is a blue jacket with pale blue jodhpurs (riding trousers) and sometimes knee-length boots (changing to a more military, combat-style dress for special assignments) is a civilian body coming under the Ministry of the Interior.

You are likely to find nice ones and nasty ones in each force, though it is the Carabinieri who have attracted most unpopularity among Italians, possibly because their officers are always outsiders, posted away from their homes.

**When you need police help, call either force: ✆ 112 for Polizia, ✆ 113 for Carabinieri.**

Another category is the *Guardia di Finanza*, dressed in grey uniforms, whose job is to regulate all financial transactions, which includes customs and excise, taxation, and currency dealing. Its officers are often involved with cases of fraud, embezzlement, the drugs industry and smuggling.

In the towns, the force you are likely to see most often is the **vigili urbani,** often directing traffic or giving parking tickets. This is the only one of the five main forces that goes unarmed, and a *vigile* is invariably polite and helpful if you need information, though it is doubtful that he or she will speak much English. Officers are dressed all in white, with tall white helmets and white bags slung over their shoulders.

Lastly, the *Polizia Stradale* look after the main highways, and are often to be seen giving speeding tickets and keeping the traffic flowing.

Outside banks you will often find armed guards, members of private security companies, and you may also see men and women in the towns doing jobs similar to those of the *vigili urbani* but dressed in white shirts and dark blue trousers or skirts: these are members of private police forces, used by the urban authorities.

## POLITICS

Since 1948 Sardinia has been an autonomous region of Italy, and, together with Sicily, Trentino-Alto Adige, and Friuli-Venezia Giulia, enjoys a special status, with independent administration of police (not Carabinieri), agriculture, industry, transport and tourism. It sends 18 deputies and 9 senators to the Italian parliament in Rome — their number directly related to population — and their political make up reflects the national balance of power rather than any unique regional pattern. Thus it shares the traditional political loyalties of southern Italy, with a strong Christian Democrat Party (*Partito Democrazia Cristiano*, or *DC*) presence, followed by the Communists (*Partito Comunista d'Italia*, or *PCI*), supported mainly in the mining areas and the cities, with the Socialists (*Partito Socialista Italiano,* or *PSI*), in third place.

Although the separatist Sardinian Action Party (*Partito Sardo d'Azione,* or *PSD'Az*) enjoys occasional surges of popularity, it has not been a significant force on the island since around 1985. Its representation at Strasbourg is better but it currently lies fourth in the island's political popularity table. You will see posters and graffitied slogans for it everywhere.

You will also see fragments of old Fascist graffiti in Sardinia, the big black letters faded but still legible, urging the people to work hard, or tread boldly, or glorify their country, or just persevere. These survivals from the past are another feature that the island shares with parts of the south of Italy, to which, for better or worse, Mussolini paid more attention than any leader before him.

## POLLUTION

Sardinia does not share the Italian mainland's notoriety as a polluter of its rivers and shores, and its distance from the peninsula has saved it from the worst effects. The purity of the seas around Sardinia was confirmed recently by a Friends of the Earth report, putting the island at the top of the list of Italian coasts for the cleanliness of its waters.

But there are black spots. Tourists don't need much telling to keep away from the few concentrations of industry on the island: the sight and smell of them is enough. On the coasts, these are the petrochemical works at Sarroch, south-west of Cágliari, and Porto Torres, on Sardinia's northern coast, and the power station at Portovesme, opposite San Pietro island. Arbatax, on the otherwise untainted east coast, has some light industry. Avoid the sea around ports, of course, particularly Cágliari and Olbia, though one only needs to travel a small distance (as far as Poetto in the case of Cágliari) to be safe.

**Cobalt 60.** The most sinister stain on the Mediterranean blue is the sea around the Maddalena archipelago, where scientists have recently recorded a higher-than-normal reading of the radioactive Cobalt 60. Whether this has anything to do with the nearby NATO base is open to question.

Outside the industrial spots mentioned above, air pollution is low compared with the smoggy mainland, and that goes for noise-pollution too. There's no doubt about it: Sards are quieter, though you should expect to suffer the occasional sound-box blasting the beach.

## POPULATION

Sardinia's population is almost 1,600,000, nearly half of whom live in the southern province of Cágliari. The town of Cágliari has a population of 233,000; Sássari of 118,000; Oristano has 25,000, and

*A parking lot on the coast at La Pelosa.*

Nuoro 37,000. With an average of 23 people per square mile (60 per sq km), the island has the lowest density of population in the whole of Italy; for contrast, Malta has 2,800 per sq mile. Indeed one of the most striking aspects of driving through the countryside of Sardinia is its emptiness: very few people live in isolated country houses, most live in villages often on hilltops and mountainsides, and widely spaced apart. Only a quarter live in the major towns.

Until very recently the island had seen as much emigration as any of the southern Italian regions, and the attitude still exists that to make good, young people must head for the mainland. Today the island offers more incentives to stay, though the tendency to leave country districts for the cities, all of which are experiencing an unprecedented growth, has meant that many villages are left with ageing populations.

Another recent development is the settlement of the coasts. In the past the Sardinian coastline had been largely empty of villages and even roads, not only because the interior offered more security against foreign invaders and raiders, but as a result of the malaria that was epidemic in the lowlands. Now the tourist explosion has reversed this movement, and many of the roads that run along the coast have been bult only in the past 30 years. Again, it is the inland villages that suffer.

## POST

**Postage rate.** Letters and post cards addressed to anywhere in the EC cost the same as internal mail, i.e. L750 for letters, L650 for post cards. Expect delivery to Europe to take anything between four and ten days, and you don't need to specify 'airmail' (*via aereo*) on the envelope. Parcels take longer, and must be efficiently sealed and accompanied by a customs declaration, available at the post office. If you want either letters or parcels to travel faster, pay another L2,000 or so and specify *espresso*. Recorded delivery which includes insurance is *racommandato*, costing about the same extra as *espresso*.

As post office queues can be lengthy and frustrating, it's worth buying **stamps** (*francobolli*) elsewhere, at shops selling cigarettes and newspapers, and some bars having a separate cashier selling cigarettes.

Letters sent **Poste Restante** should be addressed *Fermo Posta*, with the surname first, underlined and printed for maximum security.

## PUBLIC HOLIDAYS

Italy's religious calendar was recently drastically overhauled, demoting a number of saints and so striking off a handful of annual holidays. Nowadays, Italy, which used to be famous for taking dozens of saints' days off each year, has fewer public holidays than France, Germany, Austria, Belgium, Denmark, Spain, Luxembourg, Sweden and the Netherlands.

The Italian public holidays are:

| | |
|---|---|
| January 1 | New Year's Day (*Capodanno*) |
| | Easter Monday (*Lunedì della Pasqua*) |
| April 25 | Liberation Day (*Liberazione*) |
| May 1 | Labour Day (*Festa del Lavoro*) |
| August 15 | Assumption (*Assunzione* or *Ferragosto*) |
| November 1 | All Saints' Day (*Ognissanti*) |
| December 8 | Immaculate Conception (*Immacolata Concezione*) |
| December 25 | Christmas Day (*Natale*) |
| December 26 | Boxing Day (*Santo Stéfano*) |

## PUBLIC TOILETS (Restrooms)

Public toilets in Sardinia are scarce, and are usually in stations, airports, museums and archeological sites. If you're in need, ask at the bigger bars for the *bagno* or *gabinetto* — particularly if it's the sort of bar that sells snacks — or try any hotel or restaurant.

The standard of hygiene is generally good in Sardinia, and you will usually find toilet paper, and often soap and paper towels or hand-dryer too.

## RADIO AND TELEVISION

Tune in your radio or try the channels on a television-set to see the effects of the deregulation of Italy's radio and TV network. The FM airways are so crowded that it's difficult to find clear reception on any frequency for more than a few hundred metres of driving, while alongside the three state-run TV stations, there are scores of local channels in each area, as well as the handful of private networks that broadcast throughout Italy. Of these, the biggest are all owned by Italian Euromogul Silvio Berlusconi — Canale 5, Rete 4, Italia I, Tele Monte Carlo, and Capo d'Istria — and all survive on a diet of crude advertisements separated by cabaret, tasteless quiz shows, B-movies and lots of much inferior American soap (drama originally sponsored by soap manufacturers). Choice, in this case, does not mean higher standards.

The RAI channels (*Radio e Televisione Italiana*) are more discerning and show fewer adverts (none is ad-free). Their main strength lies in quality films and a news service that is mostly superior to Britain's. The channels are divided according to a broad political classification representing overall control, though these tendencies are not at all apparent to the casual viewer: RAI 1 is run by the Christian Democrats, RAI 2 by the Socialists, while RAI 3 gives more attention to local television.

In Sardinia the main private channels are Tele Costa Smeralda and Videolina, neither of them rising above the general silliness. For something different, try one of the French channels, which can be picked up fairly easily owing to the proximity of Corsica.

The **BBC World Service** is easily found on a short- wave radio, best on 12.095MHz (0500-1700 hrs) or 15.070MHz (0700-1745 hrs). Other daytime frequencies change too often to be listed here. At night and in the early morning try 7.325MHz or 9.410MHz.

## READING

If you plan to take books with you and are interested in the island and its people, here are a few recommendations for some easily-digestible insights into Sardinia.

Before D.H. Lawrence, the first Englishman to describe the island was a lawyer, John Warre Tyndale, who in the 1840s took time off to walk over every inch of Sardinia, taking many notes from which he produced a three-volume portrait of the island and its customs. Hardly holiday reading, this, and Lawrence had no intention of following his example. Instead, Lawrence's work *Sea and Sardinia* (currently published by Olive Press at £6.95, or as part of a Penguin collection, *D.H. Lawrence and Italy* at £5.99) has a much more limited scope, the fruit of a fortnight's expedition in 1921. In fact only six days were spent on Sardinia itself, following an obscure route from Cágliari through the

*The cathedral at Sássari has an ornate Baroque façade.*

*An empty stage at Nora's Roman theatre.*

*Shadow and light in the heart of Iglésias: the Piazza del Duomo.*

*Night falls over the Rosello fountain, Sássari.*

middle of the island, via Sórgono to Nuoro, and on to Olbia (then called Terranova), where he boarded a boat back to the mainland. Highly subjective, it is nonetheless an intensely visual travel-book, seeing the island through a poet's eye.

After Lawrence, the best book written in English is by Alan Ross, a cricket correspondent and author who visited the island in the period following World War II, recording his impressions in *The Bandit and the Billiard Table* (Collins Harvill 1989; £6.95). As well as being a learned writer with loads of knowledge about the island, Ross is an entertaining storyteller. He gives a good account of himself and the islanders in a time before the Aga Khan and the tourist explosion had lifted Sardinia out of obscurity, though much is still recognisable, and the background on historical figures such as Nelson and Garibaldi is good.

Virginia Waite's book, *Sardinia* (Batsford, 1977; out of print) is intended more as a travel guide, though she gives an authoritative description of the island. It suffers from being out-of-date but is a good little appetizer if you manage to track it down.

Russell King's *Sardinia* in David & Charles's *Islands* series is up to his usual efficient standard. Full of facts about the people, industry, economy and social climate, it may be another book only to be found at libraries, though nothing has superseded it.

The little town of Nuoro has produced more than its fair share of great writers. Two who have written about their native town in the early part of the century are Grazia Deledda and Salvatore Satta. Grazia Deledda (1871-1936) was a Nobel Prize-winner whose many books about Nuoro and its surrounding mountain-villages are wonderful evocations of a long-vanished rural society. Try one of her two books published in English: *After the Divorce* (Quartet 1985; £4.95) and *La Madre* (Dedalus European Classics 1987; £3.95).

Nuoro's other literary star is Salvatore Satta (1902-1975), whose *The Day of Judgment* was first published in Italy posthumously in 1979, and in this country in 1987 (Collins Harvill; £5.95). Famed as a jurist rather than a writer, Satta made this book his lifetime's work, taking 30 years to produce a kaleidoscopic portrait of Nuoro at the turn of the century, exploring its people's dreams and sufferings in a poetic, elegiac kind of mood. In fact the book became Satta's own last testament since he died before completing it.

. . . And a film. If you have not already seen it, try to catch the Taviani brothers' masterly *Padre Padrone* (1977), a bleak epic on rural Sardinia seen through the eyes of a shepherd-boy; it is hated by many Sards for its backward portrayal of the island.

## RESIDENCE AND PROPERTY

There are no restrictions on buying property in Italy, only a barrage of paperwork. For more information contact the Italian consulate; for sample prices see chapter 2 and the Costa Smeralda section.

## TELEPHONING

You can use coins of L500, L200 and L100 in all public telephone boxes in Sardinia, as well as the *gettone* tokens worth L200. In addition, almost all public call-boxes on the island are now adapted so that they can be used with a card as well as coins, an improvement on the British system of either—or. If you're phoning from Sardinia, a card (*scheda telefónica*) is the more convenient if you're using a public box, and you can buy one from any *tabacchi* cigarette shop and some bars, costing L2,000, L5,000 and L10,000.

Otherwise, if there's a telephone office handy, you might as well use it: the charge depends on the units (*scatti*) you've used, which are visible on a digital display inside the sound-proof booth. The main telephone company is the *SIP* and each town has its SIP office, open all day 0900-2200; there are other offices too, run by independent companies and keeping similar hours. Information on the main office in each town is included in the guide.

**International calls.** To make international calls from Sardinia, dial 00 for the **international access code,** followed by one of these codes:

| | | | |
|---|---|---|---|
| Australia | 61 | Norway | 47 |
| Eire | 353 | Sweden | 46 |
| Germany | 37 | Switzerland | 41 |
| Netherlands | 31 | UK | 44 |
| New Zealand | 64 | USA & Canada | 1 |

Follow with the area code you want, minus any intial 0, and finally the number. If you want to dial reversed-charge, (call collect in the USA) phone the operator (℡ 151) and ask for a call *cárico a destinatario;* e.g. *vorrei telefonare in Inghilterra al cárico del destinatario,* and give the number.

Note that hotels charge more per *scatto* than if you use a public phone.

## TIME

Italy is on GMT+1 in winter, GMT+2 in summer, which makes it always one hour ahead of British time apart from the four weeks between the last Sunday in September (when Italy comes from summer time (daylight saving time)), and the last Sunday in October (when Britain, Ireland, the USA and Canada come from summer time); during this period British and Sardinian times are the same.

All of Europe, from Iceland to Turkey (plus Cyprus) starts summer time on the same date, but Canada and the USA have their own separate starting time.

## TOURIST OFFICES

The tourist information network in Sardinia is excellent, as it is throughout Italy. As on the mainland, the service is divided into at least three parts, defined according to which administration it comes under. Thus the provincial offices, **EPT**, or *Ente Provinciale per il Turismo,* are controlled by the provincial authorities, and have offices in each of the provincial capitals of Cágliari, Nuoro, Oristano and Sássari. Then there are the independent **AAST** agencies (*Azienda Autónoma di Soggiorno e Turismo,*) which can be found in the resorts and major towns. Lastly there are small, village offices controlled by the local *Comune* dealing with all facets of local information, the **Pro Loco.**

From the tourist's point of view, all are useful, and all have access to more or less the same material, but the bigger the office, the less communication problems you are likely to have, and also the greater the chance of the office being open – the Pro Locos for example, are a bit erratic, and can be 'temporarily closed' when they are supposed to be open. Usual summer opening hours are Monday-Saturday 0900-1400, 1600-2000, mornings only in winter.

Tourist information offices are essential at whatever level you are holidaying in Sardinia. For general information about the area you are in, as well as reading about other places on the island, they provide a wealth of literature in all major European languages, and though you must not take their frequently mistranslated offerings as the literal truth, the suggestions are there, along with the practical information you might need. Independent travellers find the offices are primarily useful for supplying a good map of the town, plus a comprehensive list of available accommodation. They can also tell you whether camp-sites are shut, how to get to them, and the bus timetables.

## WATER

Water is always available in Sardinia, and the islanders savour it like wine. Theoretically it is nearly always safe to drink, and if it isn't, you should see a sign to say so, such as *acqua non potabile,* or *acqua non bevibile.* In towns it is chlorinated, and the taste is often noticeable. Some rural fountains are also treated, presumably not without good cause, though other fountains have water that is especially prized, often identifiable by the crowds of parked cars around them, with families queuing to fill their demijohns.

## WEIGHTS AND MEASURES

Sardinia, like Italy and the rest of Europe, uses the metric system. Here is a brief reminder of conversion:

| | |
|---|---|
| 1 litre = 1.8 pints | 1 pint = 0.6 litres |
| 1 litre = 0.22 Imp gallons | 1 Imp gallon = 4.5 litres |
| 1 litre = 0.26 US gallons | 1 US gallon = 3.8 litres |
| 1 kilogramme = 14 ounces | 1 ounce = 28.350 grams |
| 1 centimetre = 0.3 inch | 1 pound = 0.45 kilograms |
| 1 metre = 39 inches | 1 inch = 2.5 centimetres |
| 1 kilometre = 0.6 mile. | 1 yard = 0.9 metres |
| | 1 mile = 1.6 kilometres |

And a couple of other useful tips:

$18°C = 81°F$

31 miles per gallon = 11 kilometres per litre

| | SHIRTS | | | | | DRESSES | | | |
|---|---|---|---|---|---|---|---|---|---|
| British | 14½ | 15 | 15½ | 16 | 16½ | 10 | 12 | 14 | 16 | 18 |
| Continental | 37 | 38 | 39 | 40 | 41 | 40 | 42 | 44 | 46 | 48 |
| N. American | 14½ | 15 | 15½ | 16 | 16½ | 8 | 10 | 12 | 14 | 16 |

| | MEN'S SHOES | | | | | WOMEN'S SHOES | | | | |
|---|---|---|---|---|---|---|---|---|---|---|
| British | 7 | 8 | 9 | 10 | 11 | 3 | 4 | 5 | 6 | 7 |
| Continental | 41½ | 42½ | 43½ | 44½ | 45½ | 36 | 37 | 38 | 39 | 40 |
| N. American | 8 | 9 | 10 | 11 | 12 | 4½ | 5½ | 6½ | 7½ | 8½ |

## WHAT YOU WON'T LIKE

Sardinia must go its own way and it is not for a tourist to say what should or should not be done. But one could question how much is in the island's best interests. Does Sardinia really *need*, for example, such a heavy preponderance of military hardware and foreign personnel at the NATO base on the Maddalena islands? The authorities refuse to confirm whether or not nuclear submarines are based there, but a high level of radioactivity has recently been registered in the waters around the islands, which can't be any good for fishermen, foreign tourists or the local population.

Elsewhere the Sardinian coasts have been subject to a similar disregard for local interests. The environment-conscious development on the Costa Smeralda is one thing, but shouldn't similar criteria be used at other holiday ghettos such as Costa Rei, Costa Paradiso and La Pelosa? Each of these localities has been scarred by huge developments of uniform villas which dominate what would otherwise be some of Europe's most beautiful scenery. In each case, setting aside the bland appearance of the buildings, the appropriation of Sardinia's natural resources has taken place for the benefit of an ultra-rich minority at the expense of ordinary Sards and tourists alike who cannot afford the astronomical prices.

Sardinia is not the only part of Italy to suffer from the phenomenon of *case abusive* – houses built in defiance of local regulations designed to restrict coastal development. Ugly cement is used in abundance, rivers are diverted, woods and fields destroyed, all for the sake of the dubious but not insignificant profits of property speculation.

Let's see a little more taste and restraint here, please, before more damage is done!

# DISCOVER SARDINIA

SARDINIA IS DIVIDED into four provinces named from their main towns, Cágliari in the south, Oristano in the west, Nuoro in the east and Sássari in the north. Apart from the broad, northernmost province of Sássari, to which I've given two chapters, each province is dealt with in the guide in a separate chapter — though, for the sake of convenience, I have taken some liberties over exact provincial boundaries.

Thus each chapter contains what should be easily accessible for anyone staying in or around one of the island's five main cities, including Olbia, on Sássari's north-eastern coast, the principal point of entry for tourists in Sardinia and the biggest centre in the Costa Smeralda area. Sássari town itself, Alghero, and the area around are described in a separate chapter.

Hotels are listed for each stop, with examples given where there is a large selection. The prices given are the lowest available for a double bedroom, with or without bathroom. I have shown the range of seasonal variations, and any other features such as swimming pool, tennis courts, restaurant and crêche are mentioned where they exist.

## KEY TO MAP OF CAGLIARI on pages 104-105

1 British consulate
2 Cathedral
3 Elephant Tower
4 Hospitals
5 House of Tigellius
6 Market
7 Museums: City
8 — Citadel
9 — Nat. Archaeological
10 Police
11 Rail stn (main line)
12 Rail stn (narrow gauge)
13 Roman amphitheatre
14 St Pancras Tower
15 St Remy Bastion
16 University buildings

### KEY TO HOTELS

20 Azuni
21 Castello
22 Centrale
23 Europa
24 Firenze
25 Flora
26 Italia
27 Londra
28 Melis
29 Micheletti
30 Miramare
31 Moderno
32 Olimpio
33 Quattro Mori
34 Reina Margherita
35 Sant'Anna
36 Su Furriadorgio
37 Vittoria

# 13: CAGLIARI and the SOUTH

## Capital city

CAGLIARI HAS BEEN SARDINIA'S CAPITAL at least since Roman times and is still today its biggest centre, with the busiest port and the greatest concentration of industry. Intimidating as this may sound, Cágliari is no urban sprawl; its centre is small, compact enough to be easily manageable for the tourist on foot, and offering both chic sophistication and medieval charm in the maze of narrow lanes squeezed into its high citadel.

Viewing Cágliari from the sea at the start of his Sardinian sojourn in 1921, D.H. Lawrence compared it with Jerusalem ". . . strange and rather wonderful, not a bit like Italy." Smack in the centre of the wide Golfo di Cágliari, backed by salt pans and lagoons and crowned by its fortified citadel, the city always presents an absorbing scenario, an agreeable town to amble around and a convenient base for the surrounding country.

Nearby, Cágliari has easy access to the enormous sandy expanses at **Poetto**, while further afield, a good afternoon's ride takes you to the ancient site of **Nora**. This is also one of the many marvellous bathing spots scattered along both shores of the Gulf, which can be enjoyed at the hotel-resorts of **Santa Margherita di Pula, Villasímius,** or the upmarket **Costa Rei**, or in quiet seclusion at the beach of your choice. Off the western coast of the province are moored the islands of **Sant'Antíoco** and **San Pietro,** both worth exploring, while the inland Spanish-tinged town of **Iglésias** makes an appealing destination. Deeper inland, on the fringes of Cágliari province, the famous *nuraghe* of **Su Nuraxi** is on most tourist itineraries, a compelling sight in the midst of the brown hills of the interior.

### CAGLIARI IN HISTORY

Probably founded by the Phoenicians, who gave it the name of *Karalis,* Cágliari became a colony of the Carthaginians, and was their main base until its capture by the Romans in 238BC. As an important and flourishing *municipium,* the city was one of the major trading ports in the Mediterranean, but declined with the demise of Roman power, finally falling to the Vandals and Goths and, after a Byzantine

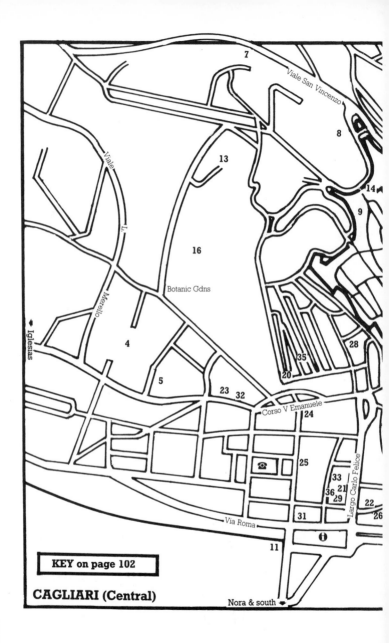

KEY on page 102

**CAGLIARI (Central)**

Nora & south ➤

interval, it was repeatedly plundered by the Saracens.

**Pisan fortress.** The city revived in the Middle Ages when, as capital of the most important of the island's *giudicati,* it became the principal Pisan base in the middle of the 13th cent. The fortifications built by the Pisans around the citadel, then called *Castello,* are one of present-day Cágliari's most prominent features – in particular the San Pancrazio and Elephant towers.

**Spanish domination.** Following the Pisan defeat at the hands of the Spanish in 1323, Cágliari kept its position as Sardinia's capital, and Philip II – Felipe to the Spanish – opened the island's first university here in the 17th cent. Even so, the Spanish domination was not a particularly happy time for Cágliari, whose population had dropped to only 15,000 by 1700 – less than when the Spanish arrived.

**British attack.** In 1708, during the War of the Spanish Succession, a British fleet under General Stanhope bombarded the city, and occupied it in the name of Archduke Karl of Austria, who had plans on becoming Carlos III of Spain. Stanhope also seized Menorca, which became a British possession under the Treaty of Utrecht in 1713 (see *Discover Gibraltar* in this series).

**House of Savoy.** When Archduke Karl's brother died, Karl became Emperor of Austria, northern Italy and Sardinia, and Belgium, as well as pretender to the Spanish throne as Carlos III. It was too much for the other European powers and in the sudden realignment of loyalties, Sardinia came under the Italian House of Savoy in 1720.

In the 18th cent Cágliari first began to creep out from behind its protective walls, some of which were dismantled, and soon came the first of today's broad boulevards along which the traffic now rumbles. Although nearly half the city was destroyed during World War II, only the occasional modern eyesore breaks the harmony of the city's centre, the real growth occurring in the last couple of decades on the outskirts, where new blocks of flats have mushroomed.

## CAGLIARI TODAY

A brisk, bustling city with a population of nearly 250,000, Cágliari still has plenty of space for idlers, amblers and holidaymakers. The humming evening promenades along Via Manno are the smartest you'll see in Sardinia, dropping down to Piazza Yenne and Largo Carlo Felice, where you will find most of the shops, restaurants, banks and hotels. At the bottom of the town, the arcades of Via Roma shelter shops and bars, between which Senegalese traders jostle for space on the ground to spread their wares. This is still the city's favourite spot for sitting down for an ice cream or a cup of coffee, in view of the port.

Behind the city and along the airport road stretch the calm lagoons – *stagni* – with their fishing boats and birdlife, including cranes and the occasional pink flamingo; look out for them on your way into or out of Cágliari. While you're in the centre you'd do well to give your car a rest, if you have one, as this is not a town for the motorist; there is too much to absorb here without the added headache of negotiating its narrow streets, one-ways and pedestrian areas.

**Via Roma.** Cágliari's main thoroughfare, **Via Roma,** is a busy dual-carriageway running alongside the ferry port between piazzas Matteotti and Améndola. Piazza Matteotti is the location of the main **rail and bus stations,** and is dominated by the very un-Sardinian *Municípío* (town hall), a neo-Gothic 19th-cent job, partly destroyed by bombing in the Second World War but rebuilt as before.

Opposite Via Roma is the *Stazione Maríttima,* the departure-point for boats and where you find ticket offices, bars, waiting areas and an information office. Behind Via Roma, and running parallel to it, is the narrow Via Sardegna, where some of the town's hotels and a good selection of its restaurants are.

**Il Bastione.** Wandering up any of the steep alleys from here you'll come to Piazza Costituzione and the monumental **San Remy Bastion.** This, too, is mainly 19th-cent and not entirely in harmony with the surroundings, its imperialist tone rather spoiled by the graffiti and weeds sprouting out of its walls. All the same it's worth the climb up the grandiose flight of steps inside to reach the wide flat expanse at the top, offering Cágliari's best views over the port, and beyond to the lagoons. Sunset is especially a good time, but it's a cool break at any hour from sightseeing-fatigue, and its shady benches are ideal for a 20-minute lie-down.

**The Citadel.** From the Bastion, you can wander off in any direction to enter the intricate maze of streets of Cágliari's citadel. This is the oldest part of the city, traditionally the seat of the administration, aristocracy and highest offices of the church. It has been little altered since the Middle Ages, and requires a good leisurely stroll through its impossibly narrow streets to soak up its atmosphere and explore its photogenic nooks.

**The Cathedral.** Cágliari's Duomo lies at the heart of the old city in the long Piazza Palazzo. It stands in one corner of the square, flanked by the 18th-cent governor's palace (formerly the royal palace of the Piedmontese kings of Sardinia, though they seldom stayed here) and the even more sumptuous Archbishop's Palace. Both were the work of the same architect, Davisto, in 1769.

**Fake front.** The cathedral's tidy Romanesque façade is in fact a fake, added in this century in the old Pisan style. The structure dates originally from the 13th cent but it has accumulated the trappings of other eras and in particular has gone through, as D.H. Lawrence put it, "the mincing machine of the ages, and oozed out Baroque and sausagey."

Inside, the greatest treasure is a couple of massive **stone pulpits,** which were originally one single pulpit, now placedone on each side of the main doors. Crafted in around 1160, this giant piece had been intended to grace Pisa's cathedral but was later presented to Cágliari, along with a set of lions by the same sculptor which now stand outside the building.

Other features of the cathedral that are worth a glance include the ornate tomb of Martin II of Aragon, sculpted in the 17th cent; the presbytery, through which you can see some paintings and ecclesiatical items in a small museum, and the **crypt.** This chamber has been hewn out of the rock, and little of its walls and ceiling has been left undecorated. Sicilian artists have cut an array of niches containing carvings of all the Sardinian saints whose ashes were said to have been found under the church of San Saturnino in 1617 (see below). Also here is the **mausoleum** belonging to the wife of Louis XVIII of France, Marie-Josephine of Savoy, who died in exile in Harwell, England, her body brought here a year later. And nearby is the tomb of the infant son of Vittório Emanuele I of Savoy and Maria-Teresa of Austria, Carlo Emanuele, who died in 1799.

**The Archeological Museum.** At the opposite end of Piazza Palazzo a road leads into a smaller square, Piazza Indipendenza, site of Sardinia's *Museo Archeológico Nazionale.* It's the best of its kind on the island, and a must for anyone interested in learning something about Sardinia's past or intending to visit its archeological sites. When I last saw it, the museum was only partially open, in the process of being transferred a short distance away, through the arch to the small Piazza dell'Arsenale. Here, the **Cittadella dei Musei,** 'Museum Citadel,' has been opened recently on the site of the old royal arsenal, with the aim of housing all the city's principal museums. The transfer of the archeological exhibits was due for completion in 1991.

Wherever you see it, the collection's main interest is in its prehistoric and classical relics. The island's most important Phoenician, Carthaginian and Roman finds are all gathered here, including busts and statues of muses and gods, jewellery and coins, and funerary items from the sites of Nora and Tharros.

**Encounter with the past.** But everything pales beside the museum's greatest pieces, from the mysterious Nuraghic culture of Sardinia. The most eye-catching of these is a series of **bronze statuettes.** Ranging from about 6 inches (15cm) to 18 in (45cm) tall, spindly and highly stylised, but packed with invention and quirky humour, these are our main source of information about this Proto-Sard phase of the island's history. Most of them show warriors and hunters in the act of drawing bows and wielding swords and spears, but others show athletes, shepherds, mothers suckling, bulls, horses and wild animals. Primitive but somehow modern too, most of these figures were votive offerings, made to decorate the inside of Nuraghic temples, and most were found buried under the main *nuraghi* at Abbasanta, Barumini, Séttimo San Pietro and Macomer, hidden from the grasping hands of foreign predators.

Among the items is a collection of votive boats, again extravagantly decorated with cow-horns, birds and animals; another display-case shows domestic items in use 3,000 years ago, day-to-day articles from the dawn of history. But it is the figurines that are most compelling. Alan Ross, wrote in *The Bandit on the Billiard Table*: "One has swum underwater and come upon an ancient ritual, or battle, arrested by an unknown act of fate. . . No one can doubt that these are real men, going about their daily business over the sun-struck plains and granite ravines of their island." See if you agree.

The *Museo Archeológico* is open Monday-Saturday 0900-1400, Sunday 0900-1300, and 1530-1830 on Wed, Fri, Sat; entry is L3,000. The *Cittadella dei Musei,* which holds an unexpected but diverting permanent exhibition of far eastern artefacts donated by a local sailor, is free, open 0900-1250, 1600-1850 daily.

**The Towers of San Pancrazio and the Elephant.** Also in Piazza Indipendenza is the **Torre San Pancrazio,** and it's only a short walk from here to the **Torre dell'Elefante** in Via dell'Università. Together these formed the main bulwarks of the city's defences, erected by Pisa in 1305-7 after it had won the city from the Genoans, though the towers didn't stop the Aragonese from walking in just 15 years later. Both have a curious half-finished look about them, with the side facing the old town completely open. The 'elephant' of the 'Elephant Tower' is a small carving of the animal on one side.

As the name implies, Via dell'Università is the core of Cágliari's old **university** district. Founded by Philip II in 1605, this was one of the few benefits which the Spanish brought to their island possession, and it was in the Physics Institute here that a physicist called Antonio Pacinotti invented the dynamo in 1875. Most of the university's faculties have now transferred to an airier part of town.

**The Roman Amphitheatre.** From the Elephant tower, Viale Buon Cammino leads to the *Anfiteatro Romano.* Cut out of solid rock in the 2nd cent AD, the amphitheatre could hold what was then the entire city's population of about 20,000. Despite much decay, with much of the site cannibalised to build churches in the Middle Ages, you can still see the cavea, trenches for the beasts, underground passages, and several rows of seats. Unfortunately, apart from some special occasions, the theatre is closed to visitors not holding a special permit, though you can see a good part just by walking round it. If you want that special permit, try asking the archeological supervisor at the town hall.

**Botanical Gardens.** Below the amphitheatre and above Cágliari's extensive hospital, the university's *Orto Botánico* offers more shady nooks,

*You won't be jostling for space on Argentiera's beach.*

open 0900-1300 daily, plus 1600-1930 (or to sunset in winter) on Monday, Wednesday and Friday only; L1,000 adults, L500 children, free on Sunday.

**Church of San Saturnino.** At Piazza San Cósimo in Via Dante, a short walk from Piazza Améndola in the newer part of town, is the oldest church in Sardinia and one of the most important surviving examples of church architecture of this period (5th cent AD) in the whole Mediterranean. Middle-eastern in appearance with its palm trees and cupola, the basilica was built on the spot where the Christian martyr Saturninus met his fate during the reign of Diocletian, later becoming the city's patron saint. Despite severe damage inflicted by bombs in World War II, the church's sturdy walls still stand. Round about lie various bits of flotsam from the past: four cannonballs, fragments of Roman sarcophagi and slabs of stone with Latin inscription still visible.

**Sanctuary of Bonária.** Not far from San Saturnino, the 14th-cent Sanctuário di Bonária stands above Viale Armando Diaz. The front of the church has recently been modernised and aggrandised by a geometric flight of steps running up to it – impressive but a bit of an overdose of cement – and no good for visitors in wheelchairs but you can follow the road around. Inside stands the legendary image of Our Lady of Bonaria, which was miraculously rescued from a shipwreck in 1370. Caught in a storm on the way from Spain to Italy, the sailors jettisoned everything, noticing one chest that refused to sink and was washed ashore. Beachcombers found the chest contained an image of the Madonna, and so this sanctuary was built in her honour.

110

**House of Tigellius and the Sepulchre of Attilia Pomptilla.** Two other Roman remains which the classical enthusiast might make an effort to see are the house of the Roman poet, Tigellius, and the Sepulchre of Attilia Pomptilla, also known as the Grotto of the Viper. Both are open to visitors only with special permission, available from the town hall, as for the amphitheatre above.

Tigellius was an obscure Sardinian poet whose singing and versifying was appreciated by the Roman emperor Augustus, but loathed by perhaps better judges such as Horace and Cicero. The poet lived in this 2nd-cent AD **villa** on Via Tigellio, just off Corso Vittório Emanuele. Still visible are the atrium (central court) with two columns and some mosaic decorations, though the overall effect is rather spoiled by the proximity of 20th-cent blocks of flats all around.

The **Sepulchre of Attilia Pomptilla** is a little further out of town on Viale Sant'Avendrace, reached by continuing along Corso Vittório Emanuele, which turns into Viale Trento before merging with Viale Avendrace at Piazza Trento. The tomb belonged to the wife of one Cassius Philippus, a Roman aristocrat who was probably exiled to Sardinia in the 1st cent AD. Its nickname, *Grotta della Vípera,* seems strange in an island famously free of these or any other poisonous snakes, but is taken from the two serpents carved into the tomb's pediment (a pediment is the triangular section on top of the columns of a classical building). If you can't be bothered with applying for a permit to see this, quite a lot is visible from the pavement. Behind, a flight of steps leads to an old Punic necropolis, the cemetery of Carthaginian *Karalis,* though there is little more to see here than a row of holes in the rock-face.

**Streetlife.** In the morning, drop in on the market in Piazza Cármine behind Piazza Matteotti. Later you could join in the evening *passeggiata* down the elegant Via Manno, a road which holds some of the most famous names in the world of Italian retailers. It's a steep walk, though, running down from the Bastion at Piazza Costituzione to the statue of Savoyan king, Carlo Felice, in Piazza Yenne. If you fetch up at Piazza Costituzione, there's a nice old-fashioned bar, *Caffé Genovese,* on the corner with Via Garibaldi, with tables outside where you can sip a granita or nibble an ice cream.

Another fashionable — but expensive — bar is the *Caffé Mediterráneo* out over at the Santuário di Bonaária, attached to the Hotel Mediterráneo. A little further on is Cágliari's *Sant'Elia* football stadium, scene of England's first-round World Cup matches in 1990.

**The beaches at Poetto.** Beyond Capo Sant'Elia, the headland jutting out into the Golfo di Cágliari, is the city's nearest **beach** at Poetto, a 10-minute drive from the centre of town (follow signs eastward out of town); buses (with a *P* before the number) leave every five minutes — 20 minutes in winter — from Piazza Matteotti: tickets L700 from the booth. The road follows the beachside strip for four miles (6km), so take your pick among the dozens of fine-sand beaches, many with small bars and showers nearby. Some are lidos, where you pay a standard daily rate (about L3,000) for entry and use of deckchairs and umbrella. Cleanliness here is guaranteed, with none of the dusty cigarette-butts that accumulate on the free beaches over the summer. See below for hotels here.

**The Devils' Saddle.** One end of the beach is dominated by the *Sella del Diávolo*, or Devil's Saddle, aptly describing the shape of the rock that rears above Capo Sant'Elia; legend claims that the Archangel Gabriel fought and won a fierce battle here against the Devil himself. The name of Cágliari's gulf, Golfo degli Angeli, favours the victor, the archangel himself. Below is a small **yachting marina,** the Marina Píccola, the smaller of Cágliari's ports for pleasure craft (see below for yachting information).

From here, the beaches begin, backed along the whole road by smart villas, alternating with a blitz of bars, pizzerias, fairgrounds and ice cream kiosks. You can imagine the scene in August but by the end of September it's a much quieter affair.


# CAGLIARI FACTFILE
## HOTELS

The *annuario,* the accommodation directory supplied by Cágliari's tourist information offices, gives the full range of 23 hotels but here's a sample:

### Four-star

**Regina Margherita;** Cágliari's poshest hotel at Viale Regina Margerita 44 (✆070.670342; L179,000) opened in 1988. Each of the rooms has shower or bath, air-conditioning, colour TV, telephone and fridge. It's designed more for the convenience of businessmen than tourists, but you can expect the best service, maximum comfort and top-quality cuisine.

**Sardegna;** Recently upgraded, this is Cágliari's only other four-star hotel, at Via Lunigiana 50 (✆ 070.286245; L99,000), on the way in from the airport and so a bit far from the centre. Full-board here is L126,000 per person.

### Three-Star

**Italia;** More central, at Via Sardegna 31 (✆ 070.655772), with doubles with bath at L83,000.

**Moderno;** This one's right on Piazza Matteotti, at Via Roma 159 (✆ 070.653971; L93,000), convenient for the station but expect a little noise. There is no restaurant here.

**Motel Agip;** On Circonvallazione Pirri (✆ 070.521373; L71,000) on the outskirts of town.

*Traces of opulence: the Roman mosaics at Nora.*

*The entrance to Neptune's Grotto, Alghero.*

*San Pietro: the view from Capo Sándalo.*

*Miles of rocky shoreline on San Pietro island.*

**Capo Sant'Elia;** A smart establishment out on the seafront at the cape (Localitá Calamosca; ✆ 070.371628) with doubles with bath at L79,000.

**Two-Star**

**Quattro Mori;** Low-key and central at Via Angioy 27 (✆ 070.668535; L41,000).

**One-Star**

**Centrale;** Via Sardegna 4 (✆ 070.654783; L21,000). A bit downbeat and noisy, and often full, but cheap.

**La Perla;** Via Sardegna 18 (✆ 070.669446; L22,000). The same comment as above.

**Flora;** Via Sássari 45 (✆ 070.658219; L33.000). Just off Piazza Cármine close by the station.

**Firenze;** Corso Vittório Emanuele 50 (✆ 070.653678; L17,000). Like most of these establishments, at the top of several flights of stairs, but it's cosy and popular (though with only five rooms, often full).

**Olimpo;** Just up the road at Corso Vittório Emanuele 145 (✆ 070.658915; L18,000), it's clean and cheap and often full.

**La Sirenetta;** Out at Poetto (Viale Poetto 192; ✆ 070.370332) so a bit dearer, with doubles at L35,000. Don't expect to find space here in the summer.

*Nuoro's Piazza Vittorio Emanuele lies at the heart of the old town.*

## RESTAURANTS

Cágliari is overflowing with good-quality trattorias and ristorantes and, because you are in a commercial city not dependant on seasonal fluctuations, you'll find most are open all the year round — but many close on Sunday or Monday for their *riposo settimanale*.

The hub of the gourmand's Cágliari is Via Sardegna. Here are clustered a selection of pizzerias, trattorias and *ristoranti;* the following are a sample.

**Il Buongustaio;** (closed Tues) is a rustic-style place at Via Concezione 7: arrive early, or else book. **Da Serafino,** with entrances at both Via Sardegna 109 and Via Lepanto 6 (closed Thurs) is extremely good value and popular with the locals. The **Trattoria-Pizzeria** at Via dei Mille 16 is a bit touristy but always open. If you want to sample seafood, you can't do better than the **Stella Marina di Montecristo** (closed Mon), specialising in lobster, swordfish, squid etc., at the end of Via Sardegna (where it meets Via Regina Margherita). Via Sardegna also has a Chinese restaurant, the **Hong Kong** at no.63, that is cheap and open daily — and there's another in Via Santa Margherita. The **Antica Hostaria** at Via Cavour 60 (closed Sun) has quality fare and takes credit cards.

## TOURIST OFFICES

For **practical information** the most useful tourist offices are the AAST kiosk in Piazza Matteotti (✆ 070.669255), the EPT desk at the airport (✆ 070.240200) and the EPT desk at the Stazione Maríttima (✆ 070.668352). The AAST has a bigger office at Via Mameli 97 (✆ 070.664195-6) and the main EPT office is at Piazza Defennu 9 (✆ 070.654811, 663207).

For **train information** the desk at the main station is open Monday-Saturday 0730-1930, Sunday closed. There is also a computerised service telling you everything you might want to know, with instructions in four languages.

Administration and **specific information** is handled either at the Regional Tourist Board's office at Viale Trento 69 (✆ 070.6061) or the ESIT headquarters, occupying the same premises as the AAST's office at Via Mameli 97 (✆ 070.668522).

## TRANSPORT

The number for **Elmas Airport** is ✆ 070.240047. See chapter 3 for flight information. The main **railway station** is at Piazza Matteotti (✆ 070.656293), but trains run by the *FCS* (*Ferrovie Complementari della Sardegna*) to Mandas, Sorgono and Arbatax leave from Piazza Repúbblica (✆ 070.491304). For main train times see chapter 4.

The ARST **bus station** is also in Piazza Matteotti; PANI's office is at the other end of Via Roma at Piazza Darsena 4 (✆ 070.652326). **Taxis**

can be found in Piazza Matteotti, Piazza Yenne and Piazza Repúbblica.

The main **shipping** terminus is at the Stazione Maríttima on Via
Roma (✆ 070.662328). There are Tirrenia ticket agencies at Via
Campidano 1, (✆ 070.666910), and the Stazione Maríttima itself (✆
070.666065).

Boats leave for **Genoa** on Mon, Wed, Sat, 1 June-30 September;
Tues and Sun, October-May, leaving at 1500. The crossing takes 16
hours. Prices per person range from L101-140,000 for a 1st class cabin
to L56-73,000 for a seat only in 2nd class. Cars cost L67-140,000
depending on season and size.

For **Civitavécchia,** boats leave daily at 1800, and there is another
departure 18 June-14 September daily at 1830;the crossing takes 13-15
hours. Prices are L69-96,000 for a 1st class cabin; L33-44,000 for a seat
only in 2nd class. Cars cost the same as on the Cágliari-Genoa
crossing.

For **Naples,** boats leave 1 June-30 September Mon, Wed, Sat;
October-May Thurs and Sat, with departures at 1830. Crossings take
16 hours. 1st class cabins cost L79-110,000, 2nd class seats L29-38,000.
Cars cost the same as Cágliari-Genoa.

For **Palermo,** boats leave 1 June-30 September on Thurs, October-
May on Fri; departure time is 1900, getting in at 0830 the next day.
Prices are L71-98,000 for a 1st class cabin, L26-34,000 for a 2nd class
seat only. Cars cost the same as on the Cágliari-Genoa crossing.

For **Trápani,** boats leave on Wed at 2100, getting in at 0830 the next
day. Prices same as for Palermo.

For **Tunis,** boats leave on Mon at 1900, arriving at 1630 the next day.
Prices are L133-160,000 for a 1st class cabin, L74-88,000 for a 2nd class
seat only. Cars cost L121-177,000 according to size and season.

## CAR HIRE

All major companies have agencies at Elmas airport. In town, *Avis*
is at Via Sonnino 87 (✆ 070.668128) with prices starting at L182,000 for
a Fiat Panda for 2 days, L513,000 for 7 days (unlimited mileage). *Hertz*
at Piazza Matteotti 1 (✆ 070.668105) charges L110,000 a day for 1-2
days, dropping to L77,000 per day for 6 or more days (also a Panda
with unlimited mileage). *Maggiore* at Viale Monastir 116 (✆
070.273692) charges L125,000 a day for 1-2 days, L600,000 for the week
(Panda; unlimited mileage).

The **smaller independent companies** might have deals which suit
your needs better: *Sina* at Piazza Gramsci 20 (✆ 070.669409) offers a
Panda for L96,000, unlimited mileage, but requires a sizeable deposit.
*Ruvioli* (Via dei Mille 11; (✆ 070.658955,666905) offers the same per
day, L486,000 for the week. Eurodollar (c/o Sardamondial, Via Roma 9;
✆ 070.668094) charges L120,000 for 12 hours, L132,000 for 24, L633,000

for a week (Panda; unlimited mileage). The cheapest that I found were *Caralis* (Via Santa Margherita 12; ✆ 070.652913) — also an undertaker's office! — charging L40,000 per day for a Panda, plus L350 per km, but the first 100km per day free, and *Autonoleggio Catte* (Via Roma 189; ✆ 070.657245) charging L30,000 a day for a Fiat Uno, plus L400 per km.

The smaller agencies have only one or two cars available so it's worth booking, or calling in early. Their offices are often closed during the day.

**Cycle hire.** If you want to rent a bicycle try the open-air shop at Piazza Paolo VI, opposite the Santuário di Bonária. Rates are L3,000 an hour, getting cheaper for the longer you take it; a day costs L15,000.


## MISCELLANEOUS

**Changing Money.** Most banks are around Piazza Matteotti and Largo Carlo Felice. There is also a bureau de change at the airport (Mon-Sat 0800-1330) and the station (Mon-Sat 0700-2000). Normal **banking hours** are Mon-Fri 0830-1330, 1500-1600, but the Banco di Sardegna in Piazza Matteotti has a 24-hour automatic money-changing machine.

**Telephoning.** The main telephone office is at Via Angioy, open 0800-2200. Others are at Via Salaris and Via Cima. The station has lots of telephones, but it's noisy.

**Post Office.** The *Posta Centrale* is at Piazza del Cármine, open Mon-Sat 0720-2020.

**Chemists.** Opening hours are normally 0830-1300, 1630-1745, but there is always one open when the others are closed, according to a rota: for information see any chemist's door.

**Emergencies.** The main Carabinieri headquarters are at Via Sonnino 111 (✆ 112). For a police emergency dial ✆ 070.4444. The emergency department at the city's hospital is at Via Peretti 21 (✆ 070.2000), or dial ✆ 070.60181 or ✆ 070.656979. For consulates, see the index.

**ACI.** The ACI office for all matters relating to cars is at Via Carboni Boi 2 (✆ 070.492881).


## CAGLIARI FOR YACHTERS

The large commercial port has plenty of space for yachts, best in the inner north-east basin, the Darsena, near the harbour-master's office. If there is no room here try the Lega Navale marina at the harbour's eastern end, administered by the Italian Yachting Club.

For something a little smaller-scale, go round the cape to the Marina Píccola at Poetto, where there are good facilities.

**Festivals.** D.H. Lawrence was especially impressed by the children's carnival costumes in 1921, and today Cágliari's **Carnival** is just as flamboyant. **Holy Week** sees processions on Good Friday and Easter Sunday, with the re-enactment of the Passion of Christ and symbolic meetings of processions headed by Christ and the Virgin Mary.

Cágliari's most impressive festival, however, is that of **Sant'Efisio,** starting on 1 May. Spread over three days and featuring a religious procession between Cágliari and the saint's church near Nora, 40km away (see later in this chapter) the festival attracts thousands from all over the island, and is an excellent opportunity to see the widest possible range of traditional Sard costumes.

## CAGLIARI PROVINCE

The province of Cágliari is Sardinia's biggest, containing about half of the island's entire population. There is nothing particularly homogeneous about this southern end of the island; it's just a collection of distinct regions each with its own historical, economic and social traditions. Apart from the plain of Campidano spreading out north-west of Cágliari, it is all hills and mountains, covered with forest and maquis, and well watered by many mountain streams.

To the **east** the Sarrabus chain rises to 1,029m (3,380ft) at the Monti dei Sette Fratelli, 'Seven Brothers Mountains.' This remote and uninhabited area, though cut through by the SS 125 road, is too desolate even for shepherds, but the jagged coastline attracts more visitors, with some unforgettable views over empty coves and rocky beaches. The holiday area is concentrated in the elite coastal tourist development of the Costa Rei, and the gaudier resort of Villasimíus.

**Campidano.** Inland of Cágliari, Sardinia's richest agricultural region occupies the plain of Campidano, the beneficiary of countless rivers as well as a vast drainage and reclamation scheme. Scenically, this is duller than the province's more mountainous zones, though there are some attractive areas bordering it, like the **Marmilla** region, holding some of the island's most important Nuraghic remains, in particular the complex of **Su Nuraxi.**

**Iglesiente.** West are the mineral rich and heavily mined mountains of the Iglesiente area, named from the picturesque old town of **Iglésias.**

**Isola di Sant'Antíoco.** Other important towns are Carbónia and **Sant'Antíoco;** the latter, formerly one of Sardinia's most important settlements, is the main town of the Isola di Sant'Antíoco, which isn't an island at all as it's joined to the mainland by a narrow isthmus. Sant'Antíoco peninsula and the true island of **San Pietro** form a small archipelago where the traces of Genoan colonisation still linger in the customs and language.

**Transport links.** Good roads exist for most areas you might want to visit, though a four-wheel drive would be useful for some of the remoter mountain areas and some of the tracks.

By **train,** there are at least ten departures a day from Cágliari to Carbónia; for Iglésias change at Villamassárgia for the ten-minute ride. For local trains north, go to Cágliari's secondary station in Piazza Repúbblica for trains on the FCS line. At Mandas, the line splits for Sórgono, in the centre of the Barbágia, or Arbatax, the port on Sardinia's east coast.

ARST **buses** run to all destinations in the province: check at the *autostazione* in Piazza Matteotti for timetables and prices.

**Ferries to Isola di San Pietro.** To reach San Pietro you need to take a ferry either from Sant'Antíoco's minor port of Calasetta, or the Sardinian mainland port of Porto Vesme; details are below.

## EAST TO SARRABUS AND THE COSTA REI

Once past the growing industrial town of Quartu Sant'Elena, the coast gets progressively emptier, and despite the closeness of Cágliari, it's easy to find isolated inlets for a leisurely dip. **Solanas** is the prettiest village, superbly situated and watched over by one of the sentinel towers that dot this entire coast, but without any accommodation at hand. Nearby, however, is the four-star *Capo Boi* (Open May-September; ✆ 070.791505), charging four-star prices (L146-224,000 for a double) for casual callers though much less for package tourists for whom it supplies all the creature comforts in splendid isolation.

The only campsites in the vicinity are the *Pini e Mare* (June-September; ✆ 070.812125) at Quartu Sant'Elena — Cágliari's nearest site in the Capitana district — or the much preferable *Spiaggia del Riso* ('Rice Beach'), located right on the beach on Capo Carbonara, below Villasimíus. It's well signposted, but difficult to reach without a car, and bus passengers from Villasimíus may have to walk the last couple of kilometres. It's open all year (✆ 070.797150, 791052).

**Villasimíus.** You can take your pick of hotels at **Villasimíus,** three miles (5km) up the road. Not so long ago a dreary little village, Villasimíus has been developed almost to death, but at least it is lively, and in summer is a hotbed of bars, pizzerias, tourist shops and nightclubs. The rest of the time it sinks back to sleep, and visitors may find it half closed between October and May. There are good **yachting** facilities here.

**Accommodation** choices range from the elite *Residenza Le Dune* out on the beach (✆ 070.791681; L624- 936,000 a week for two rooms with three beds) to the three-star *Dell'Ancora* (✆ 070.791272; L51,000) to the only one-star hotel, *Stella d'Oro* (✆ 070.791255, L47,000). Other hotels and rooms for rent are at the nearby beach. There's a tourist **information** office in Piazza Incani (✆ 070.791393).

Eleven miles (18km) north of Villasimíus, at the other end of a winding coastal road with some steep views, there are two **campsites** at Cala Sinzias open March-November: *Garden Cala Sinzias* (✆ 070.995037 summer, ✆ 070.891069 winter), and *Limone Beach* (✆ 070.995006).

**Costa Rei.** After Cala Sinzias begins the Costa Rei. This is one of Sardinia's most recent large-scale tourist developments, and has the rich international flavour of the Costa Smeralda in the north. Like the Smeralda, the Costa Rei is all purpose-built self-contained summer accommodation, with very little action in the winter months, but I feel that the six miles (10km) of beaches here are better than any you'll find on the Costa Smeralda itself, if your taste is for shimmering expanses of fine white sand. Behind the beaches nestle tourist villages, rented accommodation, bungalows, flats and villas, complete with tennis courts and some expensive bars and restaurants. Though clean and clearly carefully planned, the overall result is not just bland but highly soporific, but holidaymakers here may find just the right atmosphere for total relaxation.

If this tempts you, there's a three-star **hotel,** the *Free Beach Club* (✆ 070.991040; L89-120,000), otherwise you'll have to settle for rented or **holiday village accommodation,** which should work out a lot cheaper. Expect to pay about L260,000 a week for a two-roomed apartment, rising to more than a million lire in high season, plus supplements for electricity, cleaning, and washing; better to come before 15 June or after 15 September, when there are special offers, such as two weeks for the price of one. For more information, write to *Casa Vacanze* at Via Marco Polo 5, 09040 Costa Rei, Castidias, Cágliari (✆ 070.991102; winter ✆ 0182.88406); or *Holiday Service* at Corso Vittório Emanuele 404, Cágliari (✆ 070.669194/654720; fax 070.668159), or contact the EPT branch in Cágliari. These agencies can also provide information on **property purchases.**

A **bus service** connects Costa Rei with Cágliari at least five times daily in summer, twice in winter.

At the northern end of Costa Rei is the *Capo Ferrato* **campsite** (March-October; ✆ 070.991012), and there is another at Torre Salinas (✆ 070.99632; April-October), five miles (8km) further north as the crow flies, though much more in practice as the road doubles back inland to meet the main SS 125.

**Muravera.** The next town is Muravera, an inland citrus-growing centre that has developed as a resort because of its coastal offshoots. There are a couple more campsites in the neighbourhood, and a choice of seaside **hotels.** In town, try the *Corallo* (✆ 070.9930502; L45,000) or the cheap *Stella d'Oro* (✆ 070.9930446; L19,000).

**The inland route.** From Muravera, a newly-asphalted road curves inland through the village of San Vito into the hilly Gerrei region. San Vito compensates for its drabness with some lively **festivities** on its saint's day, June 15; there is another on the first Sunday in August, and five days of fun around the third Sunday in October − with traditional costumes, poetry and singing competitions, and concerts.

Alternatively you could take the tortuous SS 125 mountain road that cuts through the middle of the **Monti dei Sette Fratelli,** taking you from Muravera back to Cágliari. This is more scenic, bringing you through the desolate Picocca gorge, with its wind-eroded rock sculptures.

## NORTH TO CAMPIDANO, SU NURAXI AND THE MARMILLA

For 60 miles (100km) between Cágliari and Oristano, the Campidano plain extends featurelessly, its flatness exploited by King Carlo Felice in the 1820s when he routed along here the long highway running the length of the island, still named after him. Now a fast dual carriageway, the SS 131, it's useful if you're in a hurry, though you might miss some spots of historical interest.

**San Luri Castle.** For instance, San Luri, lying 24 miles (40km) up from Cágliari. The 13th-cent castle here was where Mariano IV of Arborea, father of the warrior-queen Eleanor, signed a peace treaty with the Aragonese king in the hope of getting him off his back, in vain as it turned out. As Giudice of Arborea, Eleanor spent a lifetime in arms against the Spaniards with some success, but in 1499, after her death, Martino, the son of the King of Aragon, won a definitive victory at San Luri against forces commanded by the new Giudice, Aimerico, married to the dead Eleanor's younger sister.

San Luri's castle today is well-preserved and holds a small **museum,** open only Tuesday, Wednesday and Friday evenings 1700-2000 (L3,000), displaying a private collection of curios and relics, many from the First World War and Mussolini's Ethiopian campaign. At the centre of town is the 16th-cent church of San Rocco, visible from miles away. Before leaving San Luri, why not buy a loaf of the local bread? Huge and flavoursome, it's renowned throughout the Campidano.

There are a couple of **hotels** here, the *Mirage* (℗ 070.9307100; L47,000) and the *Castello* (℗ 070.9307045; L18,000).

**La Marmilla.** North of San Luri is the district known as La Marmilla, an area rich in *nuraghi,* including one excavation known as **Genna Maria,** outside the village of Villanovaforru. Recently unearthed, the site dates from the middle of the second millenium BC. In the village a **museum** has opened, showing a selection of graceful ceramics and other finds covering a period of eight centuries, many of them artifacts for domestic use (open Tues-Sun 0900-1300, 1530-1930, winter 1530-1730; L3,000).

**Su Nuraxi.** Far more striking, however, is the *nuraghe* of Su Nuraxi, outside Barumini. It is best reached via the local SS 197 leading northeast from San Luri. This route will also give you the chance to view the extraordinary conical hill at **Las Plassas,** just south of Barumini. Clearly visible sticking up like broken teeth from the top of the hill's round peak are the remaining fragments of the 12th-cent castle — a landmark for miles around.

Nearly two miles (3km) further, turn left at the village's main crossroads and you'll quickly see Su Nuraxi. Its dialect name means simply 'the *nuraghe,'* and it is the most splendid example of this type of building that is peculiar to Sardinia. Not only that; it's the biggest Nuraghic complex, comprising a bulky fortress and defences surrounded by the remains of a village, and it's thought to be the oldest, probably built around 1500BC. Though much of its history is obscure, it is clear that this was a palace at the very least — possibly a capital city. The central tower once reached 70ft (21m), though it's now shrunk to about 48ft (14.5m), its outer defences and inner chambers all connected by passageways and stairs. Sards and Carthaginians probably covered the whole complex with earth at the time of the Roman conquest, which may account for its excellent state of preservation.

Su Nuraxi is one of Sardinia's most recent nuraghic finds, and if it weren't for a torrential rainstorm that washed away the slopes of a hillside in 1949, the site may never have been revealed at all. If you have no time to spend at any other *nuraghi,* make a point of visiting this one, just to get an idea of the primitive grandeur of Sardinia's only home-grown civilisation. The site is free and open every day during daylight hours — and there's a restaurant and bar nearby.

*Old Sardinia: the weathered walls of Nuraghe Sant'Antine.*

La Marmilla ends just north of here at the high plain of **Giara di Gésturi,** last refuge of Sardinia's wild ponies. You'll need a little luck and a lot of cunning to spot these small, shy creatures, but in any case it's an excellent spot for walking, at a height of 1,900-2,000ft (580-610m). Leave your vehicle at one of the bordering villages of Tuili, Setzu, Sini, Genuri or Gésturi and spend an invigorating afternoon tramping through the thick woods, best of all in the spring, when the area is a regular stopover for migrating birds.

## SOUTH-WEST: THE IGLESIENTE AND SULCIS

Following the minor coast road south-west out of Cágliari, keep an eye out for the flamingos that can often be seen in the shallow lagoons on the edge of town. Soon after the lagoons, the country gets a little hillier, the tail-end of the **Iglesiente** region, the name given to the area immediately below the Campidano plain. The southern section is all mountains, some rising to more than 3,000ft (1000m), and crossed by only one very minor road running through Capoterra to Santadì. In winter or spring it's worth taking this road to see the wildest and remotest part of the Iglesiente mountains, forested with oak and overgrown with a colourful array of scented maquis.

Following the coast road you have to rush through the chemical-tainted air of the island's biggest industrial complex at **Sarroch;** the SARAS refinery here is claimed to be the second-biggest in the Mediterranean, importing 18,000,000 tonnes of crude oil, mainly from Libya, and generating a number of subsidiary petrochemical industries. The sandy coves around the village of **Pula** are thankfully out of sight of the brutal industrial landscape, though for some they're still a little too close for comfort.

**Nora.** From Pula village a signposted road branches off for the promontory of Capo di Pula, where the 11th-cent church of **Sant'Efísio** stands, site of the saint's martyrdom and destination of Cágliari's famous Mayday procession. Behind it is an exquisite sandy bay which you'll find difficult to resist dipping into, though most visitors come here to see the **archeological site of Nora,** at the end of a small peninsula. Founded by the Phoenicians and settled later by Carthaginians and Romans, this is the most complete ancient site on the island, part of it under the sea, just visible below the surface close to the shore. The town was abandoned around the 3rd cent AD, possibly as a result of a natural disaster.

The remains on land include buildings – both habitations and Carthaginian warehouses – a temple, baths with some splendid mosaics surviving, and a theatre in a good state of preservation. The rest is rubble, but the site's position right on the headland makes it a vividly evocative place, full of atmosphere. The site is open 0900-2000 in summer, 0900-1230 and 1400-1700 in winter and the tickets (L3,000), which have a useful map of the site on the back, are also valid for a small **museum** back in Pula (signposted *museo*; open daily 0900-1300, 1600-1900) holding some small treasures unearthed from the site. A twice-daily **bus** from Cágliari stops at Pula and Nora.

The village has a few **hotels:** the *Sandalyon* (∅ 070.9209151; L34,000), *Eleonora* (∅ 070.9209691; L32,000) or *Quattro Mori* (∅ 070.9209124; L18,000).

For luxury-class, however, you'll have to travel a few kilometres further south to the **Santa Margherita** district, where the thick pine forest shelters a parade of top-class establishments mostly used by the tour companies, the biggest of them run by Britain's Trust House Forte. The *Forte Hotel Village* complex (∅ 070.92171) is a massive structure with beds for more than 1,200 people, and it shares its lavish beaches, pools, tennis and squash courts, stables, disco, cabaret, crêche etc, with another top-class hotel, the *Castello* (∅ 070.92171), both open May-October; casual visitors can expect to pay L245-371,000 for a double with bath.

Also here is the *Is Molas* (∅ 070.9241006; 96-116,000), open all the year round and handy for its championship **golf course,** though access to both this and its excellent restaurant is available to all.

**Bithia.** After another four-star hotel (the *Is Morus*; ∅ 070.921171), the main road curls inland towards Teulada, but it's worth turning left to take the scenic coastal road, with terrific views over a deserted cliff-hung coastline. A brief detour at the beginning of this stretch will bring you to the Punic and Roman city of Bithia, brought to light in 1933 together with the traces of a Nuraghic complex. Again, there's a splendid beach just beside it, marked by a 17th-cent watchtower.

Meeting the SS 195 just west of Teulada, the road continues past a turn-off for the small beach resort of **Porto Pino,** with two **campsites** (open in summer only) and a **hotel:** *La Medusa* (∅ 0781.967032; L23,000). At Giba you can choose to go east into the mountains or west to the sea. A third option is straight ahead along a small road that skirts the Lago di Monte Pranu − like almost all Sardinia's lakes, artifically created − passing through **Tratalias.** The only vestige of this small village's past importance is the well-restored Romanesque church of Santa Maria, consecrated in 1213 as Cathedral for the Sulcis region, the name given to the coastal strip of the Iglesiente.

**Mussolini's town.** From the uninteresting town of San Giovanni, you could continue five kilometres north to take a look at **Carbónia,** a coal-mining centre built by Mussolini in 1936 and originally called 'Mussolinia.' Today its regimented streets and planned workers' houses still carry a hint of the *Duce's* presence. On the other side of the SS 125 stands Sardinia's most important Carthaginian military site, the fortress of **Sirai,** with a watchful view both inland and out to sea.

**Sant'Antíoco.**Just off Sardinia's south-western coast lie the so-called 'islands' of Sant'Antíoco and San Pietro. The first has not been an island since the Carthaginians linked it to the mainland with a causeway, but the description has survived.

Although popular holiday destinations in summer, the islands have not yet upgraded their tourist industry to include holiday villages or mega tourist-complexes; in fact accommodation is on the scarce side, but the small scale of life here is what makes them an attractive proposition.

Access to Sant'Antíoco, which is the name of the main town as well as the peninsula-island, is along the Carthaginian causeway, built when the port was already an important outlet for the mining products of what is now the town of Carbónia and the surrounding area.

**The Monk and the Nun.** Halfway across the causeway look out for two stones sticking out of the water. These, named *Su Para* and *Sa Mongia* − 'the monk' and 'the nun' − are supposed to be the petrified remains of these two people who had fallen in love but, attempting to escape from Sant'Antíoco, were turned to stone in mid-flight as a sign of God's wrath.

The port-area of the town is just on the other side of the causeway, with **anchorage for yachts.** Nelson's flagship, **Vanguard,** put in here shortly before the Battle of the Nile in 1798, severely damaged from a storm at sea. The ship was rerigged in four days, though Nelson deplored that the ship's company was not allowed ashore, because of Sardinia's recently declared neutrality in the French Revolutionary Wars. "We are refused the rights of humanity," he wrote to Lady Nelson.

For all but sailors, however, the historical centre in the upper part of Sant'Antíoco holds the real interest. This has been inhabited continuously since Phoenician times and was an important base both for the Carthaginians and the Romans, commanding the whole of Sardinia's south-west coast. Its ancient name, *Sulcis,* was extended to cover the entire mainland coastal area.

**Catacombs.** The church of Sant'Antíoco, a Romanesque construction dating from the 12th cent, was built over Christian **catacombs,** which were in turn enlarged from an existing Carthaginian *hypogeum,* or underground burial-place. Dark and dingy but fascinating nonetheless, with authentic skeletons and reproductions of the ceramic objects found here during excavation, the catacombs are open for guided tours Mon-Sat 0900-1200, 1500-1800; Sun 1500-1900 (L2,500).

Before leaving the church look out for the statue of Saint Antiochus, who was himself interred in the catacombs − a second burial, after he had miraculously risen from the dead to convert the neighbouring people. The statue plainly shows his Mauretanian origins; his feast-day is on the second Sunday after Easter, which sees the start of a four-day affair featuring traditional songs, poetry recitations and dancing, a procession to the sea, and fireworks.

**Tophet.** From the piazza where the church stands, a signpost points down a side-road to the Punic necropolis or *tophet,* an extensive burial site dedicated to the Carthaginian goddess Tanit which once covered the entire hill where the old city now stands. Numerous urns are scattered all around, long thought to contain the ashes of first-born children gruesomely sacrificed according to the barbaric practices of the Carthaginians, though recent research has shown that much of the accepted view of the Carthaginians' religious rites was Roman propaganda, passed down through the generations to soil the reputation of their old enemies. The urns, it now seems, contained the cremated remains of terminally sick and still-born children, dead from natural causes. There is a similar *Tophet* in Carthage itself, still visible today – see *Discover Tunisia* in this series.

There are also the well-preserved ruins of a temple here, and an excellent little **museum** where a guide explains, in Italian, the most interesting specimens before taking you around the hilltop site. The museum has some notable pieces of Punic craftsmanship, and together with the site is open 0900-1200, 1530-1900 in summer, closing an hour earlier in winter (L2,500).

The best of Sant'Antíoco's **hotels** is the centrally-located *Moderno* (✆ 0781.83105; L37,800). Other hotels are out of town, mostly along the island's northern coast on the Calasetta road. There are also **campsites** here, one open all the year round: *Camping Vacanze* (✆ 0781.88218), just before Calasetta.

**Calasetta** itself is a small resort with more hotels, ranging from the *Stella del Sud* (✆ 0781.88488; L75-90,000), on the far side of town overlooking the main beach (the *Spiaggia Grande,*) to the enigmatically-named *FJBY* (✆ 0781.88444; L33,000). There are also pizzerias and restaurants: particularly good for seafood is the portside *Il Ciunco,* though I found the service was bad.

A dirt road runs south from here with access to beaches which are mostly hidden away out of view. They are better on the other side of the island, reachable from the tarmaced road that meanders down from Sant'Antíoco, skirting the island's highest point, Perdas de Fogu (890ft, 271m), from where a dramatic panorama takes in the nearby island of San Pietro.

**Isola di San Pietro.** Ferries leave from Calasetta and from the mainland industrial port of Portovesme, below Portoscuso, for Isola di San Pietro, on this daily schedule:

Calasetta-Carloforte 0735, 0930, 1050, 1320, 1450, 1720, 1850.
Portovesme-Carloforte 0605, 0700, 0800, 0850, 1000, 1030, 1335, 1440, 1520, 1550, 1710, 1900, 2020, 2150.

Crossing time is 30-40 minutes, one-way tickets L4,000 for a small car, L1,000 per person; return tickets are not available. Make sure you're in the queue in good time: summer especially sees a lot of congestion.

Barely three miles (5km) from Sant'Antíoco, San Pietro has more of a holiday feel to it, perhaps partly due to the absence of industry and the presence of a local fishing fleet. The dialect here is pure Piedmontese, two and a half centuries after the Savoyan king Carlo Emanuele III invited a colony of Ligurians (from the area around Genoa) to settle, after they were forced from their previous home on the island of Tabarca off Tunisia's north coast. The settlers were later snatched away to Tunisia in one of the last great pirate raids, but they were lucky enough to be ransomed back. The island's only town, Carloforte, is named from the king.

**Thirty-ninth parallel.** San Pietro sits astride the 39th parallel, and consequently has an observatory on the outskirts of Carloforte. Although the view from the island's eastern side is spoiled by the huge power-station opposite at Portovesme, built after coal exports dried up following World War II, San Pietro is neatly cultivated wherever the mountains allow. There are few sand beaches, but plenty of rocky shore affording some exquisite panoramas as well as great swimming and snorkelling. One famous beauty spot is at Capo Sándalo, at the end of a twisty road that leads to San Pietro's western shore, while at La Caletta, to the south, there is a cluster of houses round a beach and a campsite (see below).

**Tunny slaughter.** The Romans called the island *Accipitrum,* after the number of sparrowhawks that lived here, but its present name comes from a legend concerning Saint Peter, who was apparently shipwrecked here – a claim made by other islands in the Mediterranean – and taught the locals new fishing techniques. The most unusual kind of fishing performed on San Pietro, however, is the annual slaughter of tunny fish, the *Mattanza,* which takes place in May and June, when the tunny are passing the island on the way to their spawning grounds in the eastern Mediterranean. The fish are channeled through a series of nets ending in the *camera della morte* or death-chamber, where they are bloodily massacred as the net is slowly raised.

The practice has origins in several cultures; for example, the methods are identical to those used at other places where the Ligurians settled, such as the Egadi Islands off Sicily's western tip, but there's also a strong Arab influence in the use of titles such as *Raís,* Arab for 'chief,' for the leader of the slaughter squad, yet the name *Mattanza* is very close to the Spanish *matanza,* 'slaughter' or 'butchery.' Exactly the same method has been in use for generations off Tunisia's Cape Bon, where it's also known as the 'matanza.'

*The castle at Las Plassas is hard to miss.*

The spectacle is too brutal for many people in these environmentally-conscious times, but you will be condoning the slaughter whenever you have tunny served at dinner: it's an island speciality.

**Accommodation.** The only two officially registered **hotels** on the island are at Carloforte — the *Hieracon* (✆ 0781.854028; L59-70,000) and the *Riviera* (✆ 0781.854004; L62-71,000), both three-star; in summer, phone ahead to check on availability. Otherwise it shouldn't be difficult to find private rented accommodation. The **campsite** of *La Caletta* at La Caletta is 300m from the sea; open May-September; ✆ 0781.852112.

**Yachts.** Yachts can berth at Carloforte in the southern part of the harbour.

The **AAST,** opposite the quayside on the main Corso Tagliafico (✆ 0781.854009), has more information, and can provide maps and details on excursions.

An ideal way to see the island would be by bicycle, and you'll find a **bike-hire** shop by the Teatro Mútuo, in Via Venti Settembre.

**Iglésias.** Back on the mainland, the main town of note in the Iglesiente is its capital, **Iglésias.** The first thing you notice as you approach is the mineshafts and open castings that litter the surrounding mountains, mostly abandoned now. Gold, silver, iron, zinc and lead have been extracted here at different times, making it the chief

mining centre of Sardinia, though Iglésias itself bears little resemblance to the stereotyped image of a grimy mining town.

Below the hill where stands the crumbling Aragonese **Castello
Salvaterra,** the focus of the action is in the central tree-lined Piazza
Sella, named from the vintner whose *Sella & Mosca* wine (bottled in
Alghero) is one of Sardinia's best. Piazza Sella is the noisy meeting-
place of a throng of people every night, but for wandering the old
town's labyrinth of lanes and traffic-free squares the morning is the
best time.

**Town of churches.** Via Matteotti leads you into the heart of the old
town, where lies the secluded and elegant Piazza Duomo. The Duomo
(Cathedral) shows a mixture of Pisan and Aragonese styles, reflecting
the two dominant, and warring, powers in Iglésias during the Middle
Ages. The town got its name from the number of its churches (*iglesia*
is Spanish for 'church'), most interesting of which are the 13-14th-cent
Nostra Signora di Valverde, behind the station near the cemetery;
Santa Chiara, 13th-cent, in Piazza Manzoni, and Nostra Signora di
Buoncammino, on a hill a little way out of the centre. If you want a
meal, you could do worse than the *Ristorante Italia,* off Via Matteotti
(closed Sunday).

There is only one **hotel** in Iglésias, the three-star *Artu* (∅
0781.22492; L73,000) in Piazza Sella. The Spanish-flavoured Holy
Week celebrations would make Easter a good time to come.

**Tunnels and temples.** Inland of Iglésias, north of Domusnovas, is
the only example in Italy of a natural rock tunnel that you can drive
through, the 750m-long **Grotta di San Giovanni.**

**Temple of Antas.** North of Iglésias a mountain road climbs and
dips through a leafy valley, 9 miles (15km) along which, just off the
road, you might look in on the remote and little-visited *Témpio di
Antas,* a Roman temple built on the site of a Nuraghic sanctuary. The
curious Ionic-style columns can still be seen, along with the remains of
rooms and houses used by the priests and other members of its mixed
Phoenician-Roman population.

Further up this road, a left-turn after Fluminimaggiore leads to some
impressive beaches, and the holiday resort of **Buggerru.** South of
here, more deserted beaches beckon, though the panoramic road
around Nébida is best reached from the other side, via Iglésias. There
is a **hotel** in this beauty spot, the *Pan di Zúccaro* ('Sugarloaf')
(∅0781.47114; L38,000), named from the striking, sheer-sided rock
which dominates one end of the bay.

# 14: ORISTANO and the WEST

## The baby province

SARDINIA'S SMALLEST AND NEWEST PROVINCE, Oristano, was created in 1975 out of bits cut from the provinces of Cágliari and Nuoro. But it roughly corresponds with the much older territory of Arborea, the medieval *giudicato* which championed the Sardinian cause in the struggle against the Spaniards. Then, as now, Oristano was the region's main town, and today its crowded centre and fine buildings retain more than a hint of medieval atmosphere.

Of course the area's history goes back a lot further than the 14th cent, as you can see at the Punic-Roman site of **Tharros,** one of the best-preserved classical sites on the island. The low, heather-grown Sinis peninsula on which it stands also holds two early Christian churches, one of them with a small pagan sanctuary in its basement.

Even older traces are at Abbasanta, on the main road to Sássari, where the Nuraghic remains of **Losa** give an insight into Sardinia's prehistory. North up the coast, a visit to **Bosa** brings us back into the Middle Ages, the riverside town capped by a superb fort in the middle of a lovely unspoilt stretch of coastline.

## ORISTANO: THE TOWN

Although 2.5 miles (4km) from the sea and the mouth of the Tirso — at 90 miles (150km), the island's longest river — Oristano shares Cágliari's air of being encircled by water. This is the effect of the lagoons that surround it, and of the network of irrigation canals that have helped to make this area a richly productive agricultural zone, forming the basis of Oristano's growth and prosperity.

The southern lagoon, the Stagno di Santa Giusta, is one of the two homes of Sardinia's resident flamingo population: if they're not at Cágliari they're bound to be here. Look out, too, for the coracle-like flat-bottomed boats still used by the lagoon's fishermen, making a picturesque sight on the reed-edged lake in the early morning.

The outskirts of Oristano are unimpressive, and the town itself is not initially very striking, its old walls mostly replaced by busy boulevards. But you are quickly in the historic centre, sheltered from the traffic and ideal for wandering around on foot. Described by the travel-writer Alan Ross in the 1950s as 'essentially a country town, Oristano has long shrugged off that image and now looks every inch a smart and sophisticated provincial centre. The best time to be here is in the morning or the evening, best of all if you can see Oristano at both times, for it shows two completely different faces. Try to see as much as you can of the city's monuments in the morning, while leaving the evening free to gaze on these same buildings picked out in a soft yellow light and rising majestically amid the swarms of strollers below. Finish your ramble with a good meal, then you can sit out in one of the bars in Piazza Roma for a last glimpse of the ebbing streetlife, and squeeze the most out of the old town's charm.

**Local heroine.** At the heart of the evening bustle is, appropriately enough, Oristano's central symbol, the marble statue of **Eleonor d'Arborea** in the piazza named from her. Eleanor was the Giudice of the Arborea region from 1384 to 1404, was the best-known and best-loved of Sardinia's medieval rulers, and was the the only one who had any success in the wars against the island's aggressors. As head of the last of Sardinia's *giudicati* to remain independent of the Aragonese, Eleonor united local resistance and succeeded in negotiating a treaty in 1388 that guaranteed her a measure of independence – despite the desertion of her husband Brancaleone Doria to the Aragonese. She later strengthened her independence from the Spanish by forming a tactical alliance with the Genoans; and it was with Genoan help that the repentant Brancaleone managed to occupy Sássari on her behalf,

**Carta di Logu.** Eleonor's military achievements collapsed soon after her death from plague in 1404, though the most enduring benefit of her reign survived her by several centuries: the formulation of a Code of Laws, *Carta di Logu.* Her father, Mariano IV, first suggested the code, but it was Eleonor who introduced the laws in a legal document of 1395. Covering every aspect of civil legislation in nearly 200 chapters, this document was adopted in 1421 by the Aragonese, Sardinia's new masters, and extended throughout the island. As John Tyndale, the 18th-cent English lawyer and traveller in Sardinia, pointed out: "The framing of a body of laws so far in advance of those of other countries, where greater civilisations existed, must ever be the brightest ornament in the diadem of the Giudicessa."

**Traces of Eleanor.** Eleonor's statue in the square, carved in 1881, has her holding the scroll on which the laws were written, while small panels show her various victories; these days the statue and the *Comune* – town hall – in front of it are always crowded with dozens of schoolboys. The so-called *Casa di Eleanora* – 'Eleanor's House' – at Via Parpáglia 4 was actually built more than a century after her death, though it remains a good example of 16th-cent architecture. And Eleonor? She's buried in the 14th-cent church of Santa Chiara in

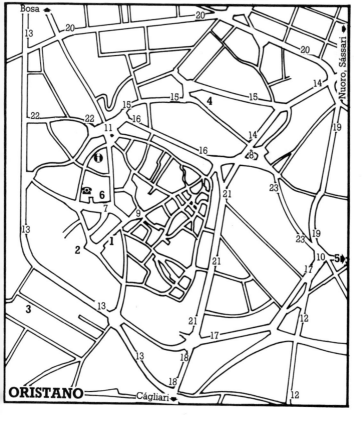

ORISTANO

*The Pisan tower of Orosei has been converted into a home.*

the parallel Via Garibaldi.

**Two towers.** From Piazza Eleonora di Arborea the narrow Corso Umberto, the pedestrianised shopping and promenading road, leads up to Piazza Roma, where pavement bars are clustered around the base of the **San Cristóforo tower** – also called *Porta Manna* or *Torre di Mariano*. This medieval bastion was the centrepiece of Oristano's fortifications, built by the Giudice Mariano II in 1291. The only other survivor of these defences is the less dramatic **Portixedda** – 'little gate' – a squat, neglected thing at the bottom of Via Mazzini.

**The Cathedral.** The Duomo stands beside its polygonal bell-tower in the spacious Piazza del Duomo. Though started in the 13th cent, most of the present cathedral is an 18th-cent Baroque renovation, retaining only parts of the apses from its original construction. All the same, it's a noble building which together with the 14th-cent onion-roofed bell-tower and the next-door seminary, the *Seminario Arborense* (1712), gives a rich theatrical flavour to this secluded square.

The fussy Baroque interior holds a few works of art, among them a wooden statue of the *Annunziata* by Nino Pisano, a 14th-cent Pisan sculptor, in the first chapel on the right.

**Sa Sartiglia.** At the other end of Via Duomo stands the church of San Francesco, built in 1838 and incorporating the remains of a much older Gothic building. The space in front, merging with Piazza Eleonora d'Arborea, forms the main arena for Oristano's annual fair of *Sa Sartiglia,* a carnival full of the pomp and paraphernalia that has built up from an unbroken tradition stretching back to the Middle Ages.

Here you'll find horseback parades and trials of horsemanship, all presided over by a judge who has previously been chosen from among the 'knight' contestants. The judge brings medieval tradition to life with his bizarre mix of medieval clothing, which he puts on in a highly formal ceremony, finished by a white mask. His title, *Su Componidori*, has Spanish origins and represents the continuation of the Giudice's role.

The judge is not the only costumed character, as all the knights wear masks and medieval clothes, and the whole performance seems to have stepped straight from the Middle Ages; the climax is the joust after which the festival is named, when the knights on horseback, charging towards a hanging ring, a *sartiglia*, try to capture it on the tip of their lance.

**Oristano's Museum.** Until recently the *Antiquarium Arborense*, containing various works of art and some archeological items collected locally, was at Via Vittório Emanuele 8, but in 1990 it was closed for two years and is due to reopen at fresh premises on the Via Parpáglia.

**Beaches.** The nearest stretch of sand is at **Torre Grande,** 3.5 miles (6km) out of town, but there are frequent buses from the ARST station, with a reduced service in winter. Other good beaches involve a trek up to the Sinis peninsula, of which more below.

**Tower.** Overshadowing everything is the 16th-cent tower after which this average resort is named, said to be the biggest of the defensive towers built by the Spaniards along this coast. It's closed to visitors and it's uninteresting.

**Hotels.** Oristano is badly off for accommodation, with just five hotels listed, only one of which could be called cheap, and that's often full. The smartest are the two *Mistral* hotels, both in Via Mártiri di Belfiore (℗ 0783.212186; L120,000) and (℗ 0783.212505; L75,000), both with bathrooms attached. Full-board is L85,000 *per person*. The modern *Ca-Ma* (℗ 0783.74374; L67,000) is at Via Vittório Véneto 119, on the way to the station. The *ISA* (℗ 0783.78040; L59,000) is nearby in Piazza Mariano, a bit rough for the price. The cheapest place, and the one with the friendliest reception, is also the most difficult to find − the *Píccolo Hotel* at Via Martignano 19 (℗ 0783.71500; L43,000), in an area of nameless (or at least unmarked) streets behind Piazza Martini, near Via del Carmine. The best bet is to ask someone in the area.

**Camping.** The nearest campsite is at Oristano's lido at Marina di Torre Grande, 3.5 miles (6km) away. The *Torre Grande* (May-October; ℗ 0783.22008), 150m from the sea, is reachable on the frequent buses from the ARST bus-station in Oristano. Otherwise you'll have to head out to the *S'Ena Arrubia* at Arborea (May-September; ℗ 0783.800552) or the *Is Arenas* on the north coast of the

*A village scene in Barbágia, where you can still see traditional dress.*

Sinis pensinsula (May-October; ℡ 0783.52284).

**Agriturismo.** Oristano's efficient and friendly agency for booking bed-and-breakfast accommodation is at Piazza del Duomo 17 (℡ 0783.73954).

**Eating.** Oristano is as short of restaurants as it is of hotels, but less choice does not mean worse fare. One of the best is *Il Faro* (closed Sunday; credit cards taken) at Via Bellini 25, with some moderately-priced dishes among the dearer ones. Easily found by following the arrows painted on the walls, is the *Trattoria del Teatro*, Via Parpáglia 11. It's a little on the pretentious side, with prices slightly above the average. The *Stella Marina* at Via Tirso 6 is a good place for seafood (closed Sunday). Via Tirso has a couple of other choices, both inexpensive: *Trattoria Gino* (closed Saturday) and *Ristorante Tirso* (closed Sunday), the latter good on fish.

For a helping of chic along with the quality food – though not particularly cheap – try the *Ristorante Craf* next to the Pro Loco in Via de Castro (closed Sunday, and the whole of August). There is another smart place, attractively vaulted, on Piazza Roma: the *Ristorante Arborea* (closed Sunday; credit cards taken) and at the other end of the same square the more downmarket *La Torre* (closed Monday), a ristorante-pizzeria with a wood-fired oven.

You might finish your meal with a glass of Oristano's celebrated *Vernaccia*, a strong, dry dessert wine that is one of Sardinia's best.

**Transport.** The **ARST** bus station is in Via Cágliari. The **PANI** bus agency is at Via Lombardia 30 on the north side of Via Sardegna. ARST buses run to **Marina di Torre Grande** and **Tharros** three or four times a day (reduced service Sundays and winter), and to **Cágliari and its airport** at 0710 and 1410 (80 minutes). There is also a service on the *Frau* line leaving at 0510 and 1610 from the ARST station, making a stop at Piazza Roma. The **railway station** is a good hike away on the outskirts of town, in Piazza Ungheria. From the station you can either take a taxi into town, or wait for the local bus (tickets on board) that passes every 40 minutes or so. There's a **left-luggage** office at the station.

**ACI.** The ACI office, for petrol coupons, car service and hire, is at Via Cágliari 50 (*Ø* 0783.212458).

**Car hire.** Apart from the ACI, the only car-hire agency is *Italia,* Via Tharros 22 (*Ø* 0783.302155). It offers a Fiat Tipo for L148,000 inclusive, for 24 hours.

**Information.** The main EPT is on the sixth floor of a modern building on Via Cágliari opposite the bus station – no.278 (*Ø* 0783.74191). A handier Pro Loco is in Vico Umberto, on the corner with Via de Castro (Monday-Friday 0900-1200, 1700- 2000, Saturdays morning only, Sunday closed).

**Money change.** Apart from the banks, the *Alerica Viaggi* agency in Via de Castro can change money; open 0830-1300, 1630-2000, Saturdays morning only, Sundays closed.

**Yachting.** Yachters in the nearby Golfo di Oristano can find good anchorages in the northern half of the Gulf: either at the resort of Torre Grande Marina, where there is a small pier, or right on the Capo San Marco near the site of Tharros.

## THARROS AND THE SINIS PENINSULA

**The Ruins of Tharros.** Many people come to Oristano just to visit the Punic and Roman ruins at Tharros which, with Nora near Cágliari, represent the best of the island's classical heritage. Like Nora, Tharros is built on a peninsula, but this headland is like a clenched fist at the end of an arm, and dominated by a sturdy Spanish watchtower from the 16th cent.

This spur of land is the southern tip of the Sinis peninsula and helps protect the Golfo di Oristano; it was the home of Phoenician settlers as early as 800BC. Tharros grew under Carthage and then, after 238BC, it flourished as a Roman city; Rome strengthened it and built the baths and streets that can still be seen today. The town withered with the demise of the *Pax Romana,* falling prey to increasing Moorish raids, and was finally abandoned in 1070 in favour of the more secure Oristano, then a small village.

**Tharros today.** Tharros, (open daily 0800-1300, 1600-1900; free) consists mostly of Punic and Roman houses arranged along a chessboard pattern of streets, of which the broad-slabbed Roman *Decumanus Maximus* is the most impressive. Another, the *Cardo Maximus*, has a deep open sewer visible alongside it. On entering the site, probably the first things you'll notice are the solitary remnants of a 1st-cent BC Roman temple, only two of the original four Corinthian style columns still upright. There are also baths and fragments of mosaics from the Roman city, and a wall and remains of a Tophet, or sanctuary, from the earlier Punic settlement. As at Nora, there is much more under the sea, flooded as a result of land-subsidence.

Ideally you should find a guide to get the most out of this site, though you need no help to appreciate its superb location, for whatever Tharros might lack in its archeological remains, it makes up for in the beauty of its position.

There are good beaches along both sides of the peninsula, though there is too much coming and going in high summer to ensure a peaceful swim.

**San Giovanni di Sinis.** At the base of the headland you will already have noticed the domed early Christian church of San Giovanni di Sinis on the side of the road. Dating from the 5th cent and quite oriental in appearance, it is reckoned to be the second-oldest church on the island, beaten only by Cágliari's San Saturnino. Byzantine in style, the interior has been stripped clean; indeed it is surprising that the church should still be standing at all, having been exposed to pirate raids for so long. Bars and toilets are nearby.

*The statue of Christ the Redeemer stands on Mt Ortobene, outside Nuoro.*

**The Sinis Peninsula.** North of Tharros is the marshy Stagno di Cabras lagoon, the biggest of several which dominate the Sinis peninsula. Flat and duny, busy with gulls, cormorants, ducks, egrets and coots, the area attracts naturalists and ornithologists — as well as gastronomes who come to sample the *bottarga,* or the roe of the grey mullet which are landed here, together with the famous local *Vernaccia* wine.

The peninsula has a string of *nuraghi* and a couple of villages at its northern end, but otherwise there is little activity other than the birds and the patient paddlings of inland fishermen in their flimsy but workable boats woven out of reeds, using methods and techniques hardly changed in centuries. Thor Heyerdal is said to have studied these reed craft for his *Ra* expeditions. Their main catch in these salt-water lagoons are eels and mullet.

A sense of profound calm lies over the peninsula's western coast, with fine sandy beaches that are rarely used, enjoying views out to the oddly-named island of Mal di Ventre — 'Stomach ache'.

**A barefoot rescue.** The largest village in the area is **Cabras,** a curious place, not exactly brimming with excitement though it is host to some wild festas, notably on 24 May in honour of the Virgin, and on the first weekend of September. In the latter, the main feature is a race run at dawn on Saturday by the town's boys, barefoot and dressed in white shirts and shorts. The boys carry aloft the statue of San Salvatore from his sanctuary five miles (8km) away, to Cabras, in a re-enactment of a frantic rescue mission undertaken four centuries ago to save the saint from Moorish attackers.

**A pagan sanctuary.** San Salvatore's sanctuary is signposted off the Tharros road. Apart from the saint there is little to see here, though if you can get permission from the custodian you can go down into a chamber below the floor of the church to look around an interesting 4th-cent AD pagan sanctuary dedicated to Mars and Venus, and with faded frescos of Venus, Cupid and Hercules.

**A slice of the West.** The slightly bizarre aspect of San Salvatore church is its location, as it is sited amid a ramshackle collection of one-or-two-roomed houses which are only used once a year when people come out for the annual Cabras *festa.* The rest of the time the place is deserted, slumbering in an eerie calm, and if it looks vaguely familiar it may be because of its use by Spaghetti-Western movie-makers as a film-set — most aptly, I suspect, as a ghost-town.

# SOUTH OUT OF ORISTANO

**Santa Giusta.** South of Oristano is another lagoon, the Stagno di Santa Giusta, named from the village standing on its shores, two miles (3km) out of town. Village-life still revolves largely around the *stagno,* though these days Santa Giusta is little more than a suburb of the provincial capital. But its **Cathedral,** crowning a flight of steps, still marks it out — an austere building of Pisan design, one of the earliest of that string of Tuscan-style constructions which went up in the 11th to 14th centuries mostly in the northern reaches of Sardinia. This one, showing Lombard touches in its stark Romanesque architecture, dates from 1135; it has been a cathedral since the 16th cent, and is today the focus of four days of celebration around its saint's day of 14 May. Some of the marble and granite columns separating the three naves inside were taken from the ruined city of Tharros.

**An Alpine colony.** A few kilometres further south of Santa Giusta is the small rural centre of **Arborea,** a 20th-cent settlement whose name is a conscious throw-back to the old Giudicato which ceased to exist three centuries ago.

Founded in 1928 by Mussolini in his effort to bring new life into Sardinia, the town of Arborea has an out-of-place Alpine appearance, reflecting the local building styles of the immigrants from the Veneto region of Italy whom Mussolini introduced as the core of his new colony. This is most noticeable in the main square, a formal flower-filled garden overlooked by the red-brick parish church and town hall.

The streets around are right-angled and tree-lined, showing the advantages of planning and orderliness. Outside Arborea, the fruits of the large-scale land-reclamation scheme that made this town possible are readily apparent: the whole district, formerly a malarial swamp, has been transformed through drainage, irrigation, and cultivation into

*Time has barely touched Sopramonte, the massif outside Nuoro.*

a rich productive zone. Fruit and vegetables, vineyards, tobacco and beetroot all thrive here, a highly visible reminder of the potential that land reclamation schemes can generate. The area also supports dairy cows, which produce most of the island's milk.

**Accommodation.** There is a comfortable **hotel** right on Arborea's main square, the cheap *Gallo Blanco* (✆ 0783.800241; L21,000), with a restaurant attached. A classier hotel is the *Ala Birdi* (✆ 0783.800512; L51,000) on Strada 24. The **campsite** on the coast five kilometres from the town is mentioned above.

# INLAND OF ORISTANO

There are two or three places inland of Oristano that are worth a look in passing, all in the former territory of medieval Arborea.

At **Fordongianus,** 17 miles (28km) further up the Tirso river, was a Roman spa town, formerly known as *Forum Traiani.* It has kept its old Roman bridge over the river, and the town's baths are still in fairly good condition and visitable.

**Wine and oranges . . . and a *nuraghe*.** Travelling up the main SS 131 you'll soon be passing through the 'Vernaccia triangle,' an area bounded by Zeddiani, Baratili San Pietro and Solarussa villages, which forms the core of the Vernaccia vine-growing region. Further on, you might stop to buy a kilo or two of what are reputed to be Sardinia's best oranges, grown around **Milis;** the season extends over ten months of the year.

Outside Abbasanta on the main Carlo Felice highway, the *nuraghe* of **Losa** makes an easy stop. Weathered and strengthened by the passage of time, this walled and well-fortified three-storey tower was probably built before 1,000BC, and gives you the opportunity to see one of the best relics of Sardinia's ancient civilisation. The opening times are a little erratic due to continuing archeological research; on my last visit they were Thurs-Sun 0800-1400 (free). Even if it's closed when you arrive, the *nuraghe* is worth the brief deviation, if only to look at it from behind the locked gate.

East of Abbasanta is **Lago Omodeo,** Italy's largest artificial lake, covering an area of 8.5sq miles (22sq km). Named from the engineer who planned it in 1923, it supplies electricity to the area as well as drinking water and irrigation.

**Two horse-towns.** Nearby, the town of **Sédilo** hosts the annual *S'Ardia* horse-race, held in honour of the Byzantine emperor Constantine in his saintly guise of San Costantino. The race takes place at dawn on 6 and 7 July at breakneck speed and over a danger-strewn course, its risks increased by people whose sole job is to harass the horses and their riders, even to the extent of shooting blank bullets at them! It's an exciting spectacle, full of hot tempers and commotion and displays of virility.

West of Abbasanta a small road leads into the Monte Ferru mountains. Rising to more than 3,000ft (1,000m), this area was once highly volcanic and is now endowed with plenty of rivers and springs which nourish its thick forests of oak, elm and chestnut. The steep village of **Santu Lussúrgiu** in the heart of the range has some lively folk traditions, best seen at its festivals. Apart from Easter, which is celebrated with choral singing, these show the local connection with breeding horses; especially Carnival, which involves horseback races; and the village's saint's day, around 21 August, which also features horseback competitions during four days of festivities. The local craftwork includes anything to do with horses . . . from saddles to pen-knives.

If you're intrigued by the prospect of a horse-fair, you'll have to drive the short distance from Santu Lussúrgiu along a mountain ridge to the hamlet of **San Leonardo de Siete Fuentes,** where 2 June sees Sardinia's most important market of this kind. The village's Spanish name is a reference to its highly-prized mineral waters which attract droves of connoisseurs at any time of the year, and there is also a crumbly old Romanesque church to see here, burial-place in 1292 of a certain Guelfo, son of Count Ugolino della Gherardesca.

Continuing along this country road you come to **Macomer,** an important road and rail junction just inside Nuoro province. The rattly old small-gauge **trains for Nuoro** leave from the station here approximately every hour. A small detour from Macomer will bring you to Silanus, outside which, signposted on the other side of the SS 129, is the charming **Santa Sabina,** a tiny Byzantine chapel standing beside a small *nuraghe.*

## BOSA

From Macomer it's a brief ride to the coast near Bosa, also in Nuoro province but more logically looked at from Oristano, 37 miles (60km) to the south or Alghero to the north. Approaching from the south, the coast road takes you past the picturesque resort of Santa Caterina di Pittinuri and through Cúglieri, scene of a defeat for the combined Punic and Sard forces against the Romans, following which the Sard leader Ampsicora took his own life.

Whichever way you come, **Bosa** appears curiously suspended, stranded in the middle of one of Sardinia's last remaining stretches of undeveloped coast. This is the only western seaboard for the province of Nuoro, but it has little in common with most of that highland, inland region, resembling more a modest Tuscan fishing village. It can hardly be said of Bosa — a town renowned for its Malvasia dessert wine — that it is 'undiscovered,' though up till now it has managed to keep a fairly low profile. It can only be a matter of time before it falls victim to mass tourism — but in the meanwhile it is a discreet and charming town, whether you're simply passing through or looking for a place for a lengthier stay.

Bosa has kept its sense of remoteness partly for geographical reasons. Surrounded by mountains, the old town lies inland from the sea, a fishing port on the edge of the Temo river. Its coastal offshoot, Bosa Marina, lies three miles (5km) downstream, a conventional minor resort with a small choice of hotels and trattorias. There is a small port here, in the lee of the Isola Rossa, once an island but now moored to the mainland by a bridge and guarded by a sullen Spanish watchtower.

**Sa Costa.** In the dangerous Middle Ages, Bosa's inhabitants preferred to live in a better-defended spot, on the slopes of the hill of Serravalle, at the top of which they built a castle. From the river, the corridor-like streets of the old district, Sa Costa, follow the contours up, one on top of the other, full of medieval gloom. To explore this packed area of back-streets, take any of the roads leading up from the **Cathedral,** on the northern side of Bosa's one bridge. This cathedral whose 15th-cent origins are hidden under layers of Baroque, is also where the main Corso Vittório Emanuele begins, leading to Piazza Costituzione; on the other side of Constitution Square the newer outskirts of town begin.

**Castle Malaspina.** To reach Bosa's castle it's a 20-minute climb through Sa Costa, but if you don't want to do it on foot, there's also a road that skirts the back of town, leading round to the castle-gate. Built by the Malaspina family in 1122, the castle today is watched over by an old lady who will lay aside her crochet-work to tell you the history of the place and guide you to the best views. It's open, therefore, when she's there, which should be 1000-1300, 1600-1900, closing earlier in the winter . . . but don't count on it, and try the Pro Loco in town if you have difficulty getting in. Entry is free.

**San Pietro Extramuros.** From the castle ramparts you should be able to pick out the ex-Cathedral of San Pietro a little way out of town. It's an 11th-cent construction, though its lovely Gothic façade was the work of Cistercian monks at the end of the 13th cent. It's a two-kilometre drive here, though if you've got the time it's a rewarding walk past groves of olive.

**Anti-Communist army.** Capo Marárgiu, north of Bosa, came into the news in 1991 with the revelation that British Army instructors had been coming here since World War II and up to the 1970s to train the Gladio, an anti-Communist army, in terror tactics in the event of a Communist takeover in Italy, home of western Europe's largest Communist Party. You may hear much more of this potential scandal.

**Information.** There is a small **Pro Loco** in Via Ciusa, off Piazza Gioberti, open 1000-1300, 1600-1900 in summer, irregular hours in winter (✆ 0785.373580).

**Accommodation.** There's a small choice of **hotels** in Bosa, more at Bosa Marina. At Bosa, they're all cheap: the *Perry Clan* in Via Alghero (℡ 0785.373074; L35,000); the *Fiori* in Viale Marconi (℡ 0785.373011; L23,000), but most atmospheric of all the *Sa Pischedda*, a fine old *palazzo* just over the river (℡ 0785.373065; L22,000).

The hotels at **Bosa Marina** are all close to the sea. The only three-star is the *Gabbiano* (℡ 0785.374123; L55,000), modern but with bad-tempered staff. It also has a **restaurant** in its basement. A smart new hotel, the *River* (℡ 0785.373400; L46,000 incl. breakfast) is only open April-September. Other hotels include the *Miramare* (℡ 0785.373400; L36,000 half-board) on Via Colombo.

Bosa Marina also has one of Sardinia's rare **youth hostels** in Via Sardegna. Recently refurbished after an eight-year closure, it's scrupulously clean and not linked to the International Youth Hostel Association, so you don't have to be a member. The charges are L8,000 a night per person in single-sex dorms (℡ 0785.374380).

If you're stuck with nowhere else to go, try **rented rooms** at Via Montresta 30, in Bosa's newer district (℡ 0785.373011).

**Holiday village.** There's no campsite in the area, although it would not be impossible to do some surreptitious 'free camping' on the beaches further up or down the coast. There is, however, a **holiday village,** the *Abba Mala* (May-October; ℡ 0785.359011) a couple of kilometres south (signposted). It offers bungalows (for two L45- 65,000, for four L90-120,000) all with their own bathrooms, and there are good beaches nearby.

**Yachters.** Anchorage is off the Isola Rossa, though boats can navigate right up as far as Bosa town; the harbour master's office is 300m upstream from the mouth of the River Temo. There is a small shipyard on the quayside.

# 15: ALGHERO, SASSARI and the NORTH-WEST

## With Logudoro

THE WESTERN PART OF SASSARI province is what used to be the *giudicato* of Logudoro, one of Sardinia's four divisions in the Middle Ages. It's a green, fertile part of the island, hilly rather than mountainous, though the hills get craggier and more dramatic as you move south and eastward from Sássari.

**Bustling.** Many visitors find the provincial capital the island's most interesting town, its crowded medieval centre teeming with life, while its wider, more modern squares are always busy, continually criss-crossed by the *sassaresi* at work or just relaxing. It has limited appeal as a holiday destination because it's inland and lacks enough entertainment to justify spending more than a couple of afternoons or evenings here. But it makes an excellent place to visit from a more permanent base by the sea — and there are plenty of such bases in the area.

Alghero is the most popular; justifiably so, as it has managed to be the island's oldest resort without losing its natural charm as a seaside fishing village. Most foreign visitors to Sardinia end up here at some point, attracted by the wide choice of beaches in the neighbourhood and, for the lovers of old buildings, some exceptionally fine examples of Pisan architecture in the old heartlands of Logudoro.

## SASSARI

Sardinia's second city, Sássari, has 110,000 inhabitants, less than half Cágliari's population, yet it feels in no way diminished by the comparison. Sássari thinks of itself as the most important, most elegant, most **swinging** city on the island, whose citizens are a cut above the *cagliaritani*. Historically, while Cágliari was Pisa's base of operations during the Middle Ages, Sássari was the Genoan capital, its importance increasing as the former principal city of Porto Torres, on the coast, was repeatedly devastated by invasion and strife. For a period Sássari was ruled by the powerful Doria family whose influence reached throughout the Mediterranean, always linked to the

SASSARI

KEY
1 Cathedral
2 Museum: Archaeological
3 Rail station
4 Rosello fountain
5 Santa Maria di Bethlehem
6 Town Hall
7 University

VIALE

Via Roma

Italia

UMBERTO

2

Via Roma

P. Fiume

Via G. Asproni

Cágliari

Emiciclo
Garibaldi

DI SAVOIA
Via Piazza d'Armi

VIALE

DANTE

AMENDOLA

VIA

NAPOLI

Cágliari

city-state of Genoa. After a brief interlude under Arborea, Sássari passed into Aragonese hands and became an important centre of Spanish rule, though Moorish pirates plundered it several times. In the end, Genoa triumphed with the coming of the House of Savoy in 1720, but the Spanish stamp is still a strong one in Sássari, not least in its churches.

**The political connection.** In the 16th cent the Jesuits founded Sardinia's first university here, and the intellectual tradition has been passed down in Sássari, particularly in the political sphere. In recent years, the city has given birth to two presidents — Antonio Segni (1962-4) and the current president, Francesco Cossiga, who took office in 1985 — as well as the late Enrico Berlinguer (1922-1984), longtime head of the Italian Communist Party and also a cousin of the Christian Democrat Cossiga. Another notable contribution of the city to Italian life was the famous Sássari Brigade, which won great distinction during the First World War.

**Back alleys and imperial grandeur.** To the outsider, Sássari seems self-sufficient and proud — even closed in on itself, an impression that becomes overwhelming once you penetrate the claustrophobic alleys and piazzas of the old quarter. A series of squares connect this with the newer city, culminating in the impressive Piazza Italia, whose generous expanse is a cure for any feelings of suffocation that the old town might induce.

The grandiose Palazzo della Provincia dominating one side of the square seems more suitable for a national palace of government at the very least, rather than a mere provincial office. In the middle of Piazza Italia, the presence of a rather pompous statue of King Victor Emanuel II, surrounded by palm trees, contributes to the somewhat colonial flavour. Today the king — not known as a bird-lover — is a favourite perch for pigeons.

**Via Roma — the museum.** Leading off the piazza is Via Roma, whose smart shops and cafés end abruptly at the massive Palazzo della Giustizia, a stern relic of the Fascist era. More inviting is the **Museo Sanna** on the other side of the road. This is Sardinia's second archeological museum and a good substitute if it is absolutely impossible for you to see the main one at Cágliari. It is housed in a modern, well-planned block with display-cases full of prehistoric and classical items.

Most interesting are the Nuraghic sculptures on the upper floor, including a small selection of bronze statuettes, which give a taste of these treasures if you can't make it to see the larger collection at Cágliari. Other exhibits from different parts of Europe show the surprisingly wide trading contacts that the Nuraghic people established.

There is a small *Pinacoteca*, or art gallery, on the ground floor (though shortly to be transferred to Via Monte Grappa) which includes a fine tryptych from the 14th cent. The museum's ethnographic section has examples of local costume, handicrafts, and types of the local bread.

Entry to the Museo Sanna is L3,000, 0900-1400 Mon-Sat, 0900-1300 Sun.

**The old centre.** The old quarter is an antidote to the right-angled regularity of Sássari's modern streets. The area is surrounded by noisy main roads, but little traffic penetrates this interior network of streets, and if you have transport you are best off lodging it in one of the city car parks or at a meter: free spaces are quite rare to find — try the station area (but make sure you have a parking ticket if required).

Just below Piazza Italia, Piazza Cavallino de Monestis is still known popularly as Piazza Castello after the Aragonese castle built here in 1331 and pulled down in 1877. It marks the beginning of the long main thoroughfare of Corso Vittório Emanuele, which descends gently through Piazza Azuni to finish up at Piazza Sant'Antonio, near the station. On each side are tiny back-streets and secluded squares: the pleasure is in the aimless wandering, the unexpected discovery, the momentary disorientation — preferably in the morning or evening, when street-life is at its best. Look out for Via Turritana and Via Rosello, both centres of gold- and silver-working, or the hidden Piazza Tola, where the Renaissance Palazzetto d'Usini stands.

*The view from 'Bean Castle,' Posada, stretches out to the sea.*

**The Duomo.** The only place in the old city worth searching out is Sássari's **cathedral.** Squeezed below the Comune, the Duomo fights for space in the cramped Piazza Duomo. Its lofty façade, though on the fussy side, is one of Sardinia's most imposing examples of Baroque architecture, a late addition to the cathedral's older elements which are in a simpler Aragonese-Gothic style from the 15 and 16th cents. The bell-tower is even earlier, a survival from the 13th-cent building, with gargoyles and other details of original Gothic decoration.

**The Rosello Fountain.** After the museum and the cathedral, Sássari has few other individual items worth looking at. There are a couple of other churches which you might see in passing: for instance, the domed, mosque-like **Santa Maria di Bethlem,** with 15th-cent Gothic vaults lurking behind a good Romanesque façade — but these are best noted as landmarks. You want a real curiosity? Then look at the **Rosello** fountain, a late-Renaissance creation from 1605-6. Standing at the bottom of a flight of dilapidated steps outside the old town, accessible from Corso Trinità, this marble fountain is fed by a perennial spring and until recently the city's womenfolk used to crowd around it to scrub their laundry. Its ornate carving, incorporating dolphins and four statues representing the seasons, was the work of Genoan stone-masons, though the statue of San Gavino which stands on top, is a copy; the original was taken away in 1975. A pity that the nearby flyover spoils the fountain's setting, but I feel it's worth a photograph.

Nearby, in Corso Trinità, are the remains of the **medieval walls** which ringed Sássari until they were pulled down in the last century.

**Two festivals.** One of Sardinia's showiest festivals takes place in Sássari on the penultimate Sunday in May (Ascension Day), which is the highlight of a month of cultural activities. The *Cavalcata* is northern Sardinia's equivalent of Cágliari's Sant'Efisio festival, attracting hundreds of richly costumed participants from villages throughout the province and beyond, though without the religious overtones of Cágliari's feast-day. It was originally staged for the benefit of visiting Spanish kings or other dignitaries, but was allowed to lapse until its revival 40 years ago by, of all people, the Rotarians.

The festival is in three stages; the morning features a horseback parade and a display of the elaborate costumes that are unique to each village, heavily embroidered and decorated with brooches, bracelets and necklaces. The second stage is a hectic *palio,* or horse-race, and the day ends with traditional songs and dances. Those necklaces, by the way, may include the famous coral traditionally gathered on the nearby coastline.

On the afternoon of 14 August there is a much more local affair — *I Candelieri,* linked to the Pisan devotion to the Madonna of the Assumption. It became a regular event when an outbreak of plague in

Sássari in 1652 mysteriously stopped on the eve of the feast of the Assumption, after which the ritual has been repeated annually as a token of thanks.

For all its religious intent, *I Candelieri* is still a crowded and boistrous event. The *gremi,* or medieval guilds of merchants, craftsmen and labourers, decked out in their traditional Spanish-style costumes, carry gigantic wooden mock candlesticks, 25ft (8m) tall, through the streets of the old town, surrounded by a mass of onlookers turning Corso Vittório Emanuele into a dense ribbon of people. The hearty *"A zent'anni,"* "May you live a hundred years," which the representative of the farmers calls to Sássari's mayor at the church of Santa Maria di Bethlem is a traditional salute to all the *sassaresi.*

**Hotels.** Sássari has nine hotels listed, ranging from the four-star *Grazia Deledda* in Viale Dante (✆079.271235; L123,000), boasting a pool, to more modest three-star establishments, for instance the *Frank Hotel* (✆079.276456; L67,000) on Via Diaz 20, the *Marini Due* (✆079.277282; L54,000) on Via Chironi; and the cheaper *Rosita* on Via Pigliaru 10 (✆079.241235; L24,000). Nice and central are the smart *Leonardo da Vinci* on Via Roma (✆079.280744; L101,000), and, at the other end of the market, *Pensione Famiglia* on the parallel Via Umberto, at no.65 (✆079.239543; L18,000).

**Youth hostels.** Youth hostels are at Alghero and Porto Torres, and **campsites** on the coast around the same towns.

**Restaurants.** Sássari has a good range of trattorias and restaurants. For a modest meal in a friendly setting try *Da Peppina* trattoria, in Vícolo Pigozzi, an alley off Corso Vittório Emanuele (closed Sunday). Nearby at Corso 148 is the *Pizzeria al Corso,* serving other things besides pizzas (closed Monday). For a bit more class, try the *Tre Stelle* at Via Porcellana 6, in the newer part of town, on the other side of the public gardens, excellent for seafood but closed Sunday and the whole of August; or *Il Senato* at Via Mundula 2, near the cathedral (closed Monday).

**Information.** The main tourist information office is on the first floor of Via Brigate Sássari 19, open Mon-Fri 0800-1345, 1530-1830 (✆079.231331/233534).

**Transport.** The **railway station** is at one end of the old city, soon after you come in on the Alghero road. There is a luggage deposit here that closes at 2045. All **local and ARST buses** arrive at and depart from the semicircular Emiciclo Garibaldi in the centre of town. The left-luggage here closes at 1630 daily. **PANI buses** leave from Via Bellieni 5, just off Via Roma. **Buses for Fertília airport** leave from the Alitalia office at Via Cágliari 30.

***ACI.*** The main *ACI* office is at Viale Adua 32b (✆079.272107).

**Car hire.** Apart from *ACI,* there is a choice of car-hire agencies. *Avis* is at Via Mazzini 2e (✆079.235547); *Hertz* Via IV Novembre

(✆079.280083); *Interrent* Viale Caprera 8a (✆079.291113); *Italia* Via Coppino 2 (✆079.238079/235244); *Maggiore* Viale Italia 3a (✆079.235507); *Punto Auto* Corso Vittório Emanuele 161 (✆079.231546); *Silanos* Viale Porto Torres 10f (✆079.260356).

**Taxis.** Taxis can be found outside the station, in Piazza Cavallino de Monestis, and at the Emiciclo Garibaldi.

# ALGHERO

Most foreign visitors will be in this corner of the island because they are staying at Alghero. One could say a lot of bad things about this tourist niche — the over-development, the fake, 'quaint' environment, the selling-out for the sake of profit — but, strangely, if any of these things are true, at least, they don't seem to matter. Although there are more restaurants, trattorias and hotels per square kilometre here than anywhere else in Sardinia, and although in these same bars and restaurants it's sometimes difficult to find anyone who isn't a tourist, the true Alghero has survived.

Alghero has saved itself by its irrepressible liveliness, its sunny, no-problems temperament, and because it is one of those very rare phenomena in Italy: a tourist town that is also a flourishing fishing port. Usually, when the package tours arrive, everything else goes — but Alghero remains the island's biggest fishing port, giving it an economic base entirely independent of the summer masses.

**Enigmatic town.** What is most exceptional about Alghero is that it

## KEY TO STREETS

1 Bastioni Cristoforo Colombo
2 Bastioni Magellano
3 Bastioni Marco Polo
4 Largo S. Francesco
5 Piazza Civica
6 Piazza San Croce
7 Piazza Sulis
8 Piazza Vittorio Emanuele
9 Via Cavour
10 Via Columbano
11 Via della Misericordia
12 Via Don Deroma
13 Via Maiorca
14 Via Manno
15 Via Roma
16 Via Sassari
17 Via Simon

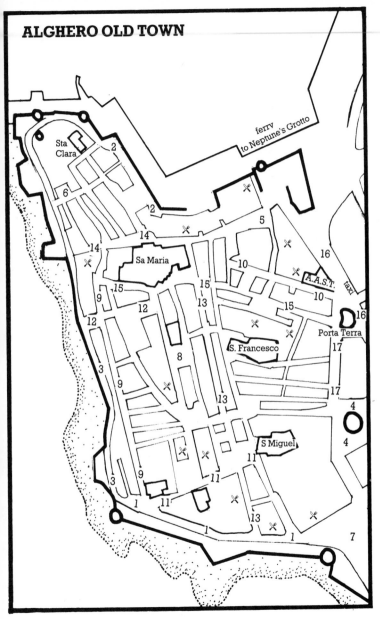

# ALGHERO OLD TOWN

Sta Clara
2
6
2
ferry to Neptune's Grotto
5
14
14
16
Sa Maria
14
10
A.A.S.T.
10
15
15
taxi
16
15
9
13
Porta Terra
12
12
S. Francesco
17
8
3
13
17
9
4
9
4
13
S Miguel
11
11
3
11
11
9
1
3
11
13
1
7
1

151

isn't really a Sardinian town at all. It doesn't feel it, nor sound it, for the Algherese don't even speak the same language. In fact its roots are Catalan, as it was settled in the 16th cent by people from north-eastern Spain. But neither is Alghero typically Catalan; its distance from Spain, from which it has been cut off for so long, gives it the flavour of a Spanish island – one of the Balearics that has drifted to the east. The result is an Alghero that is unique, detached and proudly different, neither Sardinian nor Spanish, and kept alive by a strong local identity which sets it apart from any normal tourist enclave.

The quality of life here is also distinctive. The presence of the fishermen ensures that the local cuisine is generally of the highest standard; and the nearness of some of Sardinia's most famous vineyards satisfies that other basic need of Mediterranean man. Put all these characteristics together and you have a picture of a tourist trap that's also a pleasant working town for its own inhabitants.

**Alghero's origins.** Most people agree that the town's original name was *S'Alighera*, meaning 'seaweedy' or more specifically 'place of algae' – though there is little evidence of this today in the clear blue waters of the Mediterranean. Others suggest that the name comes from the Arabic, *al- ghar*, meaning 'the cave, a possible reference to the celebrated *Grotta di Nettuno* nearby.

There was probably some sort of settlement here from earliest times, but it was the Doria family of Genoa which really put the place on the map when the promontory was fortified in 1102. They held the town for two and a half centuries, finally overthrown by Pedro IV of Aragon in 1354. Immediately the Spaniards embarked on a wholesale colonisation of Alghero, evicting many of the native population and introducing a sizeable community of Catalan Aragonese. The intruders quickly dominated the region, passing laws limiting the number of native Sards who could enter, and compelling them to leave the town at the sound of a trumpet-signal. The 'Hispanicisation' of the town was such that it became known as *Barcelonetta,* or little Barcelona.

The modern visitor to Alghero will immediately notice this foreign feel to the place. For a start, although Sardinia does not convey a particularly untidy impression by Italian standards, Alghero is much neater. And then, in the old town, not only are the narrow cobbled streets named in two languages – Italian and Catalan – but the architecture is quite distinct, from the flamboyant churches to the humbler wrought-iron balconies on houses.

**Old Alghero.** A walk around the old town should take in the series of seven defensive towers scattered through Alghero's centre and its surrounding defensive walls. From the Giardino Púbblico – the hub of Alghero, surrounded by traffic but calm and quiet within – the **Porta Terra** is the first of these massive bulwarks. Also known as the Jewish Tower, built at the expense of the prosperous Jewish

*The church of Sant'Antonio Abate at Orosei is one of several relics of the town's former glory.*

community before its expulsion in 1492, today the tower features an incongruously Art-Deco style war memorial. Further along Via Simon is Largo San Francesco, where a second tower sits, and beyond is Piazza Sulcis, site of a third tower, the **Torre Sulis,** also called Torre dello Sperone. In summer these three towers are home to many cultural events put on by the *Comune.*

Everything west of this line is a puzzle of lanes, some livened by boutiques and trattorias, others purely residential, the homes of many of Alghero's fishermen. The fact that cars are restricted makes this narrow-laned nucleus a pleasure to wander about in, and here the street names are all in the Catalan dialect: *carrer* not 'via,' *iglesia* not 'chiesa,' and *plaça* not 'piazza.'

Most of the buildings date from the 15th and 16th cents, still keeping a simple Aragonese-Gothic appearance. Some of the best examples are in Via Roma and Via Carlo Alberto, but in Piazza Civica, the 16th-cent **Palazzo d'Albis** is a good specimen of the local architecture. In 1541 it briefly hosted the emperor Charles V who was on his way to Algiers; according to popular legend, the emperor addressed the townspeople from the balcony window, dubbing the whole population *caballeros.* Later the palace became the residence of Alghero's governors and the temporary abode of Sardinia's Spanish viceroys.

Nearby, Via Sant'Erasmo has a sumptuous Jewish palace, **Palau Reial** (*palau* = palazzo), which has been well-restored to show its dignified lines and ornamentation.

At the bottom of Via Príncipe Umberto is Alghero's 16th-cent **cathedral,**with its entrance on Via Manno. The Spanish viceroys of Sardinia stopped here to take the preliminary oath before taking office in Cágliari. They would therefore see something of the palace's pleasing interior, particularly the lofty nave supported by alternating pillars and columns, rising to the octagonal dome. They would have missed the rather bland, neo-classical monument to Duke Maurice of Savoy, not because it is behind the altar but because it's 19th-cent.

Apart from the church of **San Francesco** on Via Carlo Alberto, a harmonious structure with a small cloister fronting a small piazza, Alghero's other ecclesiatical monuments are disappointing. The majolica-tiled cupola of San Michele (17th-cent), for example, is a sparkling feature of Alghero's skyline, but when you look closely at the flaky façade you're not encouraged to go inside. And that's just as well; it is dull.

Indeed, for all its elegance, the town doesn't entirely live up to the wishful thinking of its mayor's recent comparison of Alghero with San Remo. Once you get off the shopping and bar-restaurant circuit, Alghero reveals a much humbler air, suggesting how skin-deep its recent transformation into a bastion of the tourist industry really is — and perhaps this is just as well.

Much of the tourist activity revolves around the port, spreading out below the lofty city-walls, its wide quay nudged by rows of colourful fishing boats, as seen in the cover picture. This is the starting-point for excursions to Neptune's Grotto and along the coast.

Further up begin the hotels and beaches, most of them an easy walk from town. Many of the more opulent, older-looking villas here were formerly owned by a resident expatriate community, mainly central European refugees who fled to Alghero after the First World War.

**Information.** The efficiently run **AAST** (✆ 079.979262) is on the corner of the Giardino Púbblico (public garden), near the Porta Terra, open 0800-2000 May-September, 0800-1400 in winter, Sunday closed. Its multilingual staff supplies reams of maps, accommodation lists and tour details.

**Money exchange.** Banks in Alghero are open Mon-Fri 0900-1300, 1500-1600. The travel agents *Agritours* (Via Ugo Foscolo 10),*Cunedda* (Via La Marmora 34) and *Guarda Giulio* (Via XX Settembre 18) also handle transactions, and are open on Saturdays. There is an automatic currency exchange machine attached to the Banco di Sardegna in Largo San Francesco.

**Transport.** The **buses** leave from Via Catalogna, on the Giardino Púbblico. To **Sássari**, five buses leave a day (0650, 0900, 1330, 1535, 1830) taking one hour, tickets from the *Cunedda* travel agents nearby on the square (L3,300). Last return from Sássari is at 1900. Otherwise

## KEY TO HOTELS

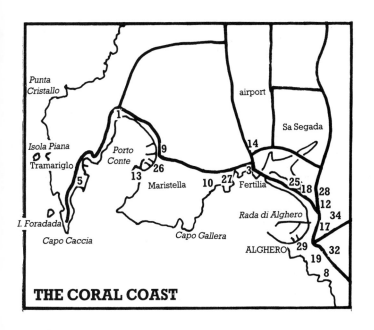

THE CORAL COAST

take a **train** (0601, 0820, 1255, 1426, 1740) from Alghero's small station. Shuttle buses connect the port with the station leaving five minutes before train departure time. (Last return from Sássari is at 2129 weekdays, 2040 Sundays and holidays.)

**Taxis.** Taxis leave from the other side of the gardens at Via Vittório Emanuele. Taxis to the **airport** should cost around L30,000 (15 minutes).

**Excursions.** The **Grotta di Nettuno** is the most popular of the boat tours you can take from the port. A fifteen-minute cruise takes you west along the coast, past the long bay of Porto Conte as far as the point of Capo Caccia. Here, sheer cliffs rear up spectacularly. Beneath them is a series of deep marine caves, among them Grotta Verde and Grotta dei Ricami (your tour may include a visit to this one), but Neptune's Grotto is the most impressive, a long snaking passage going far into the rock, into which tours are led, single-file, on the hour every hour. The dramatically-lit route takes you past an impossible array of stalagmites and stalactites, looking like rows of organ-pipes, or fairytale candlesticks, or wedding-cakes, or whatever your imagination can devise. It is one of Sardinia's most awesome grottos, and should be on your list of 'must-see' places.

**Boat tours.** Boat tours to Neptune's Grotto from the port leave hourly 0900-1900 in summer, less frequently in winter, and cost L20,000. Make sure the price includes entry into the grotto (some tickets don't). Alternatively, if you want to go under your own steam and save a little money, there are several buses a day leaving for Capo Caccia from the main bus terminal on the Giardino Púbblico (tickets at the nearby kiosk, L1,000). Bear in mind, however, that from where you leave the bus there's a 654-step descent, down the 'Escala del Cabirol,' a highly scenic route but fairly gruelling on the way back up. Its Catalan name means 'roe-deer's steps,' presumably a reference to the only animal that could negotiate what used to be a perilous path before the building of the stairway in 1954.

The descent should take 15-20 minutes (calculate five or ten minutes more for the climb up, in case you're worried about missing the return bus). Entry into the grotto costs L6,000, and guided tours — you can't go in alone — leave on the hour and last about 35 minutes (0800-1900 Easter-15 October; other periods 0900-1400). On the way back allow time before the bus leaves for a well-earned ice cream at the bar opposite the bus stop.

*Navisarda* has a booth at the port (main office Via Diez 3a) and arranges a variety of boat tours around Alghero, sailing up and down the coast and including spaghetti-lunches and suppers under the stars. These mini-cruises last from 2 hours to the entire day, costing L4,000-45,000 per person (children discounted or free).

If you want to venture further afield, there is a range of lengthier cross-country excursions you can make, to Stintino (L20,000), the Costa Smeralda (L38,000), the Maddalena archipelago (L44,000), and even Corsica (L55,000), though these involve a lot of time in coaches; contact *Algtours* at Via Garibaldi 99b for further information (✆ 079.953323).

Closer at hand, *Alghero Marisub* offers **diving expeditions** off Punta Giglio and Capo Caccia for the novice and the more experienced, at various levels with prices between L40,000 and L600,000, depending on how many dives you wish to make and the equipment you use. Contact the company for more info at Via Don Deroma 17, near the Duomo.

**Hotels.** If you're here on a package holiday you will most likely be lodged in one of the hotels running out west from Alghero towards Fertilia and Capo Caccia. But at the top end of the market, the castellated *Villa Las Tronas* (✆ 079.975390; L125-145,000) lies *east* of town, well-sited on a small promontory with beaches all around. It is full of character, formerly a baronial mansion and still keeping its aristocratic air with its old-fashioned furnishings. With only 31 bedrooms, capacity is limited, so book early.

The *Rina Hotel* (✆ 079.984240; L105-160,000 with breakfast, half-board L75-170,000 per person, full-board L85- 180,000) is one of the newest additions to Alghero, a plush enclosed complex with its own tennis courts and pool, out at Via delle Baleari 34.

Nearby, the *Hotel Oasis* (✆079.950526-46-18) offers a variety of accommodation alternatives, from 'residence' to conventional hotel rooms. For the latter, it charges L76-94,000 for a double room per night, but also offers half- and full-board which are more economical. Normal weekly rates for a 'residence' for four amount to between L495,000 and L1,170,000 according to season. Facilities for hotel or residence guests include tennis courts, pool and disco.

The *Playa* (✆079.950369;   L56-65,000), a little closer to town, charges £283-386 per person per week, half-board including flights.

Descending a notch, the *Tarragona* (✆079.952270; L38-43,000) is a slightly old-fashioned place in Via Gallura, a side street off the port. Not the most elegant of Alghero's hotels but the cheapest of the town's three-star establishments.

At the bottom end of the market is the *Normandie* (✆079.975302; L28,000), on Via Enrico Mattei in the newer part of town. But for the budget traveller Alghero's best-value hotel is the *San Francesco* (✆079.979258; L31-36,000). In the heart of the old town at Via Machin 2 (just behind San Francesco church) each of its clean and quiet rooms comes with bathroom.

**Accommodation alternatives.** If you are more comfortable in your own space, **apartments** are plentiful in and around Alghero and available throughout the year. They can be rented either in

*Gorruppu Canyon's glorious desolation as seen from a deserted hovel by the roadside.*

residence-type hotels, or through agencies. For the former, try *Residence Gli Eucalipti* (✆079.951187), a little way out from the centre on the Via Lido, separated from the sea by a pinewood. The flats are modern, airy and pine-furnished.

There is more choice with private apartments, available through *Immobiliare* agencies (estate agencies or realtors), and you can get a full list of them from the local tourist office. As an example, *Apartmenti Estivi Maria Pia* offers 4-5 bed flats with prices ranging from L300-650,000 per week according to season, including bills; minimum stay seven days, or three weeks in August. More information on these through the *Mario Cau* agency at Via Don Minzoni 159 (✆079.952478).

**Rooms to let.** Renting rooms is a cheaper option, though not always in the most interesting parts of town, and vacancies are difficult to find in high season. Try Margherita Masia at Via Roth 12 (✆079.975393).

**Campsites, holiday villages and a youth hostel.** Two kilometres out of town, *La Mariposa* **campsite** (April-October; ✆079.950480); spreads beneath a canopy of pine and eucalyptus trees and has direct access to the beach. Bungalows and caravans are also available for renting. Further out, near Fertília, is the *Calik* campsite (May-October; ✆079.930111), 50m from the beach. Beyond Porto Conte is the more secluded *Porticciolo* (May-October; ✆079.919007), also offering four-bed bungalows with bathrooms at L59-91,000 per night.

*Torre del Porticciolo* (April-October; ✆079.919007) is a campsite and holiday village 10 miles (17km) out of town, offering bungalows with and without bathrooms for L420-940,000 weekly, with its own private beach.

Alghero's *Giuliani* **youth hostel** (*☎*079.930353) is actually at Fertilia, open April-October with cooking facilities. Ring first to check availability.

**Agriturismo.** There are a number of Agriturismo options in the Alghero area. Obviously none is central, so you would need a car to use them, but they work out much cheaper than hotel-living. The tourist office has a full list: an example is *Baia Santos* (*☎*079.999053) inland from Fertilia, charging L20-23,000 per person per night for bed-and-breakfast; other arrangements including half- and full-board are also available.

**Alghero's restaurants.** Make sure you sample at least one good fish dish in Alghero, guaranteed fresh, done in a variety of ways and tastefully presented; spring and winter are the best seasons for seafood.

As with accommodation, you're spoiled for choice. The *Corsaro* on Via Columbano is well-known (closed Monday) and accepts credit cards. Also in the old town, on Via Carlo Alberto, *La Lepanto* (closed Tuesday) has superlative local cooking, seafood a speciality, and the same goes for *Da Pietro* (closed Wednesday off-season) at Via Machin 20.

For cheaper places, you're better off trying the right-angled streets of the new town. On Via Mazzini the *Ristorante Mazzini* (closed Monday) is at no.59, serving good fare at modest prices, and has a wood-fired oven for pizzas. For brief snacks, the fast-food joints by the port aren't bad.

**On the streets.** There is a lot of strolling about to do in Alghero, and plenty of bars to try; remember that most charge double if you sit.

For the homesick Briton, the old quarter has a good selection of 'pubs;' the *Mill Pub* in Via Maiorca has live music nightly at 2200. **Discos**, open in summer only, include the *Blu Moon* at Via Lido 17, by the sea, and *El Calabona* on the Viale della Resistenza on the ringroad at the back of town.

For the lover of classical music, between 22 July and 10 September there are almost nightly concerts in the cloister of San Francesco church, attracting international orchestras and soloists, tickets L10,000.

Wednesday mornings are good for a lively **fish market** on Via de Gásperi.

**Shopping.** Not for nothing is the coast around Alghero known as the 'Coral Riviera.' It is Sardinia's richest location for the gathering of this pinkish-red stone, which is then made into jewellery and gift items. Compare the prices well, but if you are going to buy coral in Sardinia, this is the place to do it. There is no shortage of shops selling it, for example the *Bottega Artigiana* on Via Roma has a good selection.

**Bike hire.** *Cicloexpress* at Via Lamarmora 39 charges L50,000 per day for a Vespa, L25,000 for a moped, L12,000 for a bicycle, L18,000 for a mountain bike, L20,000 for a tandem and L10,000 per hour for a *risciò* – a four-wheeled pedal-carriage with seats for four. Open 0830-1300, 1600-2030, till noon only on Sunday.

**Car hire.** Most agencies are based out at Fertília airport, though Avis has an office on Piazza Sulis, Budget is at Via Sássari 7, and the independent Nolauto Alghero is at Via Vittório Véneto 11. The latter charges L23,000 a day for a Fiat 126, L150,000 for a week, plus L320 per kilometre. It also offers seven days unlimited mileage at L440,000. Other cars available are Pandas, Unos and Tipos.

**Windsurfing and inflatable dinghy hire.** Windsurfing courses are held at Le Bombarde beach, beyond Fertília; otherwise contact *Alghero Marisub*, which arranges courses as well as rents out inflatable dinghies (*gommoni*) at Via Don Deroma 17, near the Duomo, or the *Baia di Conte* Hotel at Porto Conte; prices for dinghies start at L40,000 for an hour (no licence required).

**ACI.** The *ACI* office is at Via Mazzini 56 (✆ 079.979659).

**Post office.** The main post office is at Via XX Settembre 108, in the new town, open 0900-1700 Mon-Sat. (The street's name is Via Venti Settembre, always written as shown here.)

**Telephones.** As there is no SIP telephone office in Alghero, you'll have to phone either from hotels (which usually costs a little more) or from bars: try the ones at Via Vittório Emanuele 43, Via Lo Frasso 60, or Via Mazzini 21.

**Yachters.** Boats can use Alghero's marina wherever space can be found; fresh water is available from the south-east side of the marina, fuel from a nearby garage. Other options are the crowded mini-marina at Fertília and the enclosed bay of Porto Conte.

**Festivals.** As well as a range of diverse events staged throughout the tourist season, Alghero has some interesting festivals, starting with its three-day **Carnival** celebrations, when a 'guy' representing a French soldier is ceremonially put on trial and burnt on the bonfire on Shrove Tuesday. **May** sees a steady procession of pilgrims to the sanctuary of Valverde, culminating on the first Sunday after Easter. There is a range of musical and folklore events over the **Ferragosto** holiday, in mid-August, including boating competitions. Religion and secular games are mixed on Sant'Agostino's day on **28 August,** and there is more feasting at the Fisherman's Fair on a Saturday or Sunday in **September,** the precise date varying from year to year.

## OUT OF ALGHERO

**South of Alghero.** To the south, you can either go to **Villanova,** the town to which the original Algerese were banished when the Spanish took over their homes — a worthwhile drive if only for the views seaward — or follow the untrammelled rocky shore that wanders up and down almost 30 miles (45km) to Bosa. Mercifully undeveloped, though full of secret coves and inlets that are ideal for a quick or leisurely dip, this stretch needs to be driven — or ridden — over, preferably when you're not in a hurry.

**Fertília.** If you're feeling energetic you could *walk* out of town to reach Fertília, a three-mile (5-km) stroll along the seafront past the pine-fringed beaches. On the right is a long lagoon, and a medieval bridge sinking picturesquely into the water, known locally as the 'Roman' bridge and often used by fishermen as a perch. Fertília itself is nothing special, one of Mussolini's creations of the 1930s, and no doubt named by him in the same imaginative spirit that he named Carbónia ('Coal-town'). The meaning of Fertília is easy enough to guess, referring to the rich agricultural land of the surrounding area, reclaimed from swamp in the dictator's drainage schemes. Some excellent wines are produced here, notably *Torbato*, a fairly sweet white.

***Nuraghi* and more beaches.** Just off this road, six miles (10km) from Alghero, is the ***Nuraghe* di Palmavera,** a complex including a domed 'palace' from about 1100BC, though most of the surrounding 50 or so huts were added later, and the complex was abandoned because of a fire in the 5th cent BC. Finds from the site are on display in Sássari's museum. Nearby, the beaches of **Le Bombarde and Lazzaretto,** and in the lovely bay of Porto Conte, are among the best in the region, within reach of a handful of well-situated luxury hotels. Porto Conte itself was romantically named *Portus Nimpharum* by the Romans, meaning 'Lake of the Nymphs.' I haven't seen any.

**Von Tirpitz's Alghero.** From Porto Conte a road climbs up to Capo Caccia and the *Grotta di Nettuno;* another meanders north to the sandy strip where the German admiral Von Tirpitz owned a large estate before the First World War; the bays and inlets here were apparently much-used by submarines for secret nocturnal rendez-vous. Today a couple of campsites on the seashore can be reached from the minor road before it curves inland towards Fertília airport. The nearby **Lago Baratz** is Sardinia's only natural lake.

Close to the airport, six miles (10km) north of Alghero on the Porto Torres road, is the **Anghelu Ruiu necropolis,** a prenuraghic complex of tombs and one of Sardinia's most significant archeological sites. Dating back to about 1750BC, the 35 tombs excavated here are the best example of the so-called fairy- or witches'-houses (*domus de janas*) of which there are scores in Sardinia, relics of the ancient Ozieri culture. The hillside here is honeycombed with the murky chambers in which the dead were embalmed, connected by sloping passages. In some cases the lintels are carved with symbolic shapes

*Oristano by night: theatrical splendour in the Piazza del Duomo.*

including bulls' heads, but there is little else to see here: the rich
contents of the caves have been taken to Cágliari and Sássari where
they are on display in the archeological museums.

## PORTO TORRES, STINTINO AND THE PELOSA PENINSULA

Around 22 miles (35km) from Alghero, 15 miles (24km) from Sássari,
**Porto Torres** is not an obvious destination for an outing. The author
Alan Ross summed it up as "one of those places, of hang-dog,
dilapidated appearance, which create within five minutes an intense
depression, almost a panic, in case by some unforeseen calamity one
should be marooned there."

Once as important a harbour for the Romans as *Karalis* (Cágliari)
was in the south, Porto Torres declined when the Romans left and the
raiders arrived. Later caught in the struggle for power between Pisa
and Genoa, the town continued to be one of Sardinia's four *giudicati*
until the 15th cent, when the episcopal seat was transferred to Sássari
— but by then the town had long been virtually abandoned in favour
of safer inland bases. Regeneration did not come until the past 30
years or so, when it was chosen as the site for one of the island's
industrial zones, which today dominates the western side of the town.
Seven thousand workers are employed here, helping to process more
than 6,000,000 tonnes of crude oil a year. The port is active and visited
daily by ferries from Genoa, Livorno, and Toulon in France.

**Porto Torres: the sights.** Porto Torres is not the sort of place to invite much idle rambling, but it has a couple of items that are worth seeing. The first is the **Roman bridge,** its seven arches carrying modern traffic into town, an impressive testimony to Roman building techniques. The other attraction is tucked away near the town's railway station, and is a ruin consisting of baths, columns, bits of mosaic, and the remains of the so-called **Barbarian's Palace.** The barbarian in question was a Roman governor called Barbarus, who presided over the martyrdom of the town's patron saint, San Gavino, and *he* was a Roman commander of the reign of the emperor Diocletian who had been converted by two condemned Christians, Protus and Januarius. All three were beheaded together in 300AD.

Eight hundred years later, a church was built in the saint's honour, some way back from the port and originally in the open country, but now in a back street on the outskirts of town. The Church of San Gavino's humble location does nothing for its appearance as it is considered to be one of the island's finest examples of Pisan architecture – and it's also Sardinia's biggest church. But you can still appreciate the fine yellowy Romanesque façade with its three large doors, a later addition. The building has an austere, fortified appearance, which no doubt helped it to survive Saracen attacks.

Inside, 28 marble columns, dug up from the old Roman town, separate the three naves. The crypt is said to contain the sarcophagi of the three martyrs, placed here in 1614 when their exhumation was supposedly attended by various miracles and 'frequent perfumes' – but as the crypt was securely bolted when I came, I had no way of finding out.

**Accommodation.** If you have come to Porto Torres by ferry you may be looking for somewhere to spend the night. There are a handful of places, all pretty central: *La Casa* (✆079.514288; L47,000) at Via Petrarca 8, and the *Torres* (✆079.501604; L50,000) at Via Sássari 75 are both three-star; *Da Elisa* (✆079.514872; L39-44,000) at Via Mare 2, and the *Royal* (✆079.50227; L40,000) at Via Sebastiano Satta 8 are two-star. There is also a **youth hostel** here (✆079.502761), and other hotels and campsites are on the beaches east of town around Platamona (see below). Further away, beyond the petrochemical paraphernalia of the industrial zone, there are many more hotels at Stintino.

**Stintino.** This tiny village 18 miles (30km) west of Porto Torres was until recently nothing more than a remote jumble of fishermen's cottages clustered between two narrow harbours. Fortunately the discovery of its tourist potential has not drastically altered it – it remains a small, laid-back village with nothing like the development that other more accessible resorts have suffered, and most of the hotels and tourist complexes are further up the coast, right on the tip of Capo del Falcone. Stintino town's beaches are mostly rocky, and the attraction lies more in its role as the main centre of the tongue of land that forms the western arm of the Golfo di Asinara, where most of the sunning and swimming takes place.

**Stintino's hotels.** In Stintino itself, the *Geranio Rosso* (✆079.523292; L70-83,000) on Via XXI Aprile (*ventiuno*) is the smartest hotel, after which comes a range of more modest establishments such as the *Lina* (✆079.523071; L48-52,000) at Via Lepanto 38, and the Silvestrino (✆079.523007; L50,000) at Via Sássari 12. The latter has an excellent trattoria attached, specialising in lobster soup. You can **rent rooms** in Stintino for about L15,000 per person per night.

**Apartment rentals.** *Stintours* on Lungomare Colombo (✆079.523160; fax 079.523048) arranges flat and house rentals in the area, especially out at Torre Pelosa (see below). Call here, too, for **car hire** and cycles, mopeds and boats.

**Information and money change.** Stintino's *Azienda di Soggiorno* is next to the bar on the headland, open 0800-1200, 1730-1930 — though expect more limited hours in the winter. There is a *cambio* on Via Tonnara, open Mon-Sat all day till 1800.

**Yachts.** The more northerly of the two well-sheltered creeks is marginally the deeper, though its depth is no more than about 8ft (2.4m).

**The Pelosa, and the albino asses of Asinara.** Three miles (5km) up the road from Stintino you pass a collection of tourist villages at La Pelosa; here are hotels and self-catering apartments backing some of Sardinia's most de luxe beaches, with views out over a perfectly turquoise sea to the isles of Piana and the larger, elongated Asinara. Close though it is, Asinara is definitely out of bounds, having been a prison-island since the end of the last century, when its inhabitants were moved to Stintino. This is a pity, since what is visible is extremely enticing, and the island is now the only known habitat for a miniature white ass, from which the island takes its name. The promontory ends at Capo Falcone, overlooked by the Spanish Torre Falcone.

**Hotels.** All the accommodation here is on the expensive side and is open only in the summer: bear in mind, though, that you get some of Sardinia's most impressive scenery, with limpid seas lapping a beautiful coastline, along with the pools and top-quality dining facilities included in the price. *Cala Reale* (✆079.236006; L62-78,000) is one of the cheaper options, (open June-September), while the *Rocca Ruia* (✆079.236006; L111-124,000; April-October) is one of the more exclusive. Most of the others are holiday villages or 'residences,' for instance *La Pelosetta* (✆079.527188; April-October), offering two-bed apartments for L567-876,000 per week. More information is available at the agencies at Stintino (see above).

There are **no campsites** here, though discreet space could be

*The murals at Orgósolo: no effort is spared to smarten the houses.*

found for a tent.

**Yachts.** Boats can squeeze through the 10ft (3m) navigable channel between the islet of Piana and Asinara, passing under high-tension cables which have a minimum height of 82ft (25m) above the water. In fine weather, yachts may anchor just off the Pelosa beach, or off Asinara itself, near the government buildings. Landings are normally prohibited.

**Ghost-town.** If you're driving in the area, or seeking an alternative route back to Alghero that doesn't take in Porto Torres, you might consider the minor road which passes through Palmádula, giving you the chance to drop in on the old abandoned mining-town of **Argentiera.** Once the greatest producer of silver on the island, this little town sits by itself at the end of a road running down to the western coast. It has a forlorn, haunted air now, full of the echoes of its former industry. Shafts lie abandoned, miners' quarters stare blindly out, and as there are good beaches around here, the whole place will no doubt be bought up one day and converted into a holiday vilage, so you'd better get here while its lonely charm is still intact.

## CASTELSARDO AND THE SASSARI RIVIERA

Apart from the industrial blot of Porto Torres, the coast north of Sássari is an endless strip of fine sand beaches, in places heavily developed for the benefit of Sassarese and tourists. Sássari's main lido is at **Platamona,** where there are camping sites and hotels. There is a little more tranquillity eastwards, at **Marina di Sorso,** and another campsite, the *International Cristina* (May-September ✆ 079.310357).

**Castelsardo.** Continuing along this scenic coast road, the SS 200, it is about nine miles (15km) to Castelsardo, a formidable walled town dominated by its castle and surrounded by long views out to sea. Founded by the Genoan Doria family in the 12th cent — they called it 'Castelgenovese' — it was re-named 'Castel Aragonese' by the Spanish, and owes its present name to the new Savoyan kings in 1769.

**The Citadel.** Leave your car on the way up to the high citadel and walk the rest, as the lanes of the old centre are impossibly narrow and will involve you in frantic reversing. There is something grim and insular about this medieval quarter, possibly a residue of the town's ancient inaccessibility, hemmed in as it is by mountains to landward. From the battlements of the forbidding castle at the top — recently heavily restored — views open out, sometimes stretching as far as the isle of Asinara, off Sardinia's north-western point, and even to Corsica, though for that the conditions would have to be very good as on a crisp spring morning. The **castle** is open every day 0930-2030 (L2,000) and contains a *Museo dell'Intréccio* featuring the basketwork and weaving for which Castelsardo is the island's main centre.

On the cliff-edge, the 15th-cent **cathedral** does not show its age after its numerous restorations, though the interior has a good medieval canvas, the *Madonna with Angels,* by an unknown local painter. The sea-walls here are impressive, and the majolica-tiled *campanile* adds a glimmer of colour to the grey town.

**Eating and sleeping.** Below Castelsardo's castle is an excellent **restaurant** with romantic views over the sea and an impressive reputation for seafood, *La Guardiola* (closed Monday). Otherwise all the trattorias and restaurants are down below, on the main street. For a cosy atmosphere you could pick the *Trattoria Pinna* on the road going out to the port. There is also a *pensione* here (✆ 079.470168; L29-35,000); of the four or five other hotels, the *Castello* is the smartest (✆ 079.470062; L42- 48,000). The nearest **campsites** are a few kilometres east of town at Valledoria; best is *La Foce* (✆ 079.582109; May-October) with excellent facilities — especially for children — and a lake across which a small craft continually plies to ferry campers to the good sandy beach.

**Shopping.** Castelsardo has dozens of large stores along its main streets below the old town, packed with handicrafts of every description, making it a good place for shopping if you don't mind wading through a large proportion of junk to find the ideal gift or souvenir. A good purchase would be an example of the **basket-weaving** for which the area is famous, using the leaves of the local dwarf-palms. Otherwise both cork and coral goods are here in abundance, even though the areas most associated with these materials are respectively Gallura and Alghero; there are also shelf-fulls of the weird, African-looking Sard wooden masks.

Don't bother shopping around to compare prices in the different stores, since the same products are sold everywhere, with very similar price-tags.

**Easter at Castelsardo.** The medieval festival here at Easter, called *Lunissanti,* is one of the oldest known on the island, featuring holy processions on Easter Monday, accompanied by Gregorian chants. Castelsardo's other major festival is **2 August,** when the *Madonna degli Angeli* is celebrated with games and traditional dancing.

**Yachts.** Castelsardo's extensive new harbour lies to the west of town; berth off the quay of the western mole.

**The Elephant Rock.** Behind Castelsardo, near the crossroads where the coastal road meets the inland route to Sedini, look out for the **Elephant Rock.** If you are driving along here it would be difficult not to see it, as the curious elephant-shaped monolith hangs over the road, its drooping trunk practically touching the passing vehicles.

Inside the rock is a series of prehistoric burial chambers, known as *domus de janas* – fairy- or witches'-houses. One has a bull's head etched into the rock, and there are other mysterious symbols, difficult to spot but good entertainment for children.

To follow the Doria theme a little further, the lonely ruins of a **castle** belonging to the family can be viewed a short way inland outside the village of Viddalba. The solitary red redoubt watches over the silent lake of Casteldoria, a deserted craggy spot full of the echoes of a time long past.

# LOGUDORO

Inland of Sássari, few places are sufficiently inviting for the tourist to make a base, but there are several sights that are well worth stopping for, on the way to somewhere else. Most are within easy reach of the main roads, but ideally you need your own transport.

Apart from a visit to a magnificent example of Nuraghic architec-ture, the trip is a journey back into the Middle Ages and Sardinia's Pisan past, most outstandingly illustrated in a trio of superb Pisan churches that are washed up in the middle of the countryside as if marooned; the flotsam of history. Indeed the very remoteness of these monuments accounts for their immaculate condition, far from the ravagings of coastal raiders.

From Ittiri to Ozieri stretches the region known as **Logudoro,** the 'Land of Gold.' The present-day territory is much shrunken since the Middle Ages, when it covered the whole of Sardinia's north-western quarter, but it has kept the island's purest form of dialect, a softer and more rolling speech than the other Sard dialects, like an echo of the gentle landscape.

**San Pietro di Simbranos.** The smallest and remotest of the Pisan churches is near the village of Sedini, inland from Castelsardo. Like the others to come, San Pietro di Simbranos (also called *delle Immagini*) is black-and-white striped, made of alternating basalt and limestone. It's not as impressive as the other examples – for a start it's smaller and lacks a bell-tower – but it stands in a flowery meadow, and is a good reason to stop awhile along this little country road, which you might consider as a route to or from Sássari.

**Santa Trinità di Saccágia.** The next Pisan church is much more visible, right on the main Sássari-Olbia SS 597, its bell-tower riding tall as you approach. Santa Trinità di Saccágia was built in 1116; according to tradition, at the instigation of the Giudice of Logudoro who was travelling this road with his wife on the way to Porto Torres, where they were to pray at San Gavino's shrine for the baby they wanted.

While the giudice and his lady spent the night here, the wife received a visitation from a divine messenger who told her that the pilgrimage was unnecessary as she was already pregnant, so the giudice ordered the building of an abbey in gratitude. This seems the most likely explanation why anyone would want to build such a splendid monument in this out-of-the-way spot.

The striking zebra-striped façade was added some 60 years later and, like the rest of the structure, has survived remarkably well, although the abbey's outhouses are either ruined or converted into barns. Look out for the lovely Gothic capitals at the top of the the porch as you go into the main building where the simple and rather gloomy interior, open every day until dusk, shows elements of Lombard architecture. The walls are stark and undecorated apart from a gilt-decorated pulpit of white wood embedded in one wall, and only a collection of faded 13th-cent frescos brighten the church's interior.

**The heart of Logudoro.** A little further up the road, the village of **Ardara** has a history which scarcely matches its present-day nondescript appearance. This was once the seat of the judiciary of Torres and the capital of the Logudoro region – but the only traces of its former glory are a 12th-cent castle and the recently restored basilica of Santa Maria del Regno, which holds an ornate tableau of 30 panels on a gold background, the work of two 16th-cent artists. The Romanesque architecture of the church was the model for a series of lesser churches in the region.

If you are going further along this road, you might look out on your left six miles (10km) after Ardara for another relic of the Pisans in Sardinia, the church of **Sant'Antíoco di Bisárcio.** Built in 1090, rebuilt 100 years after that, it was later given cathedral status and saw the coronation of many giudici of Logudoro, though today it is in such a

*The beach at Arbatax is a stone's throw from the station.*

tumbledown state that little of its original splendour remains.

**San Pietro di Sorres.** Go 18 miles (30km) south of Sássari, on the main Carlo Felice highway (the SS 131), and you reach the third of Logudoro's magisterial Pisan basilicas by turning off for the village of Bonnánaro and climbing up beyond the village of Borutta. Or, from Alghero, follow the longer mountain road that passes through the agricultural centre of Ittiri, turning left after Thiesi. The 12th-cent church of San Pietro di Sorres soon swings into sight on a bluff with sweeping views, a tableau that might have been transplanted from the Tuscan hills.

This church, formerly a cathedral, shows more French influence in its ornate style than do the other Pisan churches; it's also grander and in a tidier state, no doubt because of its continued use. The interior does not quite live up to the promise of the outside, but the pulpit and altar are worth seeing — and there's an intriguing 12th-cent sarcophagus.

**The Sant'Antine Nuraghe.** A mile or so further on, before returning to the SS 131, the road leads straight past one of the island's grandest prehistoric monuments. The Nuraghe Sant'Antine lies in the heart of the so-called Valle dei Nuraghi, a wide area full of these ancient structures, which mimic in miniature the strange, hummocked landscape and its solitary dun-coloured hills and plateaux.

Of the dozens of *nuraghi* here in various states of decay, this Nuraghic palace is the biggest and most impressive, sometimes known as *Nuraghe Majore;* thought to date back to the 14th cent BC, it overlooks the scattered ruins of a village as well as later Carthaginian and Roman additions.

Its central complex of three external bastions connected by a defensive wall, is grouped around the original massive three-storey tower with walls 6ft to 16ft (2m to 5m) thick and reaching a height of 50ft (16m). Corridors and staircases link the different parts of the tower, and the grounds include a well in an inner courtyard. From the top you can see other *nuraghi,* though don't be fooled by the closest and most perfect specimen — it's a recent reconstruction.

The complex is normally open daily 0900-1900 in summer, closing a couple of hours earlier in winter (admission free). As it lies only a few hundred metres from Torralba station, the site is easily reached without a car.

If the *nuraghe* is closed, call at the **Museo di Torralba** in the nearby village of Torralba, just over a mile (2.5km) away, for someone to escort you around the site. In any case, if you have time the museum makes an interesting diversion as it has a small collection of finds from the site as well as a model of the *nuraghe* in its original state, and details of its excavation. There are also rooms devoted to the local costume, with fascinating old photos of the everyday dress of the people of Logudoro. This is the best of many Nuraghic museums in the zone, opened only in 1988, and now open daily 0900-1300, 1500-1900 in summer, 0800-1400 in winter (L3,000).

*Charlie Chaplin lives: even the shops come under the brush in Orgósolo.*

# 16: OLBIA and the NORTH-EAST

## Olbia, Gallura and the Costa Smeralda

THE DEVELOPMENT OF THE 'EMERALD COAST' began Sardinia's transformation from economic gloom to tourism-based boom. The area has never looked back, and its largest town, Olbia, owes its recent rapid growth to the huge yearly influx of tourists to what must rank as one of the Mediterranean's loveliest stretches of coast.

The promotion of the Costa Smeralda, and the beginning of the new age for Sardinia, was the idea of the far-sighted Aga Khan who saw the potential of this previously barren area as a high-class tourist playground. Setting new standards of environment-friendly tourism, the project pioneered the concept of carefully planned development where the lust for luxury did not intrude too much on the extraordinary natural beauty of this indented rocky coast — but at a price to be paid by the customer. The success of the enterprise started the ball rolling for Sardinia, transforming the economy of this once neglected isle and pointing the way towards a new future.

Fortunately, the Costa Smeralda is only a tiny part of Sardinia's north-eastern coast, so that you can still enjoy the area without being ultra-rich. There are miles of undeveloped shoreline, and a profusion of more than 60 islands, islets and rocks, which the non-yachter can explore on any of the various boat-tours on offer. A daily ferry-service from Palau serves the biggest islands of Maddalena and Caprera, which are linked by a causeway, while further west Santa Teresa di Gallura is the embarcation-point for boats to Corsica as well as boasting some magnificent coves and beaches of its own.

This idyllic shore is the fringe of Sardinia's northernmost region of Gallura, whose raw red and wind-sculpted granite mountains provide the ever-present backdrop without which the area would lose its unique edge-of-the-wilderness appeal. In fact these mountains should not just be admired from afar, for there is a whole hidden world within that most tourists never discover; a rugged, thickly-forested landscape which offers a welcome change to the hours of idleness, stupefied by too much sun and sand. Or is that what you came here for in the first place?

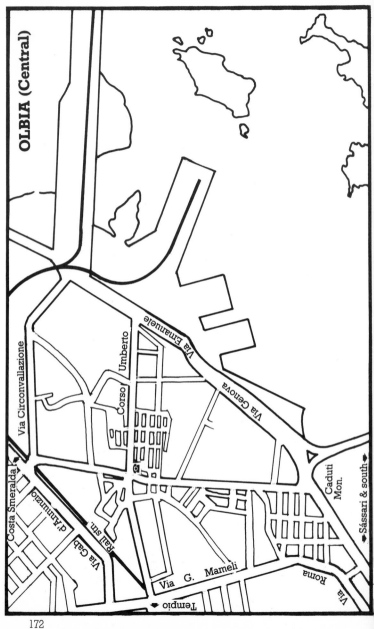

OLBIA (Central)

Via Circonvallazione

Costa Smeralda

Corso Umberto

Via Emanuele

Via Genova

Caduti Mon.

Sássari & south

Via Cab. d'Annunzio

Rail stn.

Via G. Mameli

Via Roma

Tempio

# OLBIA

When the English barrister John Tyndale visited Olbia in the 1840s, he compared its Greek name, meaning 'happy,' with the state he found it in: "A more perfect misnomer, in the present condition of the town, could not be found . . . The whole district suffers severly from intemperie. The wretched approach across these marshes is worthy of the town itself. The houses, none of which have an elegant or neat appearance, are built mostly of granite, and are whitewashed, as if to give a greater contrast to the filth and dirt within and around them."

The *intemperie* of which the barrister complained was malaria, but I can report that this scourge, along with the marshes and the filth and dirt, are long gone, vanished as a result of the land-drainage schemes and DDT-saturation of the 1950s, and the tourist invasions of the 1960s. Olbia today is once more a happy place, basking in a new-found wealth based on the traffic of tourists pouring through the docks and airport.

**Transit town.** As all those tourists are on their way to somewhere else, Olbia is essentially a transit town; though it has a charm of its own — concentrated in the main Corso Umberto and Piazza Margherita — Olbia is not a place where you will want to stay for long. But while you are here, there is no reason why you shouldn't enjoy its diversions, its many bars and restaurants providing entertainment enough to fill the odd afternoon and evening, possibly even a weekend.

**Roman rule.** Nobody knows how important Olbia was to the Greeks, but the port rose to prominence as the first Sardinian town to be taken by the Romans in 295BC, expelling the Carthaginians who had been established here since the 4th cent BC, and in the process killing the great Carthaginian general Hanno, who was buried with full military honours by the victorious Lucius Cornelius Scipio.

Surviving numerous Vandal and Saracen raids in the Dark Ages, Olbia was eventually completely rebuilt by Pisa in 1198, and renamed Terranova, a name which it kept until 1939. In the Middle Ages the city became one of the main strongholds of the *giudicato* of Gallura, somehow preserving its independence until the 15th cent. But in 1553 the Turkish admiral Dragut, fighting with the French against Charles V, Holy Roman Emperor and king of Spain and Germany, destroyed Olbia completely and took half its population into slavery, before going on to join Süleiman the Magnificent's generals at the Great Siege of Malta. Dragut appears in several guides in the *Discover* series; *Turkey* mentions his birth near Bodrum, *Tunisia* describes how he cut through the causeway to Jerba Island to save his fleet, and *Malta* tells of his death fighting the Order of St John.

In 1711, during the War of the Spanish Succession, the English Admiral Norris briefly occupied Olbia, and six years after that an Austrian army landed, took possession of the town and proposed to march on Alghero on the other side of the island. But the priest they seized as a guide led them into a trap, and a Sardinian force captured them and led them back to Olbia. This triumph of cunning over strength is still the subject of mirth among the local population.

**Olbia today.** Today numbering some 35,000, the people of Olbia seem to have shed the traumatic events of the past. Sophisticated and wily, but friendly, they are accustomed to having large numbers of foreigners in their midst; not just tourists but sailors from the port and large numbers of US servicemen from the nearby NATO base on Palau and the Maddalena archipelago, who come into town each day to spend their dollars and stalk the long Corso Umberto in search of good times. The black servicemen, with their walkmans and baseball caps, are a world apart from the Senegalese traders crouched on pavements, their wares spread before them.

The best view of the town is from the hills surrounding it, a wide panorama taking in the flat hinterland and the city at the head of a deep bay, around which cluster several islands, most prominently the immense mass of Tavolara. From close up the town is less inviting, for Olbia is the least Sardinian of all the island's centres, its appeal hardly strengthened by the untidy appearance of its back-streets. Crossed by canals and railway lines, the city is awash with traffic and flyovers and ugly blocks of flats, all of which have sprouted as a result of its recent unplanned growth, spoiling what once might have been an attractive seafront.

For the tourist there is little of historical value to see, but plenty of bars, trattorias and hotels, squeezed into the main Corso Umberto between smart clothes shops and ticket agencies. It is at least a manageable place, the airport a short bus ride away, the bus- and train-stations conveniently in the centre of town, and the ferry-port at no great distance.

**San Símplicio.** Main sightseeing item is the little basilica of San Símplicio on the street of the same name over the level-crossing. The simple granite structure is set in a piazza apart from Olbia's bustle, making it a good spot for a picnic or just to sit and relax. Justly claimed to be the most important medieval monument in the whole of Gallura — a province hardly famed for its artistic heritage — the church formed part of the great Pisan reconstruction programme of the 11th and 12th cents. The murky interior has three naves separated by pillars and columns recycled from ancient Roman constructions, and even the font for the holy water was formerly an urn that had held ashes from cremations. Along the walls is an array of Roman funerary slabs with fragments of inscription still visible on some.

The church is the site of Olbia's biggest annual festa, six days of religious processions, costumed dancing and poetry recitations, traditional games and fireworks, around 15 May, commemorating

San Símplicio's martyrdom in the 4th cent (the town's other main festivals are on Sant'Agostino's day on 24 June and Santa Lucia's day on the first Sunday of September, both lasting three days).

The only other church of note in Olbia is **San Paolo** just off Corso Umberto, easily recognisable by its multi-coloured cupola. The church, built in 1747 on the site of an old Punic temple, has little of interest within its unadorned granite-faced exterior.

**Information.** The helpful **AAST** office is on Via Piro, a side-street running off the Corso. Open 0830-1300, 1600-1800 daily except Saturday afternoon and Sunday (✆0789.21453).

**Transport.** Of Sardinia's three **airports** Olbia's is the most convenient, connected by hourly buses (no.2) to the central Piazza Margherita (tickets L1,300 from the nearby bar on the piazza); otherwise, taxis cost about L15,000). Phone ✆0789.23721 for flight information, or call in at a travel agency. For details of plane connections, see chapter three.

Trains for Sássari and Cágliari run several times daily from the **railway station,** just off Corso Umberto; here is a **left-luggage office** open 0830-1200, 1340-1730 daily. There is also a station at the ferry quay on Isola Bianca, though not all trains stop here.

The ARST **bus station** is around the corner on the Corso, with several departures daily for **Arzachena and Palau.** There are also daily departures for **Nuoro** at 0635 and 1430, and for **Sássari** at 0615 and 1950, taking about 90 minutes and two hours respectively.

*The memory of Eleanor of Arborea lives on at Oristano.*

**Ferries.** Ferries dock at the former island of Isola Bianca, now connected by a two-kilometre causeway along which you can walk or take a bus (no. 3, hourly).

Ships of the Tirrenia line leave for **Civitavécchia** (north of Rome) daily (departures 1100 8 June-14 September, otherwise 2300); **Genova** three times weekly (Tues, Thurs and Sat, departures at 2030), calling at **Arbatax**, further down on Sardinia's east coast, on Tues and Sat; tickets from the Tirrenia office either at the port (open 0830-1130 for morning departures; 1645-2300 for night departures), or at the bottom of Corso Umberto (open 0830-1300, 1630-1800; Sunday closed). Boats of the Navarma line leave for **Livorno** three or four times weekly May-June, twice daily from the end of June to the middle of September. Sardinia Ferries for Livorno now leave from Golfo Aranci, 9 miles (15km) up the coast. *Book early for all departures.*

**Car hire.** All the major companies have agencies at the airport. Agencies in town include: *Ellepi* Via Regina Elena 12 (✆0789.2390); *Hertz* Via Regina Elena 34 (✆0789.21274); *Smeralda Express* Via Piro 9 (✆0789.25512); *Inter Rent* Piazza Umberto 4 (✆0789.22163) and Via Roma 124 (✆0789.25793), and *Maggiore* Via Mameli 2 (✆0789.22131).

**Cycle hire.** *Smeralda Express* also rents out Vespas, as does *Usai* Via Regina Elena 58 (✆0789.25082).

**Boat tours.** You can take a selection of boat tours from Olbia's Marina di Porto Ottiolu, or Marina di Cugnana: look for the sign *Escursioni in batello.* Most leave at 0930 and return at about 1800, and include tours of the nearby islands of Tavolara and Molara, and the Maddalena archipelago. The price of L40,000 (reductions for children under ten) includes a spaghetti meal.

**ACI.** Via Piro 9 (✆0789.21414).

**Hotels.** There is a good selection of hotels in Olbia, though mostly on the expensive side. Most exclusive and right on the main street, Corso Umberto, is the *President* (✆0789.27501; L87,000), though the *De Plam* on Via de Fillipi, near the seafront, comes not far behind, with three stars as opposed to the *President's* four (✆0789.25777; L80-96,000). There are two other three-star places on the way out of town on the busy Viale Aldo Moro towards Palau: the *Motel Olbia* (✆0789.51456; L63,000) and the *Royal* (✆0789.50263; L80-96,000). Corso Umberto has two other two-star hotels, the *Centrale* (✆0789.23017; L52,000) and the *Gallura* (✆0789.24648; L43,000). Cheapest are the *Mastino* (✆0789.21320; L40,000), on Via Vespucci near the AAST, and the *Terranova* (✆0789.22395; L31,000) on Via Garibaldi, near Piazza Margherita.

The nearest **campsite** is outside town in Località Multa Maria (✆0789.36009), open June-September. Otherwise you must trek out to Porto San Paolo, south of Olbia, or north to Cugnana (see below).

**Restaurants.** The only problem when it comes to dining out in

Olbia is the choice. Try *La Palma,* behind the *Royal* hotel for exquisite seafood. Always crowded with locals and offering excellent value is the small but elegant *Zhanto* just off the Corso on Via delle Terme (closed Sunday).

**Yachts.** Berth at the Molo Vécchio, on the left of the long ferry causeway as you come in. The channel (minimum depth 15ft) is marked by buoys. The Capitaneria is at ✆0789.21243/21637, and there is a customs office.

## SOUTH OF OLBIA: POSADA

The coast road south from Olbia leads into a beachlover's paradise, with plenty of hotels and campsites, especially around San Teodoro and Siniscola.

The SS 125 passes the airport two miles (3km) from town and reaches the first suitable bathing beach at Lido del Sole after another four or five kilometres. The road follows the jagged coastline, always within sight of the monolithic flat-topped islands of **Tavolara** and **Molara,** which at one point are only 1.8 miles (3km) away; turn off for the Capo Coda Cavallo, or 'Horse's Tail Cape,' and you are less than two km from Molara – and you have crossed from Sássari province into Nuoro.

Hourly **tours** to Tavolara and Molara leave from the Pontile della Marina at Porto San Paolo, costing L12,000 per person, or L34,000 if you take the 8pm tour that includes supper.

There are a couple of **hotels** at Porto San Paolo: the smart *San Paolo* (✆ 0789.40001; L80-93,000) and the more modest *Franciscu* (✆ 0789.40021; L33,000), while at the nearby resort of Costa Dorata is the élite *Don Diego* (✆ 0789.40006; L86-193,000), a bungalow colony on the sea-shore.

The *Tavolara* **campsite** here is open June-September (✆ 0789.40166), and has three- or four-berth caravans for rent at L42-47,000 without bathroom, L48-55,000 with. Further down, at the popular beach-resort of San Teodoro, are two more campsites, the *San Teodoro* (May-October; ✆ 0784.86577), offering bungalows for four L51.500-61.800 and, a little further down, the *Cala d'Ambra* (June-September; ✆ 0784.865650).

**Posada.** At the mouth of the river of the same name, the Nuorese village of Posada stands on a rise a little way inland. Once a power-base for the surrounding districts, the town was prey to repeated attacks by sea-borne raiders during the Middle Ages, and now only its ruined, once impregnable castle stands witness to its former importance.

**The legend of the broad bean.** Posada's castle owes its strange name of *Castello della Fava* – Bean Castle – to a medieval legend. The story goes that when besieged here by Moors, the Giudice of

*The Tharros Peninsula was the home of Phoenicians, Carthaginians and Romans — then the Moors came.*

Gallura captured a homing pigeon, forced a broad-bean down its gullet, and tied to its leg a message addressed to a fictitious army of rescuers. As planned, the Moors intercepted the bird, read the message, found the broad bean in its stomach, and concluded that not only was there an army on the way, but that the besieged giudice had plenty of provisions — certainly enough to waste on pigeons. Whereupon the besiegers withdrew — and if you believe that you'll believe anything.

Now little more than a single upright tower ringed by some broken-down walls, the castle has been recently re-opened after restoration work; visitors must climb up iron rungs to reach the top, but are rewarded by a sweeping view of the coast and nearby river.

**Beaches and hotels.** Posada has some excellent sandy beaches a little further down the coast at **La Caletta,** where beach-bars and restaurants add a tropical air. There is a campsite at Località Su Viriarzu, *Ermosa* (May-September; ✆ 0784.854115) and hotels in the village, including the new three-star *Sa Rocca* (✆ 0784.854139; L55,000 per person half-board), below the castle in Piazza Eleonora d'Arborea. At the nearby resort town of **Siniscola** are plenty more hotels and campsites, the scene of frantic holidaying in the summer.

## NORTH TO GOLFO ARANCI

The Golfo di Olbia reaches its northern extent at Golfo Aranci, a major port whose evocative name, 'Gulf of Oranges,' has little in common with its reality. Apart from some decent beaches nearby there's no pressing reason to come here unless you need to cross on the daily Sardinia Ferries line to **Livorno,** or FS ferry to **Civitavécchia,** north of Rome. The daily crossing takes about eight hours and prices range from L50,000 to L160,000 per person, depending on season and whether you choose a cabin; vehicles cost between L40,000 for a small car in off-peak season, and L180,000 in season for a car longer than 4.5m. Ask about any possible reductions on return crossings, stand-bys, advance bookings etc. In season, *you are advised to book early*.

**Transport.** Frequent **buses** connect Golfo Aranci with Olbia. Some **trains** from Olbia run right up to the port, though most stop at the central station in town.

**Hotels.** If you need to stay at Golfo Aranci, there is a handful of hotels to choose from, most on the long main road connecting the port area with the centre of town: *Castello* Via Libertà (✆ 0789.46073; L57,000; open May-October); *Margherita* Via Libertà 59 (✆ 0789.46906; L66-77,000), and *King's* Via Libertà (✆ 0789.46075; L48-55,000; May-October). The comfortable *Gabbiano Azzurro* is just outside town directly on the beach at Via dei Gabbiani (✆ 0789.46929; L59-70,000; May-October).

**Yachts.** Golfo Aranci is not a suitable place to berth a yacht, but there are good anchorages to be found further down the gulf.

# THE COSTA SMERALDA

Legend has it that the Aga Khan almost literally stumbled upon the charms of the Costa Smeralda when his yacht took shelter from a storm in one of the narrow creeks here. In 1962 this fabulously wealthy tycoon who is also spiritual leader and Imam of the Ismaili Muslims headed a consortium of businessmen with the aim of exploiting the wild, largely uninhabited coastal strip running up the west side of the Cugnana bay as far as the Gulf of Arzachena. He had no trouble in persuading the local farmers to sell their land in this rough, unproductive terrain, paying what were then considerable sums. stories have been told of the tricks and stratagems that he used to dupe the ignorant locals into giving up their property for a fraction of its real value – but as its value at that time was only for poor land, and its owners sold willingly, this sounds like envy on the part of people lacking the Aga's vision.

The consortium's plans were on a massive scale, limited only by the conditions the regional government imposed. These included proper sewage processing and disposal, restrictions on building, and the insistence that the natural appearance of the landscape should not be unduly changed. The Aga Khan was only partially successful on this last point; although you won't see multi-storeyed hotels, advertising

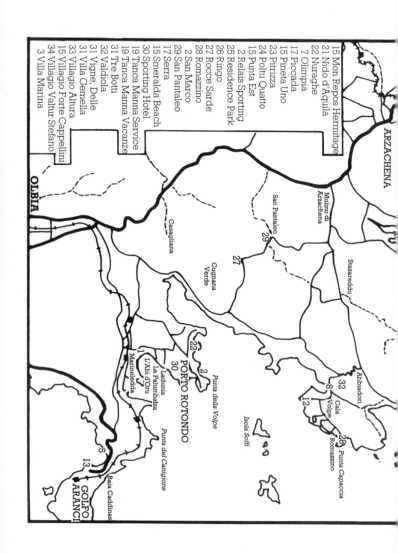

15 Mon Repos Hermitage
21 Nido d'Aquila
22 Nuraghe
7 Olimpia
17 Piccada
15 Pineta Uno
23 Pitrizza
24 Poltu Quatto
15 Punta Est
2 Relais Sporting
25 Residence Park
26 Ringo
27 Rocce Sarde
28 Romazzino
2 San Marco
29 San Pantaleo
17 Serra
15 Smeralda Beach
30 Sporting Hotel
19 Tanca Manna Service
19 Tanca Manna Vacanze
31 Tre Botti
32 Valdiola
31 Vigne, Delle
31 Villa Gemella
33 Villaggio Altura
15 Villaggio Forte Cappellini
34 Villaggio Valtur Stefano
3 Villa Marina

ARZACHENA

OLBIA

Mulino di
Arzachena

San Pantaleo

29

21

Casagliana

Cugnana
Verde

Shazareddu

Abbiadori

32

Cala
8 Volpe

12

28
Romazzino

Punta Capaccia

Marinelledda

Ladunia
L'Abi d'Oru
La Palumbalza
30

PORTO ROTONDO

2

Punta della Volpe

Isola Soffi

Punta del Cavigione

5

13

Baia Caddinas

GOLFO
ARANCI

180

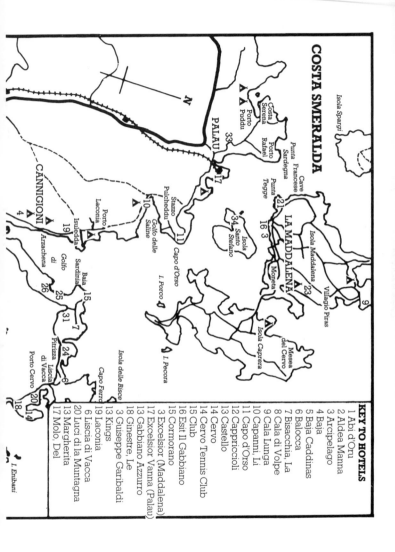

**KEY TO HOTELS**

1 Abi d'Oru
2 Aldea Manna
3 Arcipelago
4 Baja
5 Baja Caddinas
6 Balocca
7 Bisacchia, La
8 Cala di Volpe
9 Cala Lunga
10 Capanni, Li
11 Capo d'Orso
12 Cappriccioli
13 Castello
14 Cervo
14 Cervo Tennis Club
15 Club
16 Esit Il Gabbiano
15 Cormorano
3 Excelsior (Maddalena)
17 Excelsior Vanna (Palau)
13 Gabbiano Azzurro
18 Ginestre, Le
3 Guiseppe Garibaldi
13 Kings
19 Laconia
6 Liscia di Vacca
20 Luci di la Muntagna
13 Margherita
17 Molo, Del

hoardings, fast-food restaurants or even garish petrol stations disfiguring the coast's quiet inlets and rocky promontories, there is little that is *natural* about the place. True, hotels blend harmoniously with the scenery, but you will not find a genuine fishing village still surviving in these parts, or anything like the kind of bustling local market you find in other parts of Sardinia.

Even the supermarkets here are discreet. The holiday villages, for all their trappings of luxury, have a bland, almost suburban feel about them. What I find lacking is the vital human element — the local touch. Ultimately of course it's a question of taste, and you will make your own choice. If you are fortunate enough to be staying here, you will no doubt discover the virtues of this form of insulated holiday oasis, and there are few who will deny that as a hedonist's heaven, the Costa Smeralda can't be beaten.

**Porto Cervo.** The 'capital' of the Costa Smeralda, Porto Cervo, reflects the ideal. Its 'local'-style rustic red architecture is surreal, overwhelmingly artificial, embodying the dream of an idyllic Mediterranean village without any of the irritating details of real life. It's fascinating to wander around; everywhere is spotlessly clean, crime- and litter-free, and gives the impression of a child's playground inflated to huge proportions — and *that* describes the prices. Apart from the hotels and restaurants, there are banks, boutiques, phones, chemists' shops, travel agents, even supermarkets. Its tennis courts are of top-quality, used for tournaments in the summer, and open on a daily or weekly basis to the public.

On a height overlooking the rows of yachts, the **Stella Maris** church is a modern white-washed creation designed by the Roman architect Michel Busiri Vici, also responsible for the grotto-like shopping arcade in Porto Cervo's centre. Inside is a good painting by El Greco, the *Mater Dolorosa*.

**Pevero Golf Club.** The 18-hole 72-par Pevero golf course on a beautiful expanse of green above the *Cala di Volpe Hotel* is one of the best you'll find, the creation of architect Robert Trent Jones. It's linked to the *Cervo, Romazzino, Cala di Volpe* and *Pitrizza* hotels by a free shuttle service.

**Yachting.** It could be argued that Porto Cervo was designed primarily with the yachtsman or -woman in mind, as it's equipped with the best marine facilities in Sardinia. There are berths for 650 vessels, each with electricity and fresh water supplies (and rings and bollards in bronze!), and in the north-west corner is a yard with sophisticated workshops and outfitters nearby. You should, of course, expect to pay high prices for these facilities.

Elsewhere, the creeks and inlets off and around the Costa Smeralda provide numerous good anchorages, mostly with excellent bathing. Note that the Golfo di Cugnana is suitable only at its mouth, that fees are demanded at Porto Rotondo, and the small harbour at the shallow Cala di Volpe is available only to hotel-guests and berth-holders at the Porto Cervo marina.

**Beaches.** Take your pick, but don't expect the best beaches to be clearly marked — just follow any dirt track down to the sea; the rougher it is, the more promising. Try ones at Punta Cappricciolo, Romazzino and Liscia Ruia, the latter at the end of a long bumpy dirt road.

**Accommodation.** This list of hotels, residences and campsites on the Costa Smeralda includes several of the more expensive hotels managed by the Aga Khan's consortium, which are valued for their high staff-to-guest ratio. Self-catering residences normally work out cheaper and have access to the best facilities, though you need to book well ahead.

### Porto Rotondo:

*Relais Sporting*, 5★, open April-September (✆0789.34005/7) L320-580,000. One of the area's smartest hotels on a promontory enclosing a marina. Salt-water swimming pool and motor-boat rental are among its attractions. *San Marco*, 4★, open April-September (✆0789.34108) L136- 208,000. A shady villa on Piazza San Marco, serving breakfast only, though trattorias are at hand. *Aldia Manna*, 3★, (✆0789.35453) L60-110,000. Out of town, at Località Aldia Manna. *Nuraghe*, 3★, open May-September (✆0789.34436) L83-119,000; out at Località Punta Nuraghe.

### Costa Smeralda: *Cala di Volpe*, 5★, May-September (✆0789.96083) L687-971,000. Designed by celebrated architect Jacques Couelle and looking something like a mix between a medieval fortress and a peasant's eyrie, all in immaculate taste. Exceptional cuisine, a private harbour, two salt-water pools (one on the hotel's roof) plus a fine sand beach combine to make this a foretaste of heaven on earth.

*Pitrizza*, 5★, May-September (✆0789.91500) L709-995,000. A little outside Porto Cervo in the exquisite bay of Liscia di Vacca. The Pitrizza, like the Cala di Volpe, is listed in *Harpers & Queen's 300 Best Hotels in the World*, where René Lecler describes it as "one of the nicest, most informal and yet most elegant hotels I know in the Mediterranean." This has a much smaller capacity than the Cala di Volpe, with only 28 rooms, each in an independent villa overlooking the sea.

*Romazzino*, 5★, May-October (✆0789.96020) L630-942,000. Set in green grounds leading to a wide beach, this is another medieval-type complex with salt-water pool, panoramic terrace and good water-sports.

*Hotel Cervo*, 5★, April-October (✆0789.92003) L419-642,000. In the heart of Porto Cervo village, its entrance is on the central piazza but it

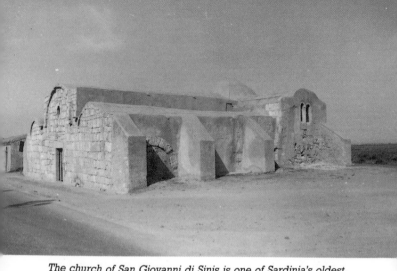

*The church of San Giovanni di Sinis is one of Sardinia's oldest.*

still projects an air of privileged quiet. There is a pool here and, for a secluded swim, a boat-service whisks guests off to a select beach 20 minutes away

*Cervo Tennis Club*, 4★, (✆0789.92244) L107-234,000. A tennis club with 16 luxury rooms available, indoor and outdoor pools, plus gym, sauna and squash courts.

*Le Ginestre*, 4★, (✆0789.92030/92474) L129-220,000. Outside Porto Cervo in lush parkland with two pools, tennis court and beach.

*Luci di la Muntagna*, 4★, February-October (✆0789.92051) L125-198,000. Good view over Porto Cervo, with pool and lifts down to private beach. Reductions for children and honeymooners.

*Balocco*, 3★, April-October (✆0789.91555) L84-142,000. Surrounded by flowering gardens, this has the air of a rustic villa; close to Porto Cervo but discreet.

*Capriccioli*, 3★, May-September (✆0789.96004) L72-96,000. Small and select, home of the well-known *Pirata* restaurant with its panoramic veranda.

*Liscia di Vaca*, 3★, April-October (✆0789.91560) L88-131,000. Again, the rustic, red-tiled look — peaceful and panoramic outside Porto Cervo.

*Nibaru*, 3★, (✆0789.96038) L66-113,000. On the Cala di Volpe bay, but close to all the facilities; low-key, with a small pool.

*Valdiola*, 3★, (✆0789.96215) L83-136,000. On the Cala di Volpe, five kilometres from Porto Cervo, with huge windows overlooking the sea.

*Residenza Capriccioli*, 3★, May-October (✆0789.96016). Three-bed accommodation for L901-1,351,000 per week, 100m from the sea between Capriccioli and Cala di Volpe. Sports facilities and gardens.

And finally a **campsite:** *La Cugnana,* May-September (✆0789.33184). At the bottom of the Cugnana bay: bungalows also available here L64,300-83,800 for three with bathroom. Expect a crowd.

### Baia Sardinia:

*Mon Repos-Hermitage*, 4★, April-October (✆0789.99011) L129-151,000. Solarium terraces over weird reefs and red-sand beach. Secluded and exclusive.

*Club Hotel*, 3★, April-October (✆0789.99006) L123-135,000. Refined, comfortable, with views out towards Caprera island.

*Smeraldo Beach*, 3★, May-October (✆0789.99046) L84-127,000. Turreted, with a rustic appearance, this large hotel has a pool, tennis courts, underwater sports facilities and a hairdresser on hand.

*La Bisaccia*, 3★, April-October (✆0789.99002) L109-121,000. Good views and private beach, with a residence attached.

*Cormorano*, 3★, April-September (✆0789.99020) L99-107,000. Private beach and tennis courts, with rooms overlooking pool. Reductions for newly-weds, the elderly and longer stays.

*Villa Gemella*, 3★, (✆0789.99303) L61-106,000. Small modern hotel on the Golfo di Arzachena, with billiard room, swimming pool. No restaurant but access to nearby *Tre Botti.*

*Villaggio Forte Cappellini*, 3★, May-November (✆0789.99057) L77−97,000. A large, fortress-like exterior fronts a complex of individual bungalows close to the sea on the end of a promontory. Stylishly furnished, with access to a large pool and open-air bar and restaurant on the surrounding lawns. No children under 15.

*Punta Est*, 3★, April-October (✆0789.99028) L80-96,000. New, white-washed appearance with pool and beach at 150m. Cruises and tours organised.

*Olimpia*, 3★, May-October (✆0789.99176) L66-89,000. Small, granite-bricked and porticoed structure, 150m from sea.

*Hotel delle Vigne*, 3★, April-October (✆0789.99411) L57-83,000. Modern-style complex with tennis-coaching, windsurfing, scuba etc. Good for children.

*Tre Botti*, 3★, (✆0789.99150) L61-82,000. Small, compact, equipped with a good restaurant.

*Residence Park*, 3★, April-October (✆0789.99016) L81-106,000. Apartments and detached bungalows (with bathrooms) with floodlit tennis courts and beach.

**Rentals and purchases on the Costa Smeralda.** There's plenty of scope here for renting or buying property, if you have deep pockets; prices go according to size and distance from the sea. **Apartment-**

**rentals** also vary according to season; typical is L420,000 per week between the end of September and the middle of June for a one-roomed apartment, rising to L1,400,000 for August rentals.

For **purchases,** the average price at Porto Rotondo is about L1,300,000 (£600) per square metre which adds up to about L62 million, or about £30,000 for a two-room apartment, twice that for a three- or four-room apartment. At Porto Cervo I saw a one-bedroomed flat with verandah and garden for L300,000,000 (£140,000) and a three-bed, two-bath apartment for L430,000,000 (£210,000).

For more details on prices and availability of rentals and purchases, contact *Agenzia Immobiliare di Baja Sardinia,* Casella Postale 49, 07020 Porto Cervo, Sássari (✆0789.99198); *Agenzia Immobiliare Porto Cervo,* Via Cerbiatta, 07020 Porto Cervo, Sássari (✆0789.92550), or *Agenzia Immobiliare della Costa Smeralda,* Centro Commerciale, 07020 Porto Cervo, Sássari (✆0789.91577).

## ARZACHENA AND CANNIGIONE

Outside the luxury zone but sharing many of the natural advantages of the Costa Smeralda, the Golfo di Arzachena is a deep narrow bay with facilities concentrated around the resort village of Cannigione. Arzachena itself is inland and not particularly inspiring, though it has its share of excitement in high season.

**Arzachena.** As the main centre of the region, it has transport links, banks and shops, though lacking the glamour of the nearby jetsetters' resorts. But it has a curiosity; the *Roccia Il Fungo,* or "mushroom rock," on the outskirts of town at the end of Via Limbara. It is one of the many strange, wind-eroded granite rocks which are scattered around these parts, this one giving good views over the coasts.

**Information.** Piazza Risorgimento at the centre of town holds the **AAST,** main tourist information office for the whole of the Costa Smeralda region. Open 0800-1330, 1500-1900 except Saturday afternoon and Sunday, it has maps and details on accommodation and excursions in the area (✆0789.81090, 82848, 82624).

**Hotels.** Arzachena has two small hotels at opposite ends of town: the *Citti* (✆0789.82662; L41-55,000; no restaurant) at Viale Costa Smeralda 197 — the main road to Palau — and *Casa Mia* (✆0789.82790; L43-47,000), with a restaurant, at Via Torricelli 3, off the Olbia road.

Or do you prefer something more rural? There are several **Agriturismo** places inland, the nearest about 4.5 miles (7km) along the Luogosanto road (✆079.669079).

**Restaurants.** There is a lack of decent eating-places in town. Apart from the *Casa Mia,* try the *Aryes Spaghetteria* below Piazza Risorgimento on Viale Costa Smeralda. There are a couple of other trattorias on this road and the main Via Ruzzittu.

**Other useful addresses.** You want to **hire a Vespa?** Then ask at

*Evening over the peninsula at Tharros.*

Raimondo Casula's scooter shop on Via Dettori, open 0900-2000; he is
a bit expensive at L65,000 for 12 hours. Arzachena's **post office** is on
the left leaving town on the Palau road.

**Transport.** All **buses** pull up on Via San Pietro, off Viale Dettori –
the road signposted for Luogosanto. At the bar here you can buy
tickets for Olbia, Palau, Cannigione and Laconia (last bus to Olbia
2145, last to Cannigione and Laconia 1945). Arzachena's **station** is
about a kilometre west out of town, with several trains stopping daily
on the Sássari to Témpio Pausánia to Palau line. **Taxis** can be found on
the central Piazza Risorgimento.

**The Giants' Tombs.** The most interesting prehistoric sights around
Arzachena are the so-called Giants' Tombs, or **Tombe dei Giganti;**
there are many examples of this type of construction in Sardinia,
made of carved granite slabs laid end-up in semicircles in the open
countryside. Why giants' tombs? The local people of long ago could
think of no better explanation, but archeologists now believe they
were linked to the Nuraghic culture, serving both as burial chambers
and places of worship. Their tall central steles (standing stones)
resemble – probably intentionally – giant doorways, perhaps
symbolising the entry into another world? The tombs reminded me of
Stonehenge, and they're only a little more recent, though opinions
differ about their exact age.

There are two more sites of Giants' Tombs worth visiting in the
area; at Coddu Vécchio and at the more spectacular Li Lolghi, the

latter is three miles (5km) west of Arzachena on the road to Bassacutena — turn left onto a track at two miles (3.5km). The 'tombs' are 12ft (nearly 4m) high and 90ft (27m) long, and at their base is a small arched doorway leading into a passage containing two chambers where the bodies were laid.

Nearby are five stone circles from about the same period, which probably once formed a necropolis; the circles range from 15ft to 25ft (5m to 8m) in diameter, each originally containing a body and votive offerings.

Not far away is **Codu Vécchio,** south-west of Arzachena and best reached from Li Lolghi by following the track until it reaches the Luogosanto road, where you turn left (east) and go 2km towards Arzachena. Taller than Li Lolghi, Codu Vécchio is also divided into two chambers, suggesting two distinct periods of construction. The site is close to Caldosa station, next down from Arzachena on the small-gauge railway from Palau.

Around both sites are *nuraghi,* with the one known as *La Prisciona,* near Codu Vécchio, the most interesting, built at any time between 2000 and 1000 BC on a height overlooking the whole Arzachena plain.

**Cannigione.** A small fishing town and yachting resort, Cannigione has a peaceful atmosphere, unruffled by the summer hordes for which it caters. Well-equipped with supermarkets and restaurants, there is a *cambio* open morning and afternoon and a small **information office** at the end of the main street. Several buses daily link Cannigione with Arzachena, where there are connections to Olbia and Palau.

**Accommodation choices in Cannigione.** In Cannigione itself is a good three-star hotel, the *Baja* (✆0789.88010; L65-70,000), open April-October, with a large swimming pool and floodlit tennis court. Open all year is the *Hotel del Porto* (✆0789.88011; L44-96,000), on Lungo-màre Dória.

Beyond Cannigione the road curves round the side of the bay with grand views and numerous small beaches, to the locality of **Laconia**. Dotted with villas, there is a hotel and a 'residence' here: the *Hotel Laconia* (✆0789.86007; L72-106,000), open March-November, and *Residenza Tanca Manna* (✆0789.86043) offering three-bed self-catering apartments for L419-837,000 per week. It's a 50m walk to the sea, but on-site facilties include bar, pizzeria, restaurant, disco, tennis courts and shops.

Cannigione also has a couple of **campsites** which positively bulge with campers and bungalowers in high summer, because (with the exception of the *Cugnana* site mentioned above) they are the nearest to the Costa Smeralda: *Golfo di Arzachena* (open May to mid-October; ✆0789.88101) and *Villaggio Isuledda* (March to end-of-October; ✆0789.86003).

At Laconia, the better-equipped *Isuledda* is popular as it's right on the shore with excellent bathing spots, while the *Golfo di Arzachena* is a little way back from the sea, though closer to Cannigtone. Both offer *tukuls* — detached or semi-detached little bungalows of varying sizes — from L50,000 per week to L127,000, according to season and size of tukul.

Beyond Laconia an unasphalted road leads round the undeveloped sandy shores of the Golfo delle Saline, where the secluded *Club Hotel Li Capanni* (✆0789.86041; L78-106,000) sits, an exclusive holiday village with excellent facilities but not open for children under 14. At the tip of the bay is a **campsite**, *Capo d'Orso* (May-October; ✆0789.708182), and a superb four-star **hotel** of the same name (✆0789.708100; L150-450,000), also open May-October. Both are named from the nearby headland, which in turn takes its name from the strange bear-shaped rock (*orso* = bear), known since ancient times and even claimed to be the dwelling-place of the Laestrigonians, the mythical cannibal tribe which destroyed Ulysses's fleet when it was docked here.


# PALAU AND THE MADDALENA ARCHIPELAGO

The group of islands scattered off Sardinia's northern tip offers opportunities for some lovely cruises — and you don't need your own yacht, though all the better if you do. The yachtless among us can choose from a variety of pleasure-cruises from Palau or from Maddalena Island itself. From Palau there is a frequent daily ferry-service to the archipelago's main island, Maddalena, from which you can drive — or walk — across to the second island, Caprera.

**Nelson's wait.** Between 1803 and 1805 Admiral Nelson stayed in these waters with his fleet for a total of 15 months while he pursued the French fleet in the prelude to the Battle of Trafalgar. Throughout this long patrol, during which Nelson never once set foot on shore, he sent a stream of letters to the Admiralty in London urging that steps be taken to secure Sardinia for Britain, as it was the only neutral shore in this part of the Mediterranean: "And I venture to predict, that if we do not — from delicacy, or commisseration of the lot of the unfortunate King of Sardinia — the French will." The French, docked at Toulon — nicknamed 'Too-Long' by Nelson's impatient sailors — eventually fled to the West Indies before returning to meet Nelson at Trafalgar, between Cádiz and Gibraltar. At this time, Britain had held Gibraltar for a century, was administering Malta after the French withdrawal, and had already taken and lost Menorca.

**Garibaldi.** The other historical figure of note who is indelibly associated with this part of Sardinia is Garibaldi, hero of the struggle for Italian unification. He spent the last third of his life on the island of Caprera, his house now converted into a museum which gives a fascinating insight not only into his reclusive day-to-day existence here, but also his long and glorious career on the world-stage.

**Palau.** Unless you are an American serviceman billeted here as part of the NATO presence, the only reason for being in this small port is for the ferry. Boats leave every 30 or 45 minutes, but *you must be here at least half an hour before departure time, more in summer.* It's a hectic bustle for tickets (L1,000 per person, L4,000 for a medium-sized car) and queues are common. And by the way, don't pick fights with queue-jumpers: the chances are they are residents of Maddalena who get priority rights as well as fare discounts.

**Information.** The **AAST** at Via Nazionale 94 (✆0789.709570) is open 0800-1400, 1600-1900 daily except for Saturday afternoon and all of Sunday.

**Accommodation.** The hotels here include *Del Molo* (✆0789.708142; L47-60,000) on Via dei Ciclopi; *Excelsior Vanna* (✆0789.709589; L35-60,000) on Via Capo d'Orso, and *La Roccia* (✆0789.709528; L36-45,000) on Via dei Mille – all three-star – and the two-star *Serra* (✆0789.709519; L36,000) on Via Nazionale.

**Transport.** Ten buses a day leave Palau for Olbia, and one for Sássari (0600, taking three hours). Two trains also leave from the station here for Sássari (at 0505 and 1628; 3hrs 45min), passing through Arzachena, Calanganius and Témpio Pausánia.

**La Maddalena.** The crossing from Palau over what Nelson called 'Agincourt Sound' takes 20 minutes. The port and only town on the island, **La Maddalena,** is a cheerful place with a population of about 15,000, swollen by the large number of Italian and US sailors which give the town a distinct garrison feel. The naval headquarters are all on the eastern side of Maddalena, a drab area of monotonous barracks guarded by armed sentries, though the main military installations and submarine base are on the neighbouring island of Santo Stéfano. The archipelago has always had a strong naval tradition, harbouring a fleet of the Royal House of Savoy long before the Americans arrived. On Via Príncipe Amedeo a **museum of naval archeology** – open 0900-1400, closing an hour earlier on Sundays and holidays, and all day Monday (free) – shows finds recovered from ancient wrecks in the area.

**Information.** The **AAST** on the seafront (Via XX Settembre) is open 0800-1400, 1600-1900 daily except for Saturdy afternoon and all of Sunday (✆0789.736321).

**Accommodation.** La Maddalena is not particularly well-off for hotels, considering the number of tourists who annually flood the archipelago. However **rooms to rent** are available: if they're not marked – look for *camere in affito* – then you'll have to ask around at the AAST or in bars. The **hotels** in town are: *Excelsior* Via Améndola 7 (✆0789.737020; L71-95,000); *Giuseppe Garibaldi* Via Lamármora

(✆0789.737314; L72-97,000); *Nido d'Aquila* Via Nido d'Aqula (✆0789.722130; L65-108,000); *Villa Marina* Via Magnaghi 12 (✆0789.738340; L76-102,000); *Arcipélago* Via Indipendenza Traversa 2 (✆0789.727328; L65,000), and the ESIT-run *Il Gabbiano* Via Giúlio Césare 20 (✆0789.737007; L39-45,000).

There are smaller places in other parts of the island, at **La Ricciolina,** the modest *Locanda de Raffaele* (✆0789.738759; L29-34,000), and at **Porto Mássimo,** the more exclusive *Cala Lunga,* open May-September (✆0789.737389; L74-132,000).

There are also two **campsites:** *Il Sole* (✆0789.727130), open all year on Via Indipendenza, and *Maddalena* (June-September; ✆0789.738333) in Località Moneta, facing Caprera island. *Punta Cannone,* on the point of the same name, is a **holiday village,** charging L56-87,000 for full-board, more if you want a private bathroom (June-September; ✆0789.737542).

On the NATO island of Santo Stéfano − briefly captured by Napoleon in 1793 in an abortive attempt to take possession of Sardinia − there is a *Valtur* 'hotel-village,' open May-October (✆0789.737061; L82,000); for Caprera see below.

**Buses and boats.** The **buses** run to various localities on the island from near the Bank of Sardinia at the end of Via XX Settembre, every quarter of an hour in summer (two hours in winter). A good way of getting around the island would be by **moped** − *motorino.* If you want to hire one try the small shop near the AAST charging L30,000 a day.

From La Maddalena it is also possible to **sail** directly to Santa Teresa di Gallura, the Sardinian port for Corsica, with daily departures (except Sunday) costing L2,000 per person, L5-12,000 for a car.

**Garibaldi and Caprera.** Between October and May half of Caprera is closed off for military purposes, but there is always plenty of space left to roam this woody protected parkland. Apart from Garibaldi's house in the centre there are no buildings.

Giuseppe Garibaldi (1807-1882) came to live in Caprera in 1855, after a 20-year exile from Italy as a result of his part in republican plots. He spent his time abroad building a career as a guerrilla leader in South America, but returned clandestinely to fight for the Piedmontese cause against the Austrians in 1848, and for Mazzini's Roman republic the following year. He later worked as a candle-maker in New York and even captained a merchant ship in the Pacific before returning to Italy, where he renounced his republican views and declared himself for Victor Emmanuel II in his struggle for a united Italy.

His decision to settle in Caprera, where he bought the northern part of the island for about £360, was no doubt determined by his wish to be in the Piedmontese Kingdom of Sardinia, and conveniently close to the naval base at Maddalena. It was from here that he set out on his spectacular conquest of Sicily and Naples in 1861, accompanied by his thousand 'red-shirts' — the *mille* whose name is given to squares and streets throughout Italy. After the successful campaign, which ended with the proclamation of Victor Emanuel as King of Italy in 1862 (though parts of Italy — notably Rome — remained independent), he retired to his simple life as a farmer on Caprera, emerging only to take part in some rash escapades meant to complete the unfinished job of unifying Italy, attempts which were disowned by the King but which did nothing to diminish his heroic stature in the eyes of Italians.

**Neighbourly disputes.** Garibaldi spent much of his time on Caprera writing his memoirs and some bad novels. His neighbour was an Englishman named Collins, with whom he had some famous disagreements concerning their wandering goat-herds, as a result of which Garibaldi built a wall dividing their properties, which can still be seen. After Collins's death a group of English admirers provided the money for Garibaldi to buy the rest of Caprera from his ex-neighbour's family.

**Garibaldi Museum.** The *Museo Garibaldi* (open Tues-Sat 0900-1330, Sun 0900-1230, Mondays and holidays closed; L4,000) is in Garibaldi's old house, the elegant South American-style *Casa Bianca*, which has been preserved much as he left it. Visitors are guided round a collection of memorabilia, including the bed where he slept, a smaller one where he died, various scrolls, manifestos and

*Little has changed in the village of San Lussúrgiu.*

pronouncements, a pair of ivory and gold binoculars given to him by the Prince of Wales (later Edward VII) and a letter from London, dated 1867, conferring on him honorary presidency of the National Reform League. A stopped clock and a wall-calendar indicate the precise time and date when he died.

The tour ends with his tomb in the garden, its rough granite contrasting with the more pompous tombs of his last wife and five of his children beside it. Apparently, Garibaldi had asked to be cremated, but following the wishes of his son Menotti, his corpse was stuffed. The tomb was opened, the guide told me, in 1932, 50 years after his death, and his body was found to be perfectly intact.

**Accommodation.** The only holiday accommodation on Caprera is a *Club Mediteranee* camp (✆0789.727078) charging L310-510,000 for seven days full-board, and a **tourist village,** *Centro Vélico* (✆0789.738529) open April-November charging L68-82,000 full-board.

## SANTA TERESA DI GALLURA

Between Palau and the port of Santa Teresa di Gallura is a succession of lovely bays, some dramatic rocky coastline, and a handful of campsites.

**Portu Puddu and Porto Pozzo.** Portu Puddu, also called Porto Pollo, is a thick knob of rock connected to the coast by a thin limb of beach where a busy **windsurfing** centre has established itself. At the end is *Isola dei Gabbiani* a **campsite** open March-October (✆0789.704024). Porto Pozzo is little more than a bar and a few houses inland, though clearly destined for greater things. Other campsites on the minor road following the coast are *Arcobaleno* (May-September; ✆0789.752040) with caravans and bungalows for rent at L50-90,000, and *La Liccia* (May-September; ✆0789.755190), also with bungalows, a little cheaper than the *Arcobaleno's*.

**Santa Teresa.** Sardinia's most northerly port, **Santa Teresa di Gallura,** is the main crossing-point for ferries to Corsica. As such it has a good collection of hotels in town, and several more outside where they are best-placed to take advantage of some of Sardinia's most alluring beaches.

**Information.** The **AAST** in Santa Teresa is on the main Piazza Vittório Emanuele (✆0789.754127), open 0900-1300, 1600-1900 except for Saturday afternoon and Sunday; there is also a booth down by the port open 0915-1315, 1520-2030 from June to the end of September.

**Sailings.** Departures on Tirrenia, Navarma or Saremar ferries for **Bonifacio,** in Corsica, are eight times daily in summer, less in winter. Crossings take an hour, and cost L12,500 per person, L30,000 for a car (with variations according to size).

Navarma also operates a service to ports on the Italian coast, leaving daily for **La Spézia** (1500); **Génova** (1600); **Livorno** (1315 and

2315); **Piombino** (1710), and **Porto Santo Stéfano** (1600).

In addition Tirrenia provides a daily service (except Sunday) between Santa Teresa and **Maddalena** island (L2,000 per person, L5-12,000 for a car).

**Buses.** ARST buses leave daily from the Post Office for **Golfo Aranci** at 1105 and 1650; **Olbia** 0625, 0845, 1220, 1650, 2045; **Sássari** 0510, 1510; **Témpio Pausánia** (inland) 0700, 0710, 1700, 1710; and **Vignola** (west along the coast) 0710, 1000, 1430, 1710, 2050. All buses make frequent stops along the coast for specific resorts. There is also a route taking in the resorts of **La Marmorata** east of Santa Teresa and **Capo Testa** west (see below), leaving seven times a day in summer, less in winter.

**Boat tours.** At the marina, **tours of the coast** are advertised at L40,000 per person. This is an excellent way to explore the varied shore, also giving you a good view of Corsica.

**Yachts.** There is good shelter in Santa Teresa's long inlet, though the main quay is often used by ferries during the day. This is a Port of Entry, with harbour and customs officials.

**ACI.** Via Genova 4 (☎0789.754077).

**Car rentals.** Apart from *ACI*, *Hertz* is at Via Maria Teresa 29 (☎0789.754247); *Happy Car* at Piazza Villamarina (☎0789.754741).

**Accommodation.** There are 21 **hotels** listed in Santa Teresa, ranging from the three-star *Bacchus* on Via Firenze (☎0789.750556; L48-56,000) to the one-star *Scano* on Via Lázio (☎0789.754447; L28-30,000). There are two other one-star hotels, ten two-star, eight three-star, all easy to find.

**Outside Santa Teresa.** Not all people who come to Santa Teresa are passing through by any means: the surrounding beaches are a draw in their own right, all with scintillating views over to Corsica, seven miles (11km) away.

To the east, Punta Falcone and La Marmorata are popular beaches with a luxury *Club Med* **hotel village** (☎0789.751520) open April-September, charging L70-87,000 for a double room with bathroom. Mini-apartments are also available.

Three kilometres west of Santa Teresa, **Capo Testa** is one of Sardinia's finest bathing localities, a rocky promontory surrounded by turquoise sea. Take your pick of the beaches here, facing Corsica on one side, or the northern Sardinian coast sloping away on the other. **Hotels** in the area include the three-star *Capo Testa e dei Due Mari* (☎0789.754333; L67-77,000) open June-September only, and the humbler *Da Colomba* (☎0789.754272; L35-40,000).

**Costa Paradiso.** You want to go farther afield? There are more beaches and plenty of privacy behind the pinewoods to be found following the comparatively new coastal road west. After **Vignola** the road tracks inland, away from the sea, where a sequence of private holiday villa developments lies tucked away. In fact, the coast in these parts is in the process of being privatised, and following the example of the Costa Smeralda has been dubbed Costa Paradiso. There are indeed some heavenly spots here, but be prepared to backtrack when you reach a barrier across the road with sumptuous villas on the other side.

Things start getting back to normal again at **Isola Rossa,** a rather mundane village named from the reddish island lying a little way out to sea. There are some decent beaches beyond, with views over to Castelsardo.

## GALLURA: THE INTERIOR

Wherever you travel on the coasts of Gallura you can't fail to be intrigued by the jagged maquis-covered mountains lying inland. The colours of the slopes change radically according to the season, covered as they are with a combination of cistus, gorse, juniper, heather, myrtle and a hundred other wild species, filling the air with a confection of herbal scents.

Higher up, the knobbly rock-strewn slopes offer scope for hill-walking, better appreciated if you have transport to take you into the higher regions. Come in winter and you'll find the peaks snow-covered and the sound of running water everywhere. Summer sees the countryside bright and still, while spring is the best time to appreciate the wonderful colours of the vegetation.

The scattered villages are few and far between, with most of the population concentrated in the large villages of Témpio Pausánia, Calangánius and Aggius, which have all become popular in recent times as cool hill-resorts. This is also one of the few areas in Sardinia where you will still see isolated farmsteads, or *stazzi,* founded by 18th-cent settlers from Corsica fleeing the strife on that island – and the inhabitants of Gallura still today a reputation for the touchy sense of honour and vengeance for which Corsicans are famous.

Large areas of the country are covered with a thick mantle of oak and cork-oak forest, the latter providing one of the few industries. Come in September or October and you are sure to notice lorry-loads of the silver and red bark being carried to processing plants in Olbia and Arbatax; come any time to the southern parts of Gallura and you can see the lower trunks of cork-oaks stripped to their rusty-red cambium (inner bark), an operation which is repeated every seven years.

People without transport could make use of the narrow-gauge railway of the *Ferrovie Complementari Sarde* that stoically burrows through this region, starting at Sássari and stopping at Témpio Pausánia, Calangiánus, and a succession of minor stations before finishing its tortuous long route at Palau. Beware, though, of some stations in remote areas: Aggius village, for example, is 4.5 miles

*Millionairesville, Porto Cervo — one of the Mediterranean's most exclusive yachting resorts.*

(7km) from its station.

**Témpio Pausánia.** The 'Capital' of Gallura, Témpio Pausánia is a calm, wooded town, its uniform granite-grey centre conserving an appearance of careful well-being.

The air here is crisp and fresh after the summer heat of the lowlands, as you might expect at a height of 1,850ft (565m). Long views stretch out on every side, most dramatically towards the region's highest mountain, Monte Limbara, rising to 4,460ft (1359m). The Rinággiu water which rises from a spring a couple of kilometres out of town is prized as a diuretic by the many islanders who come to the resort in the summer, taking advantage of the superb climate which has always kept the area malaria-free.

In the centre of town, Témpio's 15th-cent Romanesque cathedral in Piazza San Pietro seems immune to the ravages of time, though its present appearance owes much to a drastic restoration in the last century so that only its steeple and carved wooden door are completely original. Opposite, the Oratory breathes the same austere and immoveable calm.

**Accommodation.** There are three good hotels here: *Delle Sorgenti,* at Via delle Fonti 6 (✆079.630033; L47,000); *Petit Hotel,* Piazza de Gásperi 9 (✆079.631134; L47,000); *San Carlo,* Piazza Libertà 5 (✆079.630697; L30,000). On Monte Limbara is one of Sardinia's only inland **holiday villages**, *Il Léccio* (✆079.631381), offering bungalows at L18,000 per person, L48,000 full board.

If you are having a meal in Témpio, make sure you sample a glass of the local *Vermentino*, a white wine drunk as an aperitif or with desserts.

**Carnival.** Témpio's week-long Carnival celebrations have grown hugely in recent years to become one of Sardinia's main festivities. The pagan element is strong, featuring parades of outlandish allegorical floats, and the high points include the symbolic marriage of two puppets, *Re Giorgio* (King George, a sort of Carnival King) and the peasant girl *Mennena*, on Carnival Sunday, followed by a distribution of corn fritters, *fritelle*. Poor King George: on Shrove Tuesday he is burned in a ceremonial bonfire.

**Monte Limbara.** You can reach this thickly wooded peak by car along a small road branching off the main road south to Oschiri. The road passes the holiday village on the Vallicciola plain (see above) and passes within a few hundred metres of the peak, Balestrieri, at 4,460ft (1359m). There are bracing views, of course, even as far as Tavolara island, and more of the curious contorted rocks that are such a feature of the area. Before leaving, take away with you a jar of the famous **bitter honey** produced here and sold in the local shops.

South west of Limbara, **Lago Coghinas** makes a pleasant picnic-spot. One of Sardinia's many artificial lakes, this one was dammed in 1926 to provide a reservoir and hydro-electric power. Between the lake and the village of Oschiri is a site with ruins of a medieval castle and church, a Roman fort, and a *nuraghe*, all close to each other.

**Aggius.** Six miles (10km) west of Témpio, Aggius is another popular highland retreat, enlivened by its colour-washed granite houses with wrought-iron balconies. The village, which commands superb panoramic views, has a strong choral tradition and its choir has taken part in the Welsh *eisteddfod*.

**The giant's playbox.** There is plenty of exploring to do here, particularly in the amazing wilderness of rocky debris that lies behind the town. Here, boulders are strewn across an arena-like hillside, looking — as described by the travel-writer Virginia Waite — "as though a giant has pettishly emptied his playbox of rocks and thrown them carelessly about."

**A Sardinian vendetta.** In the annals of Aggius's past, the area was the hiding place of a sinister character known as *Il Muto di Gallura* — the mute of Gallura. The last in the line of a family locked in a long and deadly vendetta that claimed 72 lives and left only six survivors, the mute carried on the feud from this lonely hideout, from which he descended only to assassinate his enemies. He ended his terror with the murder of the twelve-year-old son of his main enemy, the head of the opposing family. The boy was of 'an unsurpassing beauty,' so the story goes, and was cut down while roaming the cork forests lost in song.

There is little **accommodation** available in Aggius, though there is an Agriturismo facility offered in Località Fráiga (✆079.620559).

**Calangiánus.** East of Témpio, the road skirts Limbara to **Calangiánus,** a small town surrounded by cork factories and, further up, a ring of jagged mountains. In the local shops you can see cork fashioned into a variety of unlikely objects, some of which would make excellent souvenirs, such as cards and postcards, masks, ornaments, purses and more mundane objects like kitchen utensils. There are a couple of one-star **hotels** here, *Da Simone* in Piazza Marconi (no telephone; L21,400) and *Zia Paolina* (✆079.660752; L23,000).

*Cork oaks in Gallura provide one of Sardinia's biggest exports.*

# 17: NUORO

## The heart of Sardinia

THE HUGE CENTRAL PROVINCE OF NUORO has little in common with the sun-and-sand image which most people associate with Sardinia. For many, though, it is the most interesting part of the island, one which will appeal to the inquisitive or, with its range of open-air activities, the outdoor enthusiast.

**The real Sardinia.** If you're looking for the real, 'authentic, Sardinia, look no further: this region is for you. You won't find the medieval fortresses or noble churches to be seen in other parts of the island; instead there's a collection of small and isolated villages which have never known the heel of foreign conquerors. Their inhabitants have retained a fierce sense of independence and loyalty to their traditions, and this is especially true in the ring of the Gennargentu mountains, centred on the island's highest peak, La Mármora (6,017ft, 1834m), and in ancient times almost impenetrable. These mountains form the core of the Barbágia region, called *Barbaria* by the Romans who, in common with later conquerors, were never able to subdue it, foiled by the guerrilla warfare for which these hidden recesses proved ideal. Today the region is well-connected by roads, but still offers some marvellous opportunities for leaving your car and striking out on foot.

The provincial capital of Nuoro is little different from the other villages of the region, only that it is bigger, and has developed a notable literary reputation. This was the town D.H. Lawrence made for in his Sardinian excursion of 1921, and it's perhaps no coincidence that the island's most famous writers of yesterday and today have sprung from here. Though you may not want to spend a lot of time in Nuoro, it makes a useful base for expeditions into the surrounding country.

As well as these inland areas, Nuoro province has its share of sparkling coastline, less visited by tourists than Sardinia's other coasts. Some resorts such as Cala Gonone have been developed and are beginning to find a place on the tourist map; others still wait to be explored.

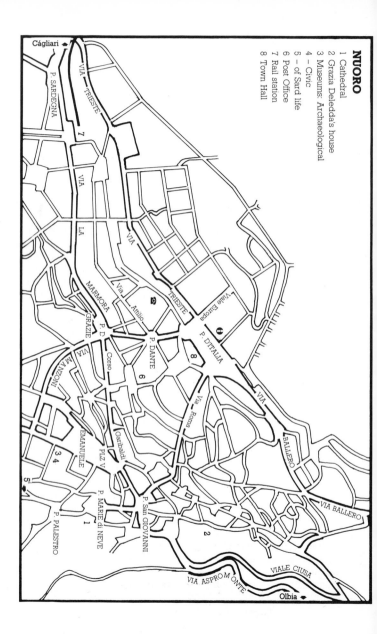

**NUORO**

1 Cathedral
2 Grazia Deledda's house
3 Museums: Archaeological
4 – Civic
5 – of Sard life
6 Post Office
7 Rail station
8 Town Hall

# NUORO TOWN

"There is nothing to see in Nuoro: which to tell the truth, is always a relief. Sights are an irritating bore." So wrote D.H. Lawrence when he passed through this way in 1921, more interested in people and places than art and architecture. But no one can deny that Nuoro has a visual impact, superbly positioned beneath the soaring peak of Mount Ortobene and the sheer and stark heights of Sopramonte.

Nowadays, Nuoro has a few sights too, not least of which is Sardinia's best museum of rural culture, which includes a dazzling collection of traditional costumes. Otherwise the town is simply a bigger version of the scattered mountain communities whose lights glitter across the valleys at night like distant constellations, sharing their self-absorbed sense of remoteness and having little contact with the outside world. However, with a selection of hotels and restaurants that you will not find in those mountain hamlets, Nuoro offers a good base, along with some fascinating glimpses into life in the old-fashioned heart of Sardinia.

**Overview.** Situated on a ledge 1,800ft (550m) above sea-level, Nuoro lies — again in Lawrence's words — "as if at the end of the world, mountains rising sombre behind." Although its origins go back to the Nuraghic age, there is little evidence today of its distant past, and your first impressions will be of a commercial 20th-cent town dominated by modern flats, administrative buildings and banks, and — like all Sardinian towns — overrun by cars. This is an unpromising first view of Nuoro, and you need to penetrate into the web of streets around the central, pedestrianised Corso Garibaldi to unearth the more attractive character of the old town. The ugly suburbs and unappealing new centre around Piazza Italia are the outward signs of the rapid, unplanned growth which began in 1926 when the provincial capital was finally established at Nuoro; the local aristocracy had been settled here for some time, along with the diocesan seat which had transferred here in 1779 from Ottana, whose marshy lowlands made it a prey to malaria.

**Literary Nuoro.** Who knows what makes one town more conducive to great art than any other? In Sardinia, Nuoro seems to have the monopoly where literature is concerned. The best-known Sard poet, **Sebastiano Satta** (1867-1914) was Nuorese, and it's not your fault that you have never heard of him, unless you have noticed his name lent to many streets and piazzas across the island? In his home-town, he is remembered not only in the street where he lived, but also the square at the top (Piazza Satta), which is filled with a collection of modern sculpture representing Nuraghic bronzes, the work of the sculptor Costantino Nivola in 1967.

A generation on, the author **Grazia Deledda** (1871-1936) was one of four Italians to win the Nobel Prize for Literature, in her case in 1926.

*Bosa — a bird's eye view from Malaspina Castle.*

It was a tribute to a steady career devoted to recounting the trials and passions of the ordinary folk in Nuoro and the villages around. Praised by Lawrence and currently undergoing a minor revival in the UK with new translations or republications, she has been compared with Thomas Hardy in her style and subject matter, though has much more in common with the Sicilian Verga.

Grazia Deledda's house can be seen at Via Deledda 28, now a **museum** showing some manuscripts, personal belongings, photographs and first editions of her works, open 0900-1300, 1500-1900 in summer, 1500-1800 in winter, closed Sunday afternoon and all of Monday (free). Her simple marble **tomb** is in the church of Santa Maria della Solitúdine, often mentioned in her books, at the end of a tree-lined path at the base of Mount Ortobene, where the road up the mountain meets the main road to Siniscola and Olbia.

**Salvatore Satta.** Nuoro was "nothing but a perch for the crows," for the town's greatest modern writer, Salvatore Satta (1902-1975, no relation to his poetic namesake Sebastiano), as he wrote in his semi-autobiographical masterpiece, *The Day of Judgment*. Though talking of life at the turn of the century, much of this book — his only work, published posthumously — still rings true today. The meandering descriptions of the townsfolk and the antagonisms between Nuoro's shepherds, peasants and aristocrats have a universal relevance. Satta's impact is too recent to have earned him any memorial in his home-town but I suspect his fame is likely to eclipse both of Nuoro's other literary figures.

**Nuoro's Cathedral.** The 19th-cent Duomo lies at one end of Corso Garibaldi in the spacious Piazza Santa Maria della Neve. You'll see it on the local postcards but it lacks impact if you see it from close up. If you can, try to persuade someone to let you into the belvedere (lookout) to one side of the cathedral; there's a fine view of the town and the valley.

**The Ethnographic Museum.** More compelling than the Duomo is the *Museo Etnográfico* on Via Antonio Mereu, set apart on a rise at the edge of town. Easily reached on foot from Piazza Vittório Emanuele, the museum has Sardinia's most comprehensive and imaginative range of local costumes, jewellery, masks, carpets and other examples of handicrafts, arranged in 20 rooms in a modern purpose-built complex that also houses the offices of a study team. Open every day except Sunday afternoon and Monday 0900-1300, 1500-1900 (0900-1300, 1500-1800 in winter), the museum is free and is easily the most interesting thing to see in Nuoro.

**Nuoro's *festa*.** Nuoro's biggest annual *festa*, the *Sagra del Redentore*, is linked with the Statue of the Redeemer on nearby Mount Ortobene. This is the site for the religious part of the festival, when a procession from town weaves up the mountain on 29 August, the date when the finished statue was put up in its present position. Down at street level on the penultimate Sunday in August, the real fun begins when people from all over the island, but especially the villages of the Barbágia region of Nuoro province, parade in costume, with popular dancing and dialect singing. It may be a little contrived and institutionalised for some, but it's a good opportunity to see the 3,000 or so costumes taking part.

**Transport and information.** All **ARST** buses arrive at and depart from the bottom of the lively Piazza Vittório Emanuele, off the Corso. The **PANI** agency is at Via Brigata Sássari 15. The **railway station,** linked with Macomer to the west, is a couple of kilometres west of the Corso on the shop-lined Via La Mármora. Here, and at the ARST terminus, there is a **left-luggage** deposit. The well-stocked **EPT** is on Piazza Italia, open 0900-1300, 1600-1900 daily except Saturday afternoon and Sunday.

**Accommodation.** Nuoro is ill-equipped for the casual visitor travelling on a budget, though it has a couple of grander hotels that are decent enough if you don't mind spending more. The *Grazia Deledda* (✆0784.31257; L70,000) on Via La Mármora opposite the station doesn't quite justify its four stars but is comfortable. All the following are three-star: the *Sandalia* (✆0784.38353; L57,000), near Nuoro's conspicuous hospital on Via Einaudi, is best of the bunch, with good views and an excellent restaurant. Behind the station on Viale Trieste, the *Motel Agip* (✆0784.34071; L57,000) offers the usual motel facilities. The *Nuovo Grillo* (✆0784.38678; L57,000) is on the southern edge of town on Via Monsignor Melas. The *Paradiso* (✆0784.35585; L58,000) on Via Aosta, near the *Campo Sportivo* on the outskirts west of the station, doesn't altogether live up to its name. The two-star *Mini Hotel* (✆0784.33159; L38,000) is more central on Via Broféemio, off Via Roma, but often full.

Apart from these, you must ask around: try Signora Iacobini's unofficial hotel at Via Cedrino 36, off Piazza Italia (✆0784.30675; L30,000). See below for a good three-star hotel on Monte Ortobene.

**Eating out.** As with accommodation, Nuoro is not particularly well-off for restaurants. If you can't afford the upmarket *Sandalia Hotel,* best choice and most popular with the Nuorese locals (and therefore often crowded) is the excellent Ristorante-Pizzeria *Da Gesuino,* at Viale Ciusa 53, on the western end of town (closed Monday). Near Corso Garibaldi at Via Broffémio 31, the rather mysterious *Da Chicchino* is a modest trattoria where you take what you are given and don't ask questions (closed Sunday). Outside town, delicious — but pricy — local fare can be had at the *Fratelli Sacchi* on Mount Ortobene (see below).

For a lunch-time snack between sights, there's a handy and clean sit-down bar on Via Mereu, between the Museo del Costume and the Duomo (closed Sunday in winter).

**Transport connections.** From Piazza Vittório Emanuele, there are buses for **Cágliari** at 0710 and 1345, stopping at Elmas Airport; six daily for **Olbia,** and one at 1610 for **Sássari.** Of the local destinations, six a day leave for **Dorgali,** three for **Lanusei** (one on Sunday); 11 for **Oliena** (one on Sunday); 11 for **Orgósolo;** six for **Posada,** and one at 1430 for **Tortolì,** from where there are frequent connections with the ferry-port of **Arbatax.**

**Car hire.** The only car-hire agency in town is *Maggiore* at Via Convento 32.

## AROUND NUORO

Most of the areas north of Nuoro, in the Barbágia region south, and those on the coast which are worth visiting, can be explored from Nuoro in one day if you have a car; if not, you must rely on buses which may require a night or two away. When driving in these mountains make sure your trip back is in daylight, not only because the winding, narrow roads are not easy to negotiate, but also because to travel in these parts at night would be a terrible waste of some stupendous scenery — and that, surely, is what you've come to see.

**Mount Ortobene.** Right outside town, the switchback road for Monte Ortobene starts its five-mile (8-km) ascent through woods with dizzy views down. Best vantage point is at the top (3,134ft, 955m), where the bronze statue of *Cristo Redentore* (Christ the Redeemer), sculpted in 1901, stands poised in an attitude full of swirling motion.

The woods round about are perfect for walks and picnics, and there are possibilities for horse-riding at the *Locanda Sedda Ortai*, 0900-2100.

From Piazza Vittório Emanuele, ten buses a day ply the road up in summer, only three in winter, at 0855, 1300 and 1530.

Near the top, the *Fratelli Sacchi* **hotel** charges L35,000 for a double without bath in a lovely bucolic setting (✆0784.31200). You can eat well here too.

**Travelling North.** North of Nuoro, on the other side of the Oristano-Olbia SS 131, the borderlands between Sássari and Nuoro provinces are largely flat and uninhabited. Shepherds are the only travellers on these wide and empty expanses, and the few villages have become well known as centres of rustic craftsmanship. **Buddusò,** for example, is associated with the chestnut or oak-wood wedding-chests known as the *cassapanca,* while Sards know **Pattada,** to the west, where the elegant shepherd's penknife called the *pattadesu* or sometimes *leppa,* is made. Supposedly unbreakable, the knife's handle is a beautifully crafted piece of horn, originally from mouflon until that species of wild mountain goat came under special protection, and now from the ram.

**Bandits.** The eastern border of the region is at **Ozieri,** and is a local centre for cheese production and horse-breeding. The village is also famous for its almond-cakes known as *suspiros*. . .and for crime. The locals here amuse themselves with tales of past exploits by desperados on the wrong side of the law. At a road-block outside Ozieri, for example, bandits robbed 250 people in broad daylight in October 1952 while the entire local police force was celebrating its annual festival. More recently, in March 1973, thieves stole 230 sheep from the state agricultural penal colony near Lodè, a small hamlet west of Buddusò. As in the Barbágia (see below), larceny, delinquency and murder were the symptoms of a rural society struggling to adapt to rapidly changing circumstances. Little of the kind takes place nowadays, and you can feel safe in your travels hereabouts − but looking at the bare, featureless landscape it is easy to understand how such a state of affairs could have come about.

**Local hero.** South of Ozieri is the Gocéano range of mountains, at the heart of which lies the village of **Bono.** This was the birthplace of an outlaw even further back in time, but revered on the island today more strongly than almost any other Sard apart from Eleanor of Arborea. **Giovanni Maria Angioy** was an 18th-cent aristocrat who fought for the peasants' cause against the evils of feudalism. He was also an early campaigner for Sardinian independence, and following his lead − and with French support − the people rose up throughout the island, forcing even the viceroy to flee from Cágliari. But in 1796 Angioy was driven out of Sardinia, leaving behind a name which has been immortalised in streets and squares in every island town and village on the island.

**South of Nuoro: Oliena.** Seven miles (12km) away, Oliena is the nearest village to Nuoro, nestling on Mount Corrasi and easily visible across the deep valley below the provincial capital. This dramatic, rugged limestone massif which rises to 4,426ft (1349m), forms part of the Sopramonte massif, famed in Sardinian folklore as the haunt of bandits until relatively recently. But Oliena prefers its reputation as the producer of one of the island's best wines, a dry, deep black brew which turns lighter and stronger over the years.

The local traditional dress for men and women is an elegant black and white costume which these days comes out only on Oliena's feast days. Most interesting of these is the Easter *s'incontru,* or meeting, between the processions following the figures of the Virgin Mary and Jesus, though the costumes are also given an airing for the four days of revelry around San Lussório's day on 21 August.

**Excursions on Sopramonte.** Organised trips around Sopramonte's caves and crags start from Oliena. Contact Fabrizio Serri on Via Fala e Nodi in the village (✆0784.285222 – after 1330), or the *Cooperativa Turística Enis* in Località Maccione (✆0784.288363).

There are two hotels in the area, both outside the village, and both used by trekkers. The *Ci Kappa* (✆0784.288733; L48-53,000) is nearer, on Via Martin Luther King, also providing a good restaurant. Four miles (7km) from Oliena, the *Su Gologone* (✆0784.287512; L68,000) is

*The Maddalena archipelago as seen from Garibaldi's home.*

better known, well-equipped with swimming pool and tennis courts in a rustic setting next to some therapeutic spring waters. Though remote, this is a popular destination both with nature-lovers and those who enjoy its good restaurant. The hotel organises horse-riding and jeep expeditions onto Sopramonte, starting at L20,000 per person. Some deals include a 'lunch with the shepherds' (L50,000), a contrived open-air affair also offered by other tour organisations, where tourists are offered a succulent succession of typical local dishes cooked over an open fire — vegetarians might prefer to stay away!

**Bandit country.** Deeper into the mountains, at the end of a straggly 11 mile (18km) road from Oliena, **Orgósolo** is stuck with its label of bandit-capital of the island. Though the bandits have gone, there is no denying the village's gory past. Historically, the clans of Orgósolo, whose members spent the greater part of the year away from home following their flocks across the mountains, have always nursed an animosity towards the settled crop-farmers on Barbágia's fringes, which occasionally broke out into open warfare. One famous incident was a night-time 'invasion' of the low-lying village of Tortolì, near the coast at Arbatax, in 1897.

The ill-feeling was not only directed at outsiders but also against rival clans, expressed in large-scale sheep-rustling and bloody vendettas, such as the *disamistade,* or enmity, which engulfed Orgósolo at the beginning of this century. The feud arose over the inheritance of the village's richest clan-chieftain, Diego Moro, who died in 1903, and lasted for 14 years, virtually exterminating the two families involved. Between 1901 and 1954, Orgósolo (population 4,000) had an average of one killing every two months.

**A Sard Robin Hood.** One of the village's most famous — or infamous — sons was the romantic Graziano Mesina, who won local hearts in the 1960s by robbing only from the rich to give to the poor, and killing only for revenge those who had betrayed him. Roaming at will through the mountains, he became something of a media legend, even granting interviews to reporters and television journalists. He was eventually caught and locked in Sássari prison, but he escaped in 1968, and his recapture near Nuoro was hot news all over the island, to the extent that he was taken by helicopter that same day to appear on television in Cágliari.

**The murals.** Saddled with this semi-legendary background, Orgósolo inevitably attracts visitors who come in the hope of finding some traces of its violent past. Of course, there is nothing to see, only a rather shabby collection of breeze-blocked grey houses whose poverty seems a world apart from the white-washed luxury of the Costa Smeralda, just a couple of hours' drive away.

But the villagers have obliged the tourists by providing a vivid collection of **murals,** some of them covering whole houses and showing an impressive range of talent. Other Sardinian villages have also caught onto this idea, but few reach the heights of imagination on display here. Most of the murals have a political theme, illustrating the oppression of the landless by the landowners, or demanding Sardinian independence. One of them seems ironically intended to shock unsuspecting newcomers, a scarlet face cleverly painted onto a rock below the entrance to the village, as if a bandit is lurking behind it. Come to Orgósolo to see these colourful examples of folk-art, but don't expect anything more. The days of shoot-outs on the main street are over!

**Into Barbágia.** There are dozens of small villages like Orgósolo, connected by twisting mountain roads and still, as Salvatore Satta described them in the early years of the century, "miniscule settlements as remote from one another as are the stars." Each village is separate and self-sufficient, each the orbit of quiet industry until the evening when their populations spill out for a brisk, cheerful *passeggiata* before disappearing behind closed doors. Night in these villages is sudden and profound.

It is in these tight communities that you are most likely to come across the few remaining local costumes still worn by elderly folk. Otherwise your best chance is to come during one of the numerous small festivals that punctuate the year, each village having at least one, for which preparations are made months in advance. **Mamoiada,** 7 miles (11km) west of Orgósolo, is the scene of a highly pagan Carnival romp, when masked *mammuthones* representing hunted animals march through the streets, dressed in sheepskin with their backs covered in rows of jangling goat-bells. **Ottana,** on the northern fringes of the area – and reckoned to be the dead centre of Sardinia – vies with Mamoiada for its masked and horned Carnival horrors. **Fonni,** at 3,200ft (1000m) the island's highest village, has a less gruesome costumed procession in its festival devoted to the Madonna dei Mártiri, on the Monday following the first Sunday in June.

Each of these villages is primarily a shepherding community, whose isolation and poverty in the post-war years led to widescale emigration and, among those who stayed behind, a crime-wave. Sheep-rustling and family feuding gave way to the much more lucrative practice of people-rustling, or the kidnapping and ransoming of wealthy industrialists or their families. This phenomenon reached epidemic proportions during 1966-8 when scores of Carabinieri were regularly drafted into the area to comb the mountains for the hideouts, though seldom with any success. Recently, the kidnappings in Sardinia have declined and the cases reaching the newspapers nearly all come from the southern Italian region of Calabria.

**Skiing in the Gennargentu.** Nowadays, shepherds send their children to university, others go to mainland Italy for work and don't come back. They leave behind dwindling village communities whose salvation may lie in a greater awareness of their tourist potential, catering for outdoor activities and winter sports. The **Gennargentu** chain of mountains — the name means 'silver gate,' referring to the snow that shrouds them every winter — have benefited particularly, with the island's only **skiing** facilities established on Monte Bruncu Spina (6,001ft, 1,829m).

For **accommodation** here, ask at Nuoro's EPT for the *rifúgio,* or mountain shelter, close by; alternatively stay at **Desulo,** where there are two three-star hotels, the *Gennargentu* (✆ 0784.61270; L45,000) and the *Lamármora* (✆ 0784.61126; L44,000), and one two-star, *La Nuova* (✆ 0784.61251; L25,000). At **Fonni,** a little further away, there is the three-star *Cualbu* (✆ 0784.57054; L46,000), while **Aritzo** has a choice of six hotels. **Tonara** has a youth hostel and campsite next to each other at the top of the village — for these, enquire first, as neither is registered in the province's accommodation-list and neither was open when I was last there. In any case there is a trio of small hotels in Tonara, the *Belvedere* (✆ 0784.63576; L38,000); *Il Noccioleto* (✆ 0784.63923; L33,000), and *Su Toni* (✆ 0784.63420; L36,000).

These villages all make good bases for **mountain treks,** best undertaken in spring and summer; for fuller details, ask for the handy trekkers' booklet from Nuoro's EPT. From Desulo, for example, it is possible to reach the area's highest peak, La Mármora, along a 7.5 mile (12km) path. On the way you may see wild pigs, vultures and deer, though you would be lucky to spot one of the rare mouflon, an elegant wild goat with long curved horns, its numbers decimated by hunting; these days its only western European habitats are the remotest areas of Corsica and Sardinia.

## NUORO'S COAST

The province of Nuoro briefly touches the west side of Sardinia at Bosa, already described in chapter 14. Its long eastern seaboard is highly developed around Siniscola and Posada (see chapter 16), but further south it preserves a desolate beauty, virtually uninhabited apart from a couple of isolated spots around **Orosei** and **Cala Golone,** and there is some light industry further south at the small port of **Arbatax**.

**Orosei.** Some 25 miles (40km) east of Nuoro, Orosei stands two miles (3km) from the sea, though historical archives describing Turkish raids here suggest that it must have had a harbour in the Middle Ages, after which the silting-up of the nearby River Cedrino thrust the shoreline eastwards.

The surrounding country is all fertile and flat, planted with vines and citrus groves, a contrast to the landscape you have left behind.

*Garibaldi's tomb at Caprera: the great man looks on.*

Orosei's back streets shelter an interesting old quarter with some fine examples of Spanish architecture, not least the church and towers of **Sant'Antonio,** 15th-cent but much restored and remodelled. Other churches worth looking out for (and well-signposted) are San Giácomo, San Gavino and the ruin of San Sebastiano.

There are two three-star **hotels** here – *Maria Rosária* on Via Grázia Deledda (✆ 0784.98657; L54,000) and *Su Barchile* on Via Mannu (✆ 0784.98879; L38,000) – and a couple more further north on the coast, at the area known as **Cala Liberrotto.** Here is the four-star *Tirreno* (✆ 0784.91007; L80,000) and the three-star *Cala Ginepro* (✆ 0784.91047; L63,000); there are also two **campsites** in the vicinity, *Cala Ginepro,* open all year (✆ 0784.91017), and *Sa Prama* (June-September; ✆ 0784.91072). Cala Liberrotto has some extremely swim-worthy **beaches,** as does Orosei's Marina, and from town another small road leads a little further south to some more secluded bathing spots.

**The Ispinigoli Grotto.** Between Orosei and Dorgali, the *Grotta di Ispinigoli* is signposted a little way off the main road. This deep cave contains one of nature's most magnificent works of art, in the form of a mind-bending collection of stalagmites and stalactites, dominated by one 125ft (38m) column that appears to hold the whole lot up. Inside have been found traces of some distant human presence – jewels, amphorae and bones, probably dating from Phoenician times. The local name for the cave, *Abisso delle Vergini,* hopefully owes more to popular imagination than to fact, but it is likely that such an impressive natural phenomenon would have attracted some kind of religious ritual.

Tours inside the grotto leave on the hour 0900-1800 in summer; between October and April visitors must contact the Pro Loco in Dorgali (✆ 0784.96243) for access; the half-hour tour costs L4,500 per person. There is a good restaurant close to the entrance.

**Dorgali and Cala Gonone.** The centre of the renowned *Cannonau* wine-growing region, Dorgali attracts a lot of tourists in summer, both for its craftwork and for the recent growth of the small port of Cala Gonone as a resort, six miles (10km) away on the coast. Dorgali's restaurants and hotels are generally cheaper, and you will find banks and shops too. In Dorgali, the hotels are *S'Adde* (✆ 0784.94412; L53,000); *Querceto* (✆ 0784.96509; L47,000), and *San Pietro* (✆ 0784.96142; L30,000) − respectively three-, two- and one-star.

**Cala Gonone** is reached going south out of town and turning left into the tunnel that brings you through the mountain wall, from which the road plunges down to the bay. Beautifully sited at the base of the 3,000ft (900m) high mountains, this once tiny settlement was cut off from the rest of the island until quite recently, accessible only by boat. Now hotels and villas dominate the scene, though these have not entirely spoilt the sense of isolation, and it's worth a visit if only to take advantage of the numerous boat-tours to the secluded coves up and down the cliffy coast. Among the favourites are Cala Luna and Cala Sisine, though if you are here for a short time you would do well to choose a tour that combines pauses at these swimming-stops with exploration of the deep grottos that pit the shore.

**The Sea-Ox Grotto.** Most famous of the grottos is the *Grotta del Bue Marino* − touted as the last refuge of the Mediterranean monk-seal, or 'Sea-ox' in Italian. I suspect these creatures must have moved on a long time ago, as would any wildlife confronted by the boatloads of trippers descending daily. Still, it's a good expedition to one of Sardinia's most remarkable caves, a luminescent gallery filled with natural sculptures, the delicate stalactites and stalagmites forming organ pipes, wedding-cakes and even human heads (one of them is known as *Dante,* after an imagined resemblance to the poet). Fresh and salt-water lakes are hewn deep inside the mountain, and the continual dripping allows you to study the never-ending act of creation taking place before your eyes.

**Hotels in Cala Gonone.** There are 13 **hotels** listed for Cala Gonone, so no shortage of choice. Most luxurious is the *Palmasera* − also a residence − open April-October (✆ 0784.93191) on Viale Bue Marino, offering double rooms at L110,000, or two-bed, one-roomed apartments at L870,000 a week. Another panoramic choice is the *Mastino delle Grazie* (✆ 0784.93150; L57,000), but some way from the seafront. The modern *Pop* (✆ 0784.93185; L65,000) is right on the port, and nearby is the *Cala Luna* (✆ 0784.93133; L39,000), the *Bue Marino* (✆ 0784.93130; L42,000) and the *Píccolo Hotel* (✆ 0784.93232; L42,000). Most others don't have seafront views.

**Yachters.** Though blessed with a perfect setting, the port of Cala Gonone is cursed by gusty winds blowing off the mountains. Berth in the northern corner of the breakwater, stern to a short quay.

**The Gorruppu Canyon.** South of Cala Gonone lies one of Sardinia's last truly unspoilt tracts. Swerving inland along the ridge of the Flumineddu river, which is walled on the other side by the Sopramonte massif, the new road brings you into a mountain landscape of rare majesty. There is no dwelling, no shepherd or other form of human life, and it is only after passing through the Genna Silana Pass at more than 3,300ft (1000m), taking you into a second wide valley, that there are a couple of hamlets off the main road. Even here you are unlikely to see more than the occasional car until you reach the end of the stretch at Baunei, by which time you are within sight of the sea.

**Two hikes.** Stefano Ardito, in his *Backpacking and Walking in Italy* outlines two long-distance hikes in these wild parts, which he describes as among the best in the whole Mediterranean basin. For both, good maps and supplies are necessary, as there is little hope of meeting people to ask directions or refreshment.

One of them − a three- or four-day hike − follows the coast from Cala Gonone as far as Cala Sisine, at which point the route wanders inland, up the Sisine river canyon, as far as the solitary church of San Pietro, from where a track leads down to Baunei.

The second and shorter hike follows the course of the Flumineddu river from Dorgali and takes you into the Gorruppu canyon, though further exploration requires mountaineering skills and even dinghies to cross the small inland lakes buried in the heart of the gorge. You could complete the first part of this itinerary in a day, given good maps or a guide to locate the paths.

From Baunei and the next village of Lotzorai, the road descends steeply to Tortolì, an inland town from which the port of **Arbatax** is a brief three-mile (5-km) drive. Arbatax is little more than a paper factory, a few bars and a port. The small beach here is famous for its red rocks, but there are better bathing spots north and south of town (see below).

**Ferries from Arbatax.** Ferries link the town with **Genova,** leaving Arbatax 1 October−31 May on Tuesdays and Saturdays (departure time 1400); 1 June−22 July and in September on Thursdays and Saturdays (departure time 1400), and 23 July−2 September on Thursdays and Saturdays (departure time 1600).

For **Civitavécchia,** north of Rome, ferries leave 3 September−2 July on Tuesdays and Sundays (departure time 2400), and 23 July−2

September on Tuesdays (departure time 2200), Fridays and Sundays (departure time for both 2400).

**Information and excursions.** There is an **AAST** kiosk on the seafront in town open 0900-1900 in summer but only irregularly in winter. Here you will find information on **excursions** possible from Arbatax, up and down the coast, including the Grotta del Bue Marino for L30,000 (reductions for children under ten).

The **Tirrenia agency** is in town, on the right after the AAST kiosk, open 0900-1300, 1600-1930, Saturday morning only, and also open Sunday and Wednesday 2200-2400. Otherwise buy tickets on the day of departure from the booth at the port.

**Transport.** All **buses** stop on the seafront, with regular departures for Tortolì, from which there are frequent daily connections to Cágliari and Nuoro. The small **railway** station, right on the headland, is useful only for Tortolì, unless you are interested in going inland at a leisurely pace. The full journey to Cágliari takes seven hours.

If you want to **hire a car,** the *Rent A Car* agency at Tortolì is on Via Mons Virgílio, ✆ 0782.623352.

**Accommodation.** There are several small hotels in the Arbatax area, most a taxi-ride away. Best is the *Cala Moresca* (✆ 0782.667366; L81,000) in Località Cala Moresca, and all the others have comparable prices and standards of comfort, apart from the cheaper *La Bitta* (✆ 0782.667080; L45,000) and the *Supersonic* (✆ 0782.623512; L35,000), both in Località Frailis. Tortolì, five kilometres inland, also has a small selection, mainly two-star.

**Around Arbatax.** If you want to get the best out of the Arbatax area, you need a car. The road north leads to the tiny village of **Santa Maria Navarrese,** which has a picturesque watch-tower, and a church founded by the King of Navarre's daughter, who was shipwrecked here; there's also a beach of fine sand.

**Somewhere to stay?** Options in the neighbourhood include a quartet of hotels and a pair of campsites. The hotels are the three-star *Santa Maria* (✆ 0782.615026; L57-62,000), the two-star *Mediterráneo* (✆ 0782.669544; L48,000) and *Stella del Mare* (✆ 0782.669510; L44,000), and the one-star *Agugliastra* (✆ 0782.615005; L26,000). The campsites are in Località Is Orrosas and are both open May-September: *Le Cérnie* (✆ 0782.669472) and *Cavallo Bianco* (✆ 0782.669499).

South of Arbatax is a series of sand and rock beaches at **Lido Orri**.

**And finally.** But the road west climbs to the mountain village of **Lanusei,** capital of the Ogliastra region, named from the quantity of wild olives that grow here. At 1,937ft (590m), it's a picturesque gateway to the Barbágia mountains and gives you that final chance to travel through the Gennargentu range. Or continue southward on the sinuous SS 198, following the narrow-gauge railway down towards Cágliari, where our journey of discovery began.

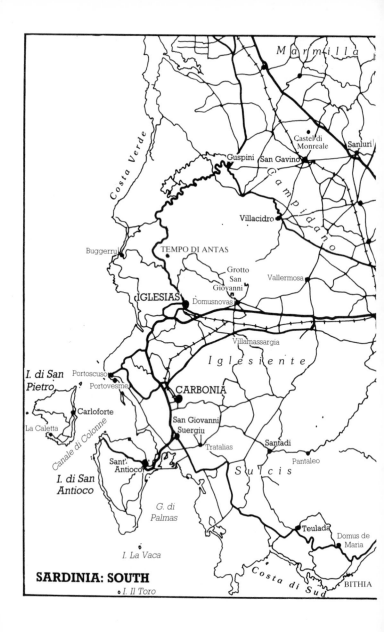

SARDINIA: SOUTH

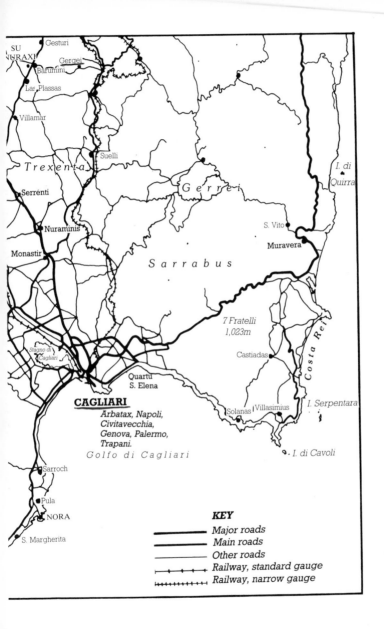

SU
NURAXI
Gesturi
Gergei
Barumini
Las Plassas
Villamar
Suelli
*Trexenta*
*Gerrei*
Serrenti
Nuraminis
S. Vito
Muravera
Monastir
*Sarrabus*
*I. di Quirra*
7 Fratelli
1,023m
Stagno di
Cagliari
Castiadas
*Costa Rei*
Quartu
S. Elena
**CAGLIARI**
*Arbatax, Napoli,*
*Civitavecchia,*
*Genova, Palermo,*
*Trapani.*
Solanas
Villasimius
*I. Serpentara*
*Golfo di Cagliari*
*I. di Cavoli*
Sarroch
Pula
NORA
S. Margherita

**KEY**

| | |
|---|---|
| ▬▬▬▬ | Major roads |
| ▬▬▬ | Main roads |
| ─── | Other roads |
| ┼─┼─┼─ | Railway, standard gauge |
| ╫╫╫╫╫ | Railway, narrow gauge |

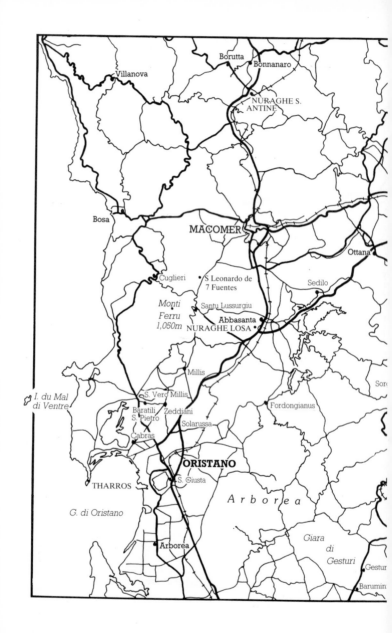